The Psychology of Global Citizenship

The Psychology of Global Citizenship

A Review of Theory and Research

Stephen Reysen
Iva Katzarska-Miller

LEXINGTON BOOKS
Lanham • Boulder • New York • London

Published by Lexington Books
An imprint of The Rowman & Littlefield Publishing Group, Inc.
4501 Forbes Boulevard, Suite 200, Lanham, Maryland 20706
www.rowman.com

Unit A, Whitacre Mews, 26-34 Stannary Street, London SE11 4AB

British Library Cataloguing in Publication Information Available

Library of Congress Cataloging-in-Publication Data Available

LCCN 2018947265 | ISBN 9781498570299 (cloth: alk. paper) | ISBN 9781498570305 (electronic)

∞™ The paper used in this publication meets the minimum requirements of American
National Standard for Information Sciences Permanence of Paper for Printed Library
Materials, ANSI/NISO Z39.48-1992.

Printed in the United States of America

Contents

Acknowledgments

We are grateful to many people who have been part of our lives and helped us along the way in the creation of this book. Iva Katzarska-Miller thanks her Transylvania University colleagues for their support and encouragement, and the administration for grants that allowed conducting some of the research described in this book. I thank my mentors in University of Kansas for nurturing my intellectual growth, and Glenn Adams, who set me on the path to study global citizenship. I thank my wonderful students who helped with and participated in the research over the years. I am grateful to Carole Barnsley, and all my friends who have been there with a kind word when things were not easy. Special thanks to my Bulgarian family for living aspects of global citizenship in a different cultural context. This book, however, is dedicated to my son Justin, with all my love.

Stephen Reysen thanks his wonderful coauthor, family, friends, colleagues at A&M-Commerce, and mentors (Faye Crosby, Constance Jones, Robert Levine, Nyla Branscombe). I also thank students (Lindsey Pierce, Jamie Snider, Marion Blake, Shonda Gibson, Natalia Assis, Ida Mohebpour) who have worked on various projects related to global citizenship over the years and the many individuals who participated in this research.

Finally, we thank the anonymous reviewer of the book, who provided us with invaluable feedback, and the people in Lexington Books for their commitment to this book, in particular Kasey Beduhn and Becca Rohde.

Introduction

According to a poll conducted by GlobeScan (2016) for the BBC, surveying 20,000 people from 18 countries between December 2015 and April 2016, 51% of the people surveyed said that they see themselves more as global citizens than a citizen of the country they live in. Polling has been conducted by this organization since 2001 with 14 of the 18 countries. Over time there has been a general trend of more individuals viewing themselves as global citizens over nationality. However, in the midst of the global financial crisis in 2009, a new trend emerged where OECD countries (member countries of the Organization for Economic Co-operation and Development, which tend to be considered "developed" countries) began showing a decrease in global citizenship, while non-OECD countries began a marked increase in global citizenship. In 2016, 43% of U.S. residents sampled reported that they agree with viewing themselves as more of a global citizen than a citizen of the United States.

The results of the poll are both surprising and not. The term *global citizen* has been part of the social discourse, with politicians endorsing or disavowing such an identity. Both presidents Ronald Reagan and Barack Obama claimed to be global citizens. In his speech at the UN General Assembly on June 17, 1982, President Reagan declared, "I speak today both as a citizen of the United States and of the world." Similarly, then-candidate Barack Obama, standing before a crowd in Berlin on July 24, 2008, described himself as a "proud citizen of the United States, and a fellow citizen of the world" (Associated Press, 2008). At the other end, Republican Presidential candidate Newt Gingrich declared in 2009, "I am not a citizen of the world. I think the entire concept is intellectual nonsense and stunningly dangerous!" (Gerzon, 2010, p. 11). The current President, Donald Trump, also disavows the concept, stating at a rally on December 1, 2016, "There is no global anthem, no global currency, no certificate of global citizenship" (Ip, 2017).

Global citizenship is also becoming increasingly mentioned in popular culture. For example, there is a Global Citizen music festival held each year in New York City. In between musical acts like Coldplay, Jay-Z, Stevie Wonder, Beyoncé, and Pearl Jam, activists, celebrities, and politicians speak about global issues (e.g., poverty, lack of clean water) and call for action. Although the concert is free, there are tickets. The organizers hold a lottery where individuals can increase their chances of getting tickets by participating in acts of social justice (e.g., sign a petition, volunteer, donate to charity) which are tracked on their website. The concert's audience size, and the number of events run by the organization, continues to grow each year. Furthermore, with webcasts live streaming the festival, fans around the world are exposed the message regarding the importance of global citizenship.

Is the global citizenship that some politicians embrace and others renounce the same as the global citizenship embodied in the Global Citizen music festival? What did the 43% of U.S. residents who view themselves as more global than national citizens have in mind when defining themselves as such? Why would global citizenship in non-OECD countries increase while in OECD countries decrease? What is a global citizen after all, and what cultural forces drive its existence today? In the book we will attempt to provide the answer to similar questions in detail. Here, however, we would like to acknowledge that global citizen identity (although not new) has increased in present years, the main reason for which is the era of globalization in which we currently exist.

Although globalization has been defined in various ways, in essence it is "a process of interaction and integration among peoples, companies, and governments of different nations (Chiu, Gries, Torelli, & Cheng, 2011, p. 664). In effect, the world has been, and continues to become more interconnected. Globalization is not a new phenomenon. Although researchers may debate about the origins of globalization, with some suggesting international trade in the 1490s, O'Rourke and Williamson (2002) suggest that globalization truly started with the world economy becoming more integrated in the 1820s. Many researchers discuss globalization with respect to economies and trade, but it also includes social components such as spread of cultural patterns, ideas, and technology. While globalization has been around for some time, it may feel to many as if it has intensified in recent years. Indeed, with the spread and adoption of technologies (e.g., Internet, video conferencing, cell phones), people are more connected now than any time in history. Although globalization does impact the movement of people and things, it also has an impact on psychological aspects of our lives. For example, individuals in various countries are increasing in their self-reported degree of individualism (Beugelsdijk, Maseland, & van Hoorn, 2015). With greater interconnectedness, psychologists have begun questioning how globalization has changed our sense of self (Arnett, 2002).

One impact of globalization is the effect it has on peoples' identities (Arnett, 2002). Along with thinking of oneself in more local terms (e.g., family member, city or state resident), or one's national identity, individuals are increasingly viewing the self in terms of being a citizen of the world (Norris & Inglehart, 2009) and taking on a more global identity (Moghaddam, 2014). Moving away from national identity and concerns related to one's country, people are able to view the self as a global citizen with concerns that are beyond one's nation. For example, the various environmental crises are viewed as global problems rather than solely national problems, with the need to work with others around the world to solve them. We conceptualize global citizenship as a superordinate identity afforded by globalization, one that subsumes multiple other identities (e.g., ethnicity, nationality). Indeed, any person can view the self as a global citizen; however not all do. Exploring the reasons of why one would take on the identity (or not) is one of the topics covered in the book.

APPROACH TO THE BOOK

Global citizenship, and similar concepts, has a long history of theory and discussion in academic circles. For example, education theorists have decried the need for global education (Oxfam, 1997), legal scholars note the need for global citizenship to address and mitigate global problems (Falk, 1993), philosophers have stressed the connection between global citizenship and global ethics and social justice (Dower, 2014), business scholars have expounded on the connection between global citizenship and socially responsible business practices (Waddock & Smith, 2000), political scientists have striven to understand how global citizenship has impacted various societal organizations (Schattle, 2008), and geographers discuss global citizenship and global education as the suggested approach for teaching students about the world (Gaudelli & Heilman, 2009). The current state of global citizenship theorizing and research would best be described as fragmented and disorganized. Despite this fragmentation, which is predominantly driven by lack of conversation among academic perspectives, common themes do exist. For example, common questions being posited concern how individuals come to view themselves as global citizens and what it means to be a global citizen.

The primary goal of the book is to present a comprehensive review of theory and research of global citizenship. As already mentioned, presently, the literature regarding global citizenship tends to be fragmented with theorists approaching the concept through disciplinary lens, leading to the lack of integration of concepts and perspectives from multiple disciplines. Thus, we have attempted to write a book that is multidisciplinary in nature, by highlighting the common themes across the literature to assess the key components of global citizenship from various academic and non-academic perspectives. Much of the academic work on global citizenship is theoretical. The majority of books focusing on global citizenship, particularly in education, often lack empirical support for the proposed ideas. Since we come from a discipline that is scientific in nature and relies on empirical evidence, the main focus of the book is a review of the empirical research that has been conducted. Since, research is usually based on underlying theories, which we present, where applicable, throughout the book. We include both qualitative and quantitative work. Qualitative research is a necessary and complementary side of quantitative research to provide a fuller understanding of a concept (Onwuegbuzie & Leech, 2005). Thus, we use multiple methods to explore the nature of global citizenship.

A second goal of the book is to present a social psychological perspective of global citizenship but also integrating components of the concept from other disciplines. We highlight the view of global citizenship as an identity, or a psychological connection to an identity label. Such an approach solves much of the problematizing of the concept from some disciplines (e.g., lack of legal world citizenship). We present a model of global citizenship identification that includes the components of global citizenship highlighted by academics and lay persons alike. The model, thus, brings together the disparate lines of theory and discussion, and places them within well-grounded theoretical frameworks. Although researchers have only begun to empirically examine the model, there is a growing body of empirical evidence to support it.

As with any research, there are caveats to our presentation in this book. The authors of this work are social psychologists, and our interpretations and presentation are colored by this position. One practice/assumption that is being challenged in recent years is psychologists' tendency to present research as universal, even though it is conducted predominantly with U.S. undergraduate students (Henrich, Heine, & Norenzayan, 2010). Indeed, the majority of research in psychology is conducted in the United States, by U.S. researchers, and published in U.S. journals (Arnett, 2008). This is a problem since cultural and cross-cultural researchers show that psychological phenomena can vary when studied with culturally diverse samples. Thus, in the present work we have attempted to emphasize the importance of context for global citizenship and specify the participant samples while reviewing the research.

OVERVIEW OF CHAPTERS

In Chapter 1, we provide a brief review of the history of cosmopolitanism and global citizenship, explore definitions of the construct, and list different "types" of global citizens derived by both theory and research. Since global citizenship grew out of the concept of cosmopolitanism in the history review, we track that thread and highlight the relatively recent emergence of the global citizenship notion in academia. As mentioned above, many academic disciplines have discussed the concept of global citizenship through disciplinary lenses, thus leading to an ambiguous concept. We emphasize some common themes in definitions (e.g., felt responsibility to act for the betterment of the world). Lastly, theorists and researchers have proposed types of global citizens (e.g., economic global citizen, moral global citizen). We review research that suggests there may be merit in making such distinctions as the types do correspond with associated behaviors and values.

In Chapter 2, we review research concerning superordinate identities and global orientations that are oftentimes used interchangeably with global citizenship (e.g., cosmopolitan, world citizen, and human). We give attention to the measurement of the construct, the category label used in the measures, and other variables the measures are associated with. While most of the research focuses on identities, we also review global orientations. We draw conclusions about how similar these identities and orientations are based on their associations with shared variables.

In Chapter 3, we review lay conceptualizations of global citizenship and related concepts. There are consistent themes in how participants define and describe global citizens from individuals at different ages, cultural contexts, and roles in life. We discuss the seven most commonly expressed themes, which were found regardless of whether participants have ever heard of global citizenship or if they see themselves as global citizens. Despite the commonality in themes, however, cultural differences are also observed. Lastly, we review lay perceptions of related concepts (e.g., cosmopolitanism, globalization) and find similar themes highlighting their connection to global citizenship.

In Chapter 4, following a review of models and measures of global citizenship, we present Reysen and Katzarska-Miller's (2013a) model of antecedents and outcomes of global citizenship identification. Building upon Shweder's (1990) notion of intentional worlds, the model posits two antecedents to viewing the self as a global citizen—normative environment and global awareness. Based on social identity approach (Tajfel & Turner, 1979; Turner, Hogg, Oakes, Reicher, & Wetherell, 1987), the model shows global citizenship identification predicting six clusters of prosocial values, including (1) intergroup empathy, (2) valuing diversity, (3) social justice beliefs, (4) environmental sustainability, (5) intergroup helping, and (6) felt responsibility to act for the betterment of the world. We review theory and research supporting the model.

In Chapter 5, we review research that focuses on the exploration of variables that influence the model. In particular, we highlight aspects of educational content (e.g., number of words related to global citizenship in class syllabi), educational environment (e.g., professors' opinions of global citizenship), culture (e.g., individuals' perception of culture as dynamic and fluid), media and technology (e.g., social network usage), politics and religion (e.g., liberal political orientation), and perception of self (e.g., possible selves). Across this research we show multiple variables that indirectly predict global citizenship identification and prosocial values. Furthermore, these studies provide consistent empirical support for Reysen and Katzarska-Miller's (2013a) model of antecedents and outcomes of global citizenship identification.

In Chapter 6, we review research examining global citizenship in educational settings. Highlighted in this review are theorized dimensions and goals of global citizenship education, and the reasons some teachers do not incorporate global citizenship in their classes. Review of research providing support, or lack of support, for strategies for greater inclusion of global citizenship in educational contexts, including curriculum changes, language learning, study abroad, service learning, classroom activities, and a whole school approach follows. We note areas of global citizenship education that need further empirical examinations.

In Chapter 7, we review research utilizing global citizenship and related constructs in the field of business. We begin by reviewing global competencies and the impact of a job candidate's global citizen identity in hiring decisions. We also explore research demonstrating the type of employees global citizens are. From a marketing perspective we review research examining consumers' global identities and orientations as factors that influence product evaluation and purchase. Lastly, we review a business' global citizenship—corporate social responsibility—from multiple perspectives (e.g., consumer, employee). As individuals spend a significant amount of time at work, we examine what aspects of the normative environment influence global citizenship.

In the conclusion, we review the positive and negative sides of global citizenship as a concept. Furthermore, we note areas across the literature where further research is needed, as well as some areas that future researchers may explore.

Chapter One

Global Citizen History, Definitions, and Types

In this chapter we present a short history of cosmopolitanism and global citizenship. We start with cosmopolitanism because the concept of global citizenship grew out of the long history of the construct (Schattle, 2008, 2009). Cosmopolitanism as a concept has morphed over the years, and theorists often credit the eventual emergence of global citizenship from the notion of belonging to a common group, a tenet at the heart of cosmopolitanism. We have strived to keep the review short as there are published histories on cosmopolitanism and related concepts that we do not wish to repeat (e.g., Falk, 1993; Heater, 2002; Hicks, 2003; Inglis, 2014; Nussbaum, 1997; Schattle, 2009). However, we would be remiss if we did not present the cliff notes version of the history. A review of past definitions of global citizenship, highlighting commonalities and differences in how theorists and researchers have approached the conceptualization of global citizenship, follows. We include as well theorizing of different types of global citizens as these are often a reflection of the conceptualizations of global citizenship.

A SHORT HISTORY OF COSMOPOLITANISM AND GLOBAL CITIZENSHIP

Intellectuals having a theoretical focus on global rather than local affairs have a long history. When Socrates, a Greek philosopher, was asked where he was from, "he replied not Athens, but the world" and that he "embraced the universe as his city" (Montaigne, 1958, p. 116). Later, another Greek philosopher Diogenes was "asked where he came from, he said, I am a citizen of the world" (Diogenes, 1965, p. 65). The term *cosmopolitan* as used

1

today is credited to him (Bayram, 2015). In more recent times, another philosopher—Kant—noted that "the idea of a law of world citizenship is no high-flown or exaggerated notion" (Kant, 1963, p. 105). Yet, mentions of citizenship beyond one's nation are not limited to classical or modern philosophers. Recently, the former President of the United States, Barack Obama, called himself a citizen of the world (Croucher, 2015).

The concept of global citizenship grew out of the longstanding philosophical tradition of cosmopolitanism. Although there are many definitions of cosmopolitanism, at its core is the notion that an individual is not bound by a place and can live and function in any society (Waldron, 2000). As noted by Inglis (2014) there is a standard presentation of the history of cosmopolitan thought, although rather brief.[1] The story begins with Diogenes and the Cynics who professed being citizens of the world due to feeling at home irrespective of country or place. The notion of cosmopolitanism, however, was not fully formed, before the Cynics were largely absorbed into the Stoics (Zeller, 1889; for a review of the connection between Cynics and Stoics see Dudley, 1937). The Stoics were the first to widely disseminate the notion of cosmopolitanism (Pangle, 1998). The founder of Stoicism was Zeno of Citium, a student of the Cynic Crates, who often praised the moral virtue of the Cynic beliefs (Zeller, 1889). Many of the concepts that the Stoics placed heavy emphasis on such as virtue, moral responsibility, connection with nature, and the interconnectedness and unity of all things in the world (Zeller, 1962) are observed in contemporary conceptualizations of global citizenship. In essence, the message of the Stoics and cosmopolitanism was that while individuals are born in a particular community, they are part of, and share an interconnection with, a larger world which contributes to a felt obligation to other human beings and morals including respect for others (Nussbaum, 1997). However, the Stoic teaching regarding cosmopolitanism changed over time, such as when the school of thought moved to Rome (Arnold, 1971) and took on a more political application (Nussbaum, 1997). Yet, even in its Roman political embodiment, the cosmopolitan ideas were not about the establishment of a world form of government but giving allegiance to "the moral community made up by the humanity of all human beings" (Nussbaum, 1997, p. 8).

Beyond the Stoic cosmopolitanism appearing in legal treatises in Spain (Inglis, 2014), the Enlightenment philosopher Immanuel Kant was the next key figure in the development of the concept. Nussbaum (1997) notes that while there are clear Stoic influences on Kant's notion of cosmopolitanism, there are also pronounced differences. First, a less notable difference, while the Stoics lived in an era with normalized colonialism and their vantage point of cosmopolitanism viewed aggression and oppression as sometimes justified, Kant was strongly opposed to colonialism as morally unacceptable. Second, while the Stoics advanced the notion that there is a wise deity that designed nature for the good of all, Kant explicitly notes uncertainty about the presence of such a deity, removing theology from the notion of cosmopolitanism. However, as Nussbaum notes, theology may have been more relevant to Greek philosophers and the connection to God was dropped or sidelined by the Roman philosophers from which Kant drew inspiration. Regardless, the change indicated that cosmopolitans' respect and cherishment of all things was not because these things were created by God. Third, the Stoics strived to ultimately rid themselves of emotions, believing them to be learned, separate from the self, harmful to decision making, and an impetus to war. Thus, to be a cosmopolitan was also to be without emotion, with the exception of love of humanity, an attitude that should be shared by all. However, Kant viewed emotions as an innate aspect of human nature and instead argued for the suppression of evil in humans. Despite these differences, the core message of Stoic cosmopolitanism remained—the notion that we are all part of the same ingroup (i.e., humans) and have an obligation to respect each other.

The notion of cosmopolitanism then largely rested, with a short-lived appearance during the formation of the United Nations, until the 1990s as academics started debating the concept anew (Inglis, 2014). Meanwhile, a strain of discussions, built upon cosmopolitan notions, emerged within the field of education. These discussions were relatively detached from the prior philosophical and/or political debates and instead focused on global education. Much of the subsequent theorizing of global citizenship was a result of the discussions of global education. As noted by Hicks (2003) global education began in the UK in the 1920s, but did not pick up steam until the 1970s–1980s. Around the same time other nations were also beginning to discuss inclusion of global content into school curricula: Japan in 1954, South Korea and Australia in the 1960s, America in the 1960s–1970s, China in the late 1970s, and Russia in 1991 (Zhao, Lin, & Hoge, 2007). Currently, global citizenship, as part of educational standards, is prevalent in various countries (Canada, Australia, Europe), but not in the United States (Beltramo & Duncheon, 2013). The discussions, or maybe more appropriately debates, in the education literature (mainly in the United States and UK) often revolve around whether or not inclusion of global content is necessary (e.g., Standish, 2012). The terminology used to describe the concept of global education varies, with terms such as *cosmopolitanism, transnationalism, world-mindedness, international citizen,* or *world citizen.* The vast array of synonymous concepts used to define, operationalize, and measure global education leaves the concept ambiguous at best. From cosmopolitanism to global education, a common thread of human interconnectedness impacted the later theory and research of global citizenship.

Although various terms have been used interchangeably in the past, such as *cosmopolitan* and *world citizen,* we sought to discover when the specific term *global citizen* first entered academic circles. We are sure that some industrious researcher will correct us in the future; however, this is what we found. Numerous searches with Google Scholar produced a book review published in 1944 by an author only identified as "R. C." (R. C., 1944). The first sentence, "A distinguished experimental embryologist grapples in this book with the problems of being a global citizen in the 1940's" (p. 118), is the only reference to global citizenship in the review. The book that R. C. reviewed is a collection of essays by Needham (1943) titled *Time, the Refreshing River*. The essays include the author's musings regarding philosophy, science, religion, politics and international events, being part of a larger commonwealth, emergence of a world society, and taking a larger worldview. Interestingly, the term *global citizen* is not used by Needham in the book. From there the term is used sparingly across the years with some time periods showing no reference to global citizens. In the early nineties, academic references of global citizenship increased into the forties and since then the number of books and articles referencing global citizens have increased exponentially (see Figure 1.1).

One potential explanation for the explosive rise in usage of global citizenship by academics is the growing recognition and study of globalization. Indeed, references to globalization begin to increase rapidly starting in the 1990s (Buckner & Russell, 2013) along with the usage of the term *global citizenship*. Globalization brought on discussions regarding post-nation states, universal human rights, and education for an interconnected world. Buckner and Russell (2013), in their analysis of usage of global citizenship in secondary education, history, and social studies textbooks over the years, suggest that global citizenship usage emerged from the rise of discussions and media coverage pertaining to human rights post Cold War. The relationship between global citizenship and human rights is evidenced by the finding that discussion of global citizenship was more prevalent in social studies and civics books which include large sections of discussion regarding human rights. Another potential explanation for this growth is the increased debate of global citizenship in education circles. In 1997, Oxfam, an international organization of charities focused on mitigating poverty, released a guide for teachers wishing to incorporate global citizenship in the classroom. Indeed, the definition of global citizenship provided in the book has become one of the most cited. The push for global education, and related usage of global citizen as a term, has been further bolstered in recent years by educational governing bodies (e.g., UNESCO) adopting the term. Thus, the evidence suggests that both globalization and global education conjointly and reciprocally drove the growth of global citizenship usage in academia.

To summarize, based on the historical review of the literal term, the concept of global citizenship appears to be relatively recent. However, tied to the longstanding discussions and debates of cosmopolitanism and global edu-

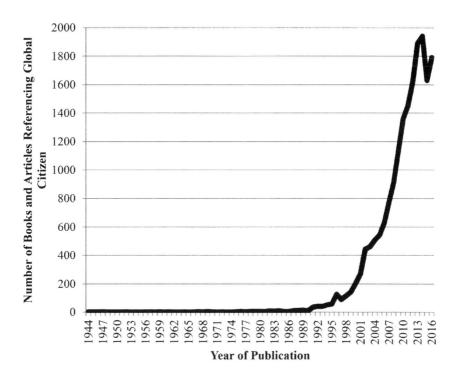

Figure 1.1.   Number of books and articles referencing global citizen by year.

cation, there is a long thread of thought about viewing the self as part of the whole world rather than tied to local or national groups. In recent years, the concept of global citizenship has spread from philosophy and education to areas such as political science and more recently psychology. However, as is common in academic circles, there is a wide variety of conceptualizations and understandings of the notion of global citizenship. This is especially evident across definitions from various academic disciplines.

DEFINITIONS OF GLOBAL CITIZENSHIP

A noted criticism of global citizenship (both term and concept) is that it is meaningless because currently it is impossible to legally be a citizen of the world. Banks (2008) notes that there are three components to citizenship: citizens are (1) granted individual rights (e.g., freedom of speech), (2) given the opportunity to participate in the political process, and (3) granted various forms of aid (e.g., health, education, welfare). Thus, individuals as citizens have particular rights, but also duties, to a government. This strict adherence to the current definition of citizenship leads theorists (this line of argument mainly arises from political scientists) to state that global citizenship is a fallacy due to the impossibility for an individual to be a citizen of every nation (Bowden, 2003), or due to a lack of a single world government (see Dower, 2008). Woolf (2010) notes that when individuals describe themselves as global citizens they are implying that they are open-minded, engaged with other cultures, aware of international interdependence, and respectful of cultural differences, however, he suggests that these are characteristics of a good citizen, with no need to attach global to the phrase. To be a citizen means to be part of a nation or group with rights, duties, boundaries, and outgroups. As there is not a globe in anything other than a geographical sense, people cannot be citizens of that globe. And thus because people cannot legally be citizens of a globe, the term *global citizenship* is faulty. However, even when criticizing this aspect of global citizenship, Bowden and Woolf acknowledge that there is a possibility to conceive of globally minded citizens. This acquiescence is in line with other conceptions that describe global citizens more in terms of attitudes and mindset rather than any notion that they are legally citizens of all nations. In other words, global citizenship is a psychological category or construct, rather than a legal recognition of being a citizen of the world. We certainly would not argue for the legal viewpoint, but criticizing global citizenship on this legalistic argument fails to acknowledge the power of identities in shaping attitudes and behaviors, regardless of fundamentalist adherence to the notion of citizenship.

Due to the various disciplinary backgrounds from which theorists and researchers approach the concept, there are a variety of global citizenship definitions and little consensus as to how to define the construct (Clark & Savage, 2017; Sperandio, Grudzinski-Hall, & Steward-Gambino, 2010). For example, a political scientist may focus on the duties and rights of citizens, an education theorist may focus on skills and competencies, while a forestry researcher may highlight environmentalism and sustainable behaviors. Below are a few examples of definitions of global citizenship from various academic fields.

> . . . a citizen who is influenced by the local as well as global incidents. (political science: Ahmad, 2013, p. 42)

> Global citizenship is the recognition that individuals in the 21st century have rights, duties, identity and the potential for representation on a global scale. (political science: Langran, Langran, & Ozment, 2009)

> . . . a moral disposition which guides individuals' understanding of themselves as members of communities—both on local and global levels—and their responsibility to these communities. (political science: McDougall, 2005, p. 6)

. . . knowledge and skills for social and environmental justice. (sociology: Andrzejewski & Alessio, 1999, p. 7)

. . . the attitude and behavior of holding a commitment to the whole of planet earth and the human family, not in place of, but in addition to and indeed even in priority over, one's more localized self-understandings and loyalties (tourism: Canton, Schott, & Daniele, 2014, p. 124)

Global and moral citizenship refers to the ability to function effectively, efficiently and responsibly as a person in communicating and interacting with people from diverse cultures, backgrounds and authority levels, both globally and locally. (industrial and organizational psychology: Coetzee, 2014a, p. 1087)

. . . global awareness, caring, embracing cultural diversity, promoting social justice and sustainability, and a sense of responsibility to act. (social psychology: Reysen, Larey, & Katzarska-Miller, 2012, p. 29)

Oxfam sees the global citizen as someone who: is aware of the wider world and has a sense of their own role as a world citizen, respects and values diversity, has an understanding of how the world works, is outraged by social injustice, participates in the community at a range of levels, from local to global, is willing to act to make the world a more equitable and sustainable place, takes responsibility for their actions. (education: Oxfam, 2006, p. 3)

. . . global or world citizenship is defined as a set of key elements: knowledge, skills, and attitudes that equip a person to function as a citizen in the globalized world. (curriculum and instruction: Gibson, Rimmington, & Landwehr-Brown, 2008, p. 17)

. . . global citizenship is about individuals' considering themselves as part of this world without losing their national feelings, feeling responsible to other species, and contributing to the world by following the developments and innovations that emerge. (education: Günel & Pehlivan, 2016, p. 54)

. . . a political concept, an active commitment to the world, which all living beings have in common and for which all humans must take responsibility. (education and social work: Castro, Lundgren, & Woodin, 2015, p. 192)

Global citizenship involves the rights and duties of considering oneself as belonging to a global community, in addition to local, regional, and national forms of citizenship. (communication studies: Kuehl, 2011, p. 236)

The above examples demonstrate some of the similarities, but also differences, in how academics define global citizenship. For example, the majority of the quoted definitions speak to a larger responsibility toward the world and all of humanity; meanwhile some specific topics emerge such as skills for environmental sustainability or social justice. This trend is consistent with much of the theorizing on global citizenship with some theorists highlighting single issues such as cultural equality (He, 2005), social justice (Che, Spearman, & Manizade, 2009), environmentalism (Tarrant, 2010), sustainable consumerism (Haugestad, 2004), or civic action (Pitty, Stokes, & Smith, 2008), and others providing multiple aspects. For example, research by Schattle (2008), in which he interviewed over a hundred self-proclaimed global citizens, highlights multiple components of global citizenship such as global awareness, responsibility, participation, cross-cultural empathy, personal achievement, and international mobility. In the construction of their measure of global citizenship, Morais and Ogden (2011) noted three components including social responsibility (justice, interconnectedness, empathy, responsibility), global competence (awareness, intercultural communication, global knowledge), and civic engagement (involvement, activism, political voice). Despite global citizenship's short academic history relative to the notion of cosmopolitanism, a growing convergence of the notion of felt responsibility or an obligation/duty to act for the betterment of the world appears. Needless to say, to date there is yet to emerge an agreed-upon definition of global citizenship.

TYPES OF GLOBAL CITIZENS

Theorists have also suggested different types of global citizens, which complicates the definitional conceptualizations further.[2] For example, Falk (1993) details five categories: (1) global reformers, (2) elite global business people, (3) global environmental managers, (4) politically conscious rationalists, and (5) transnational activists. Ahmad (2013) also suggests five types of global citizens: (1) a person who consumes information about the world through various technologies (e.g., social media), (2) a person who travels to other countries, (3) a person who makes a lasting connection with another country such as through marriage, (4) a person who obtains permanent resident status in another country, and (5) a person who belongs to a larger supranational (e.g., European Union) group and can move freely between nations. While Falk describes different ways in which individuals engage with others in business or political activities, Ahmad's types of global citizens appear to be distinguished by the types of individuals' connection with different nations. Those by Falk, and especially Ahmad, are heavily influenced by the notion of citizenship from a traditional sense (i.e., citizens of a nation state).

While reviewing approaches to the internationalization of higher education, Stein (2015) notes four positions, or types, of global citizenships: (1) entrepreneurial (competition in world market), (2) liberal humanist (recognition of humanity), (3) anti-oppressive (inclusion of discussions of power and opposition to top-down globalization), and (4) incommensurable (similar to anti-oppressive, but without any particular desired outcomes). Schattle (2005) also notes the divergence of discussion of global citizenship, which he categorized into two types, the first concerning a civic republican discourse (with topics including awareness, empathy, and responsibility) and the second a libertarian discourse (with topics including global mobility and competitiveness). To highlight how a country can express one of these views, Schattle (2014, 2015) reviewed public discourse in South Korea to find that there is a general promotion of a top-down approach to global citizenship that emphasizes national advancement rather than moral obligations to the rest of humanity. Thus, in the South Korean national discourse, global citizenship is approached from a libertarian view. The civic republican and libertarian perspectives distinguish global citizenship along moral lines. The former includes felt responsibility and promotion of human rights, similar to Stein's liberal humanist and anti-oppressive, while the latter links global citizenship with economic global competition, similar to Stein's entrepreneurial. Both are worldviews not necessarily tied to strict legal perspectives of global citizenship.

Other theorists have conceptualized global citizen types along attitudinal perspectives. For example, Veugelers, de Groot, and Nollet (2014) suggest three types: (1) an open global citizenship in which people recognize greater interconnectedness of the world, (2) moral global citizenship which focuses on equality, human rights, and felt responsibility for the world, and (3) social-political global citizenship in which people work politically for equality and appreciation for cultural diversity. Heater (1997) suggests four categories, of world citizenship (note the term) that vary with respect to specificity: (1) felt interconnection to others, (2) felt responsibility to act for the planet (e.g., working with an NGO), (3) adherence to international laws (e.g., human rights), and (4) support for a world government. Although there are aspects of these types of global citizenship that share similarities with the more legalistic notions such as those proposed by Ahmad (2013), these types do not necessarily suggest legal citizenship, but rather focus on the different attitudes or degrees of individuals' participation and engagement with the world.

After interviewing 29 undergraduate students at a U.S. university who had participated in study abroad, Streitwieser and Light (2016) propose five different types of global citizens that differ in terms of increasing complexity. The first type—global existence—reflects the acknowledgment that everyone is a human being, born on Earth, and are therefore global citizens. The second type, termed *global acquaintance*, concerns international travel through either family connections or work. The third type—global openness—reflects an inclusive view of others along with a desire to seek mutual understanding. The fourth, termed *global participation*, reflects individuals who believe that active engagement with other cultures and peoples is required to be considered a global citizen. Lastly, the fifth type—global commitment—concerns individuals' commitment, and felt responsibility, for action to improve the world as a whole. Although the researchers used the term *types* to describe characteristics of global citizenship, we view this hierarchical and increasingly complex description to better reflect degree of global citizenship embodiment. In other words, students begin with global awareness (Type 1) and end with a felt responsibility to act for the betterment of the world (Type 5).

Two studies conducted with South Korean school teachers distinguished between types of global citizenship using cluster analysis of attitudes. First, in a study of 253 South Korean secondary school teachers, Seo (2016) examined teachers' perceptions of global citizenship. Participants completed 15 items measuring global citizenship developed by Morais and Ogden (2011) that purportedly taps three factors (social responsibility, global competence, global civic engagement; see Chapter 4 for further discussion of this measure). Following cluster analysis, Seo proposes the existence of six types of global citizens. The types include: (1) sociable citizens (high intercultural communication skill but low level of global knowledge; 8.91% of sample), (2) responsible citizens (low communication but high responsibility; 16.19% of sample), (3) anti-intercultural citizens (low communication but high civic engagement; 13.77% of sample), (4) less interested citizens (low on responsibility, communication, knowledge, and doesn't particularly engage in civic activism; 31.17% of sample), (5) anti-political citizens (high civic engagement but low political voice; 12.96% of sample), and (6) active citizens (high engagement and intercultural communication skills; 17% of sample). Second, Cheon (2017) surveyed 300 primary school teachers in Seoul, South Korea, to also examine teachers' perceptions of global citizenship. The researcher included 18 of Morais and Ogden's (2011) global citizen scale items. Based on cluster analysis results of those items, Cheon proposed six types of global citizens. The types included: (1) global leader (high on civic engagement, responsibility, and competence; 14.4% of sample), (2) indifferent elite (high on competence but low on engagement; 14.6% of sample), (3) non-informed activist (high engagement but low on responsibility and competence; 19.9% of sample), (4) incompetent citizen (high on responsibility but low on engagement and competence; 9.6% of sample), (5) pessimist (moderate levels on the three dimensions; 18.3% of sample), and (6) outsider (low on all three dimensions; 16.6% of sample).

Both Seo (2016) and Cheon (2017) conducted both factor analysis and cluster analysis on Morais and Ogden's (2011) measure. Although the original Morais and Ogden measure resulted in three factors (social responsibility, global competence, global civic engagement), Seo observed five factors and

Cheon observed four factors (which was reduced to three after removing two items that showed cross-loading). One plausible explanation for the different factor structure is that Seo used 15 items and Cheon used 18 items out of the 30 original items. A second plausible reason is that the original measure was developed with U.S. college student participants, while these studies were conducted with South Korean primary and secondary school teachers. As discussed in more detail in Chapter 3, the cultural context and participant characteristics influence their understandings of global citizenship. Additionally, both studies show six clusters or types of global citizens. However, although the samples are relatively similar, the clusters differ between the studies. In both studies the majority of participants are categorized into types that do not strongly endorse values related to global citizenship, at least the way Morais and Ogden conceptualize and operationalize the construct. Thus, across two samples in the same region of the world, different types are observed; however, both showing the majority of teachers falling into a disinterested or uninformed type of global citizenship.

In the most detailed description of global citizen types, Oxley and Morris (2013) reviewed prior theorizing and arrived at eight different types. The types are broken down into two broader categories representing cosmopolitan-based and advocacy-based types. The cosmopolitan types include: (1) political global citizenship with a focus on the relationship between the person and state, (2) moral global citizenship with a focus on human rights, (3) economic global citizenship with a focus on international development, and (4) cultural global citizenship with a focus on cultural symbols that are similar and different across societies. The advocacy types include: (5) social global citizenship with a focus on interconnectedness of all peoples, (6) critical global citizenship with a focus on challenging oppression and social inequalities, (7) environmental global citizenship with a focus on environmental sustainability, and (8) spiritual global citizenship with a focus on emotional connections between individuals. In recent research attempting to empirically measure endorsement of the eight types, Katzarska-Miller and Reysen (in press) using U.S. participants found that the types are distinguishable with the exception of the social dimension. The items measuring social global citizenship loaded on multiple factors showing the concept of interconnectedness implied in the social dimension is a component of multiple dimensions of global citizenship.

To summarize, building upon the diversity of definitions, there also exists a diversity of different types of global citizens. Theorists have proposed global citizen types according to roles in society (e.g., Falk, 1993), how one interacts with the world (e.g., Ahmad, 2013), moral versus economic values (e.g., Schattle, 2014), the degree of commitment or action for the world (e.g., Streitwieser & Light, 2016), and endorsement of attitudes related to global citizenship (e.g., Seo, 2016). The different types add to the complexity of understandings of global citizenship. In almost half of the reviewed studies, the most divergent global citizen type is the economic one. This type is distinguished, as suggested by Schattle (2005), by a focus on global mobility and competitiveness in the world market rather than a focus on moral values such as empathy and responsibility. Indeed, Katzarska-Miller and Reysen (in press) find that economic global citizen type is the most distinct compared to the others, evidenced by positive correlations with ethnocentrism, right-wing authoritarianism, and valuing tradition, whereas these values are not associated with the other global citizen types. The types appear to be meaningful in predicting related attitudes and behaviors. The results of Katzarska-Miller and Reysen (in press) show that the different types are related to endorsed behaviors and values that tend to match the type. For example, political global citizenship is associated with activism within the political arena and endorsement of values of law and order, while critical global citizenship is related to battling oppression and supporting civil rights issues. The variety of types reviewed begs the question of whether there should be a single definition of global citizenship. Is it even possible to define the construct? Are all these different types parts of the larger construct of global citizenship, or are these types constructs on their own?

CONCLUSION

In the present chapter we provided a short history of cosmopolitanism and global citizenship. Growing out of the long-standing philosophical tradition of cosmopolitanism, the concept of global citizenship with an emphasis on felt responsibility to act for the betterment of the world has expanded exponentially in the recent decades. However, the proliferation of global citizenship across academic disciplines, most notably education, has spawned a variety of definitions, measures, and conceptualizations. This diversity in perspectives has generated bountiful but fragmented and ambiguous knowledge base of theory and research. Adding upon this problem is the variety of purported types of global citizens. Ranging from activity-based to attitude-based distinctions between different types further muddies the water regarding what global citizenship is and how best to measure the construct. From the root of viewing the self as part of a larger community to including a variety of values and attitudes, such as social justice and environmentalism, the picture of global citizenship is only beginning to be better understood in academia. Moving one step further on the confusion ladder with respect to the current disarray that is global citizenship theorizing and research, in the next chapter we provide a selective review of research of synonymous terms used in the literature. For example, what is the difference between a global citizen and a cosmopolitan? Although reviewing research of synonymous terms may seem to perpetuate the confusion surrounding global citizenship, we see it as an opportunity to examine the similarities and differences among the various concepts.

NOTES

1. Inglis (2014) further argues that the standard narrative of cosmopolitan history of Greece–Rome–Enlightenment–1945–Now, overlooks sources of cosmopolitan ideas both within and outside of the Eurocentric bias of the standard account.

2. In the literature, some theorists use global citizen types and others use types of global citizenship. Although one can make the argument that those are distinctive concepts, we view the two as interchangeable because in both cases individuals can be placed, or place themselves, into a category (i.e., type).

Chapter Two

Superordinate Identities and Global Orientations

As noted in the previous chapter, the notion of global citizenship grew from the concept of cosmopolitanism, or the larger idea of belonging to something greater than one's nation state. Cosmopolitan ideals also gave rise to a variety of other concepts that on occasion are either differentiated from or used interchangeably with global citizenship (Singh & Jing, 2013). Terms such as "citizen of the world", "global identity", or "human" are commonly used to represent similar concepts, yet they may not mean the same thing. For example, Clifford and Montgomery (2014) suggest that the key distinction between cosmopolitan and global citizen is the sense of moral responsibility to others. While cosmopolitans tend to travel internationally and are knowledgeable about the world and other cultures, global citizens feel a moral obligation to help others in the world. Similarly, de Jong (2013) notes that while cosmopolitanism is characterized by a disposition of openness to other cultures that transforms into practice, global citizenship is characterized by recognition of the complexity of the world that transforms into a felt obligation to act responsibly. Scholte (2014) suggests that global citizenship emerged to fill in the gaps and fix the shortcomings of past conceptions of cosmopolitanism. In this chapter we review research, examining constructs similar to global citizenship. We have divided the chapter into two parts by grouping the constructs representing identities, and values/orientations. We should add a note of caution that some measures, which we interpret to measure identity, are not described by the researchers as such. Yet, they do represent superordinate identities that are measured (at least partially) by identification with the group.

SUPERORDINATE IDENTITIES

The notion of superordinate identity emerges within the framework of social identity and self-categorization theories (Tajfel & Turner, 1979; Turner et al., 1987). This framework argues that identities fall into one of three levels of inclusiveness: personal identity (e.g., me vs. person next to me), intermediate (e.g., male vs. female), and superordinate (humans vs. other forms of life). In the original work (Turner et al., 1987), human was designated as superordinate identity because all humans are included in the group. However, any identity that is inclusive of various subgroups (e.g. American is both inclusive of Texans and New Yorkers) is a superordinate identity to the subgroup ones, meaning that any intermediate can be a superordinate identity. Identities can shift depending on the context in which a person is embedded, and which identity becomes cognitively activated depends on an interaction of the person and the environment. Furthermore, people can vary in their degree of connection to a group (i.e., ingroup identification). When a group identity is salient, individuals will depersonalize, or self-stereotype, in line with the content of the group. Ingroup identification predicts greater adherence to the prototypical, or normative, content of the group. All of the identities that we review below are superordinate identities because they are inclusive in that they span across all subgroup identities (e.g., gender, ethnicity, nationality).

World Citizenship

In constructing a global-mindedness scale within the Thai socio-cultural context, Lawthong (2003) identified a dimension, which she termed "world citizenship". She defined it as "feeling that oneself is a citizen of the global society in addition to being a member of his [sic] society or country. One should behave as a good citizen, view people of all nations and languages as equal, realize the value of fellow human beings as well as respect their rights and freedom" (p. 60). In empirical research the best exemplar of the notion of world citizenship is assessed in the World Values Survey (WVS). The WVS is a large-scale survey with participants from numerous countries that is conducted every few years. Since 2005 the survey has included an item asking participants to rate their agreement with the statement "I see myself as a world citizen" (from 1 = *strongly agree* to 4 = *strongly disagree*).

As the data from the WVS is publicly available, researchers have utilized this dataset to examine a variety of topics. WVS data have shown that identifying as a world citizen is associated with higher education, income, and younger age (Birdsall, Meyer, & Sowa, 2013; Smith et al., 2016; Wang, 2015). However, nations with greater affluence and globalization show age and education as stronger predictors of identification with world citizens (Zhou, 2016). Beja (2013) found that citizens in both rich and poor countries view themselves as citizens of the world and that identification with world citizens predicts endorsement of mitigating global problems (e.g., child mortality rates, ensuring primary education, housing for the poor). Similarly, Alvarez, Boussalis, Merolla, and Peiffer (in press) using WVS data from 12 countries found greater identification to predict more positive attitudes toward humanitarian aid for other countries.

Other researchers have also noted the association between identification with the world and endorsement of aid for both people and the environment. Contorno (2012) examined data from seven industrialized Western nations to explore predictors of environmental attitudes. The world citizen item was combined with other items (e.g., attitudes toward humanitarian aid, attitudes toward immigrants) to form a cosmopolitan index. Higher scores on this index were positively associated with concern for the environment. Similarly, Rosenmann, Reese, and Cameron (2016) found identification is associated with a willingness to donate or direct tax money toward environmental causes. Further research shows that identification with world citizens is associated with support for the United Nations (Diven & Constantelos, 2011), membership in charitable organizations (Longhofer, 2011), happiness and life satisfaction for Australians (Vinson & Ericson, 2014), and endorsement of postmaterialism values emphasizing protection of freedoms (Kennedy, 2013).

In an effort to examine values related to viewing the self as a world citizen using WVS data, Bayram (2015) examined Schwartz's (1992) 10 universal values as predictors of identification with world citizens. The researcher notes that over 30% of respondents indicate that they strongly identify as citizens of the world. Although, Bayram treats the world citizen identity label as synonymous with cosmopolitan, for the present context we should note that the survey measured identification with world citizens, not cosmopolitanism per se. The results show that the values predicting identification with world citizens differed depending on the country under investigation. For example, universalism is an important predictor in Europe, while resistance to conformity is the strongest predictor in the United States. This suggests that the meaning of world citizen may change depending on the cultural context. Additionally, values related to self-transcendence, self-enhancement (excluding the power value), and openness to change were strong predictors of viewing oneself as a world citizen overall. Notably, these are similar to the values related to cosmopolitanism discussed later (Cleveland, Erdoğan, Arikan, & Poyraz, 2012).

Thus, across the research utilizing the WVS, self-categorization as a world citizen is associated with desire to help others, environmental sustainability, and endorsement of supranational organizations. However, there is some variability depending on the country sample under examination. What appears to be consistent is that individuals across various countries endorse and identify with world citizens. These individuals tend to be younger, with a liberal political orientation. Furthermore, identification is associated with prosocial causes. Based on the research in the chapters that follow, world citizen identification appears to be very similar to global citizen identification.

Identification with the World as a Whole

Buchan and colleagues (2011) asked participants from six different countries to complete a token assignment task in which the outcome would help themselves, their local community, or people in the world. Following this behavioral task they completed measures tapping ingroup identification with their local community, nation, and the world as a whole (e.g., "How strongly do you define yourself as a member of the world as a whole?"), as well as concern for global issues (e.g., global warming, bird flu). Identification with the world as a whole was associated with greater world contributions (i.e., token task) and concern for global issues. Buchan et al.'s identification with the world as a whole measure also was positively related to anger about a social injustice, identification with a campaign and online behaviors related to the injustice in a sample of Australians (Thomas et al., 2015).

Using a somewhat similar measure assessing attachment to local, national (Australia), and global places ("To what extent do you feel a weak or a strong sense of belonging to the earth/the whole world"), Walker, Leviston, Price, and Devine-Wright (2015) examined models of place attachment (global, nation, local), predicting environmental concern mediated by relative deprivation (felt sense of injustice about the current state of the environment). A difference score of global over local attachment predicted environmental policy support through relative deprivation. A difference score of global over nation attachment predicted both individual and collective environmental behaviors through relative deprivation. In effect, feeling a sense of belongingness to the whole world over less inclusive identities (local, nation) predicted greater support for environmental actions mediated by relative deprivation.

Similar to identification with world citizens, the above studies demonstrate that identification with the world as a whole is related to prosocial outcomes. The difference between the WVS and the above research is the category label used (i.e., world citizen vs. world as whole). However, the results are consistent in that identification was related to concern for global issues and environmental sustainability.

Global Identity

Türken and Rudmin (2013) define global identity as "the notion of belonging to the whole world rather than some narrow territorial part of it. It is the idea of identifying with all human kind. It can also be understood as consciousness of an international society or global community transcending national boundaries, without necessarily negating the importance of state, nation or domestic society" (p. 74). The researchers developed a 10-item measure of global identity tapping factors related to cultural openness and non-nationalism. The researchers reviewed past measures of cosmopolitanism, examined open-ended responses regarding the definition of global identity and characteristics of people with weak and strong global identities, and whittled down the initial items to a final scale with participants sampled in three countries (Norway, Turkey, United States). The final measure showed a mix of items that reflect identification from a social identity perspective (e.g., "I identify with a world community") along with items concerning ethnocentrism, nationalism, and desire to learn about other cultures. Global identity was positively correlated with cosmopolitan behaviors (e.g., reading international news and foreign magazines) and number of languages spoken by participants. Subsequent research shows that global identity is negatively correlated with social dominance orientation, right-wing authoritarianism, and conscientiousness, and positively correlated with positive attitudes and efforts to integrate ethnic minorities, openness/intellect, agreeableness, and social desirability (Phelps, Eilertsen, Türken, & Ommundsen, 2011).

In an examination of the reliability and validity of Türken and Rudmin's (2013) global identity measure in Nigeria, Edwin, Obi-Nwosu, Atalor, and Okoye (2016) found the scale to be positively related to openness to experience, moral reasoning, and self-reported altruism. While developing a measure of acculturation in India, Ozer and Schwartz (2016) observed that the openness subscale of the global identity measure was positively correlated with Western and hybrid styles of acculturation. Thus, in this particular cultural context, openness reflects an enjoyment and appreciation for Western and hybrid (i.e., local and Western) artifacts (e.g., food, friends, music, celebrations). Kunst and Sam (2013) examined associations between experienced discrimination, ethnic and global identity, sociocultural adaptation, and well-being in a sample of European Muslims. Global identity (only the five items that tapped identification with the world) was positively related to experienced discrimination, perceived marginalization as an acculturation strategy, and life satisfaction, and negatively associated with stress. Furthermore, high scores on marginalization and global identity predicted better sociocultural adaptation. In other words, global identity moderated the negative relationship between marginalization and adaptation.

Using different measures of "global identity," other researchers have found comparable results with respect to the association between global identity and prosocial values. Barth, Jugert, Wutzler, and Fritsche (2015) examined predictors of solidarity with people impacted by climate change and collective action intentions in German samples. Global identity (e.g., "I feel connected to all humanity") and a belief that climate change is morally unjust predicted solidarity, which in turn predicted willingness to engage in collective action for environmental causes. In a study of antecedents and consequences of global identity, Renger and Reese (2017) combined items to form a "global identity" scale in a sample of German participants. We use quotes here as the measure of global identity contained four items and referenced categories including global citizen, all humans of one world, whole earth, and part of the earth. The model of antecedents and consequences contained one antecedent (equality-based respect) and one consequence (intention to engage in environmental activism).

The researchers above use the term "global identity" to refer to their constructs, yet the items used contain category labels ranging from global citizen to world community and all humans of one world. Because of this, these measures are in an ambiguous position with respect to what category label or group is being referenced and rated by participants. Despite this, the results suggest that global identity, at least as measured above, is similar to identification with world citizens and the world as a whole in tapping a superordinate global identity showing positive correlations with prosocial values.

Identification with the World Community

Reese, Proch, and Cohrs (2013) introduced a five-item (e.g., "I feel strongly connected to the members of the world community") measure of identification with the world community (defined as "the exhaustive ingroup of humanity" p. 6). Identification with the world community among German participants was positively related to agreeableness, openness to new experiences, justice sensitivity (e.g., "I am upset when someone is treated worse than others"), and behavioral intentions to reduce global inequality. The measure was negatively correlated with social dominance orientation, right-wing authoritarianism, and justice of inequality (perception that inequality is just). To examine the relationship between identification with the world community and ethical consumptive practices, Reese and Kohlmann (2015) asked participants to complete measures related to identification and justice. Following a filler task, participants were offered a reward for participating; a choice between a regular sized mainstream chocolate bar or a smaller sized fair trade chocolate. Participants who highly identified with the world community were more likely to choose the fair trade over the mainstream chocolate. Furthermore, in two separate mediation analyses, attitudes toward global injustice mediated the relationship between identification with the world community and choice of chocolate, as well as behavioral intentions to mitigate global inequality.

The above findings add to the previously discussed research showing superordinate global identities as negatively related to authoritarianism and positively related to prosocial values and behaviors. In other words, identification with the world community shows a similar pattern of associations as global identity, identification with the world as a whole, and world citizenship.

Identification with all Humanity

Based on prior theorizing by Adler (1927/1954) and Maslow (1954) regarding a oneness with humanity and self-actualizing reflecting human kinship, McFarland, Webb, and Brown (2012) published the Identification with All Humanity (IWAH) Scale. The scale consists of nine items assessing an active caring and concern for others. In a series of ten studies the measure was negatively correlated with ethnocentrism, social dominance orientation, blind patriotism, and ethnocentric valuation of human life, and positively related to empathy, impression management, moral identity, social interest, globalism, support for human rights, positive emotionality, openness to experience, conscientiousness, agreeableness, extraversion, honesty-morality, universalism, global humanitarian knowledge, selection of articles related to humanitarian issues, and donations to charities. In effect, identification with all humanity was positively related to a variety of prosocial and negatively associated with nationalistic values and behaviors. Despite the consistency in the results across the ten studies, issues concerning the measure were observed by other researchers.

In the first two studies, McFarland et al. (2012) reported the measure as unidimensional. In the remaining studies, the researchers removed an item and replaced it with a different one and did not report any factor analyses with the new item in the measure. Reese, Proch, and Finn (2015) examined the factor structure of the published version of the IWAH Scale (with the replaced item) in two studies with German samples. Rather than a single factor, a two-factor solution was found to fit best. Additionally, one item double loaded and was dropped from analyses. Based on prior research concerning the measurement of ingroup identification from a social identity perspective (Leach et al., 2008), the researchers termed the two factors global self-investment and global self-definition.[1] Compared to the global self-investment dimension, the global self-definition factor showed significant but weaker correlations with variables such as empathy, right-wing authoritarianism, social dominance orientation, and moral identity. This suggests that the associations observed by McFarland et al. (2012) may have been driven by the items constituting the global self-investment dimension rather than global self-definition.

Furthermore, in three studies with U.S. participants, Reysen and Hackett (2016) also observed the same two-factor structure, with the same one item that double loaded (this item should be dropped in any future research using the IWAH). However, the researchers renamed the factors Adler/Maslow (rather than global self-investment) and ingroup identification (rather than global self-definition). The ingroup identification items are similar to those used previously to measure identification (from a social identity perspective), while the Adler/Maslow items best reflect outcomes of ingroup identification (e.g., commitment, loyalty). Similar to Reese et al. (2015), the ingroup identification factor, in comparison with the Adler/Maslow factor, showed significantly weaker correlations with various prosocial measures and scales used by McFarland et al. (2012). Furthermore, in a series of regressions, the Adler/Maslow factor predicted the prosocial measures while the ingroup identification factor did not. In effect, the IWAH Scale contains two dimensions, with one item that should be removed. Global self-investment or Adler/Maslow is largely driving the positive relations with prosocial outcomes that were observed in prior studies. An additional ambiguity concerning IWAH is the category label being examined. Participants are asked to rate the items that refer to "people all over the world," "all humans everywhere," "people anywhere in the world," "a responsible citizen of the world," "all mankind," and "people all over the world." Thus, across the different items there is not a clear or consistent identity category that participants are rating. The ingroup identification subscale does contain items from a social identity perspective, although McFarland et al. (2012) do not conceptualize them as such.

In what follows is a brief review of correlates of IWAH. We have omitted studies that presented the IWAH correlations controlling for identification with nation and community (i.e., we only include studies where raw scores were reported). McFarland and colleagues (2012) suggested that controlling for community/nation scores would provide a more accurate measure of IWAH. However, controlling for only two subgroups, or any specific groups, within the larger humanity group should be done only if there is a very specific reason to do so. All of the research that follows uses the unidimensional measure of IWAH. Most researchers have presented the results with the two factors combined into a unidimensional scale with the double-loaded item. It appears the only researcher to have acknowledged and begun analyzing IWAH as two factors and stopped conducting partial correlations is McFarland himself (McFarland & Hornsby, 2015).

The unidimensional IWAH has been shown to be positively associated with intrinsic and orthodox religious orientation, extraversion, agreeableness, openness, social dominance orientation (Sparks & Gore, 2017), expansive moral concern for others (Crimston, Bain, Hornsey, & Bastian, 2016), intergroup forgiveness (Hamer, Penczek, & Bilewicz, 2017), a liberal political orientation (Iyer, Koleva, Graham, Ditto, & Haidt, 2012), empathetic concern, universal orientation, willingness to control prejudice, willingness to volunteer to combat Ebola (Stürmer, Rohmann, & van der Noll, 2016), cosmopolitan helping (Faulkner, 2018), need for uniqueness (McCutcheon et al., 2015), perceived similarity between humans and animals, solidarity with animals, inclusion of animals in the self, and engagement with natural, artistic, and moral beauty (Diessner, Iyer, Smith, & Haidt, 2013). The IWAH is also positively related to religious and spiritual beliefs, and negatively related to critical reasoning (Jack, Friedman, Boyatzis, & Taylor, 2016). Furthermore, travel abroad and frequent interaction with outgroup members predicts higher IWAH (Belt, 2016).

Although, there are theoretical and empirical issues with the IWAH measure, identification is positively related to prosocial values and behaviors. However, researchers should heed the warnings regarding how to use the measure (McFarland & Hornsby, 2015; Reese et al., 2015; Reysen & Hackett, 2016) to ensure consistency in measurement and reporting and interpretation of results in future research. In general, the Adler/Maslow factor is more strongly related to prosocial values compared to the identification with humanity factor.

Human Identity

Human identity has received the most attention within psychology compared to other superordinate identities (see Reysen & Katzarska-Miller, 2015). Much of this research shows rather mixed conclusions concerning whether or not thinking of the self as a human (i.e., human identity salience) predicts prosocial outcomes. The research focusing on human identity tends to fall into three categories: prejudice reduction, intergroup forgiveness, and images of humanity.

Prejudice Reduction

Following a social identity perspective, Nickerson and Louis (2008) examined Australian attitudes toward asylum seekers and the associations with identification with national and human identity. The results showed that identification with humans is positively related to more positive attitudes toward asylum seekers. For example, greater identification with humans is related to a greater likelihood of writing a letter to the government opposing a tougher stance on asylum seekers. In a qualitative study, Antonis, Lia, Nikos, Antonis, and Pavlos (2012) examined the utilization of spontaneous recategorization rhetorical strategies by Greek participants regarding immigrants to Greece. Results showed that participants use human identity to signal a common ingroup shared between native Greek respondents and the new immigrants. Yet, beyond acknowledgment of a superordinate group, participants also note differences of ethnic/national origins of immigrants suggesting some may be more Greek than others. As noted by the researchers, use of a common ingroup by these advantaged participants may have been utilized to buffer against accusations of prejudice. Palasinski, Abell, and Levine (2012), in a qualitative study of Polish Catholic men residing in the United Kingdom, indicate that the spontaneous use of a common humanity can be used to avoid any negative self-representations of prejudicial responses. In other words, evoking common humanity is less about actual attitude change and more about self-presentation.

Intergroup Forgiveness

Wohl, Branscombe, and Klar (2006) summarized research showing that when harmed and perpetrator groups are recategorized into a more inclusive ingroup, the level of collective guilt among members of the former perpetrator group increases. On the other hand this recategorization leads to more forgiveness on the part of the formerly harmed group. In a series of studies, Wohl and Branscombe (2005) showed that among Jewish participants, thinking of oneself as a human (vs. subgroup identity) leads to greater forgiveness toward Germans for the Holocaust. Furthermore, the association between categorization (subgroup vs. human) and outcomes (assignment of collective guilt, forgiveness) is mediated by perceptions of the pervasiveness of genocide. In effect, salience of human identity leads to greater forgiveness because individuals view genocide as pervasive and not necessarily linked to Germans. This outcome was also replicated in a different historically victimized group (i.e., Native Canadians) with the mediator of the perception of the pervasiveness of intergroup harm. Similar results were obtained by Greenaway, Quinn, and Louis (2011), who found that among indigenous Australians, appealing to common humanity increased forgiveness of the perpetrator group (White Australians); however it also led to lower intentions of the harmed group to engage in collective action. This research shows that saliency of human identity can have positive outcomes (i.e., intergroup forgiveness), but also lessen one's willingness to act for social change.

In a related set of studies, Greenaway, Louis, and Wohl (2012) examined a perpetrator group's (White Australians) expectations of forgiveness when either human or subgroup identity was salient. The results across their studies showed that perpetrator group members reported higher expectations of forgiveness when thinking of harmed members as fellow humans rather than as members of a different group. However, the results also showed that higher expectations for forgiveness interacted with the temporal distance of the wrongdoing. When the wrongdoing was temporally close, categorization had no effect. However, when the wrongdoing was temporally distant, human categorization led to higher expectations for forgiveness. Morton and Post-mes (2011a) also found that perceived shared humanity with a harmed group (Africans) led British participants to experience less collective guilt and have stronger expectations for forgiveness. In a follow-up study, these effects occurred only when the perpetrator group was seen as unwilling to apologize for the harm doing. Together, this research shows that viewing the self as a human (vs. subgroup) is associated with greater forgiveness; however there are caveats, which suggest less than noble intentions related to forgiveness.

Images of Humanity

In the majority of the above studies, the concept of humanity is perceived in rather malevolent terms. For example, Wohl and Branscombe's (2005) results indicate that members of harmed groups were more likely to forgive genocide when categorizing on a human level, because they perceived genocide not as something unique done by Germans to Jews, but as a more pervasive phenomenon among the category of all humans. However, human nature can also be perceived in more benevolent terms. Luke and Maio (2009) conducted a study suggesting that perceptions of humanity can have implications for intergroup relations. They developed a scale (humanity-esteem) measuring evaluations of humanity (positive and negative). They found that participants with high humanity-esteem (i.e., more positive evaluation of human nature) exhibited lower levels of group differentiation. Similarly, drawing upon a social identity approach, the content of identity and its manifestations is influenced by group norms (Turner et al., 1987). Thus, positive and negative norms will result in corresponding relatively positive and negative outcomes (e.g., intergroup relations). Making human identity salient and manipulating the content of what it means to be human will moderate the effects of human identity on intergroup outcomes. For example, Greenaway and Louis (2010) examined the effects of categorization of human vs. intergroup level (White and Indigenous Australians) and images of human nature (benevolent vs. hostile) on perpetrators of historical atrocities. Surprisingly, it was the combination of hostile view with salient shared humanity that led to less perceived legitimacy of inequality and less prejudice toward the harmed group. The second effect was mediated by the perception that intergroup inequality is less legitimate. In a follow-up study, the effect was replicated when the intentions of the perpetrator were seen as unambiguously negative.

In a similar study, Morton and Postmes (2011b) examined human category salience and images of humanity on intergroup harm. In two studies British participants thought about acts of terrorism against their ingroup (Study 1) or the torture of Iraqi prisoners by British soldiers (Study 2). The image of human nature (benevolent vs. malevolent) and categorization (human vs. intergroup) was manipulated. Similar to Greenaway and Louis' (2010) findings, it was the combination of malevolent image of humanity with shared humanity that resulted in participants' more lenient attitudes toward terrorism (Study 1) and less guilt and greater justification of torture (Study 2). Both Greenaway and Louis' (2010) and Morton and Postmes' (2011b) studies suggest that the image of humanity matters. When thinking of humanity in negative terms and sharing a human category with previous outgroups, both ingroup and outgroup negative actions may be perceived as normal and legitimate. When thinking of humanity in benevolent terms, negative actions may not be legitimized to the same degree when human category is made salient.

Together, the research examining human identity shows a mixture of results pointing to both positive (e.g., intergroup forgiveness, prejudice reduction) and negative (e.g., normalization of genocide, lenient attitude toward terrorism and torture) outcomes. It is important to note that researchers examining human identity often manipulate salience rather than measure identification with humans. Measuring identification with human identity may show different relationships with the above constructs. For example, while Wohl and Branscombe (2005) show that making human identity salient results in greater intergroup forgiveness, Reysen and Katzarska-Miller (2017a) find that identification with humans shows not statistically significant to small correlations with measures of intergroup forgiveness. Compared to the other identities discussed in this chapter, human appears to differ the most with respect to associations with prosocial values and behaviors. We suspect that human identity is more ambiguous for participants or does not have as clearly defined group content. As the research on images of humanity demonstrates, being human can be seen in two opposing ways (negative or positive) that have very distinct content from each other. A related ambiguity is the potential outgroup for human identity. Haslam and Loughnan (2014) proposed two ways in which humanness can be defined. One is in opposition to inanimate objects (e.g., robots) and the other is non-human animals. This does not appear to be the case for the other identities discussed. Thus, human identity seems to hold a unique position within the superordinate identities.

Psychological Sense of Global Community

In samples collected in the United States, Malsch (2005) adapted a prior measure of psychological sense of community (Chavis, Hogge, McMillan, & Wandersman, 1986) to examine antecedents and outcomes of one's psychological sense of a global community (PSGC)—"a transcendent community that reflects a psychological process involving a sense of connectedness that extends beyond local communities and personal relationships" (p. 12). Based on the factor structure of the original measure, the PSGC was predicted to contain four dimensions: membership, influence, needs fulfillment, and emotional connection. However, only one factor emerged. Universal orientation, empathetic concern, and humanitarian values predicted PSGC, and PSGC mediated the association between these variables and prosocial outcomes (e.g., activism, civic participation). McFarland and Hornsby (2015) also examined the factor structure and correlates of PSGC. They found three factors: sense of world community, global fatalism, and human similarity. It should be noted that global fatalism had only one item, and human similarity had two items. The remaining 11 items loaded on the first factor. Combining all items in a single factor, the researchers found that PSGC was positively correlated with endorsement of human rights.

Using two items from the PSGC measure ("I feel a sense of connection to people all over the world, even if I don't know them personally," "I feel a sense of belonging to a human or world community, one that extends beyond where I live and includes more than just people I know"), Hackett (2014) surveyed attendees and protesters of a religious event. This short measure, collapsed across sampled groups, was positively correlated with valuing equality and social justice, liberal political orientation, and negatively related to social dominance orientation, and endorsement of entitlement reform (e.g., social security reform) and conservative concerns (e.g., illegal immigration). Hackett, Omoto, and Matthews (2015) used four items from Malsch's (2005) PSGC. The measure contained the two items from Hackett (2014) along with two additional items ("People all over the world have a shared fate," "At the end of the day, all people living in the world want the same things"). The PSGC mediated the relationship between self-transcendence values and human rights concern and involvement.

Although the original research on PSGC was meant to extend the research of psychological sense of community to the global community, all attempts to replicate the factor structure (Chavis et al., 1986) were unsuccessful. One explanation is that the items are not measuring a sense of community, but rather a sense of belongingness to a global community similar to identification with the world. This is further highlighted by the shortened versions of the PSGC. Another explanation is that one's PSGC is markedly different than connection to one's local communities. For example, the influence factor of psychological sense of community is understandable for a local community (e.g., participating in an organization that has a direct impact on one's community), but potentially difficult for participants to conceptualize when speaking of the world where a direct impact may not be immediately observable. Similar to the prior superordinate identities discussed, the results of research with PSGC point to positive prosocial outcomes (e.g., endorsement of human rights). Further research is needed to examine both the measurement of PSGC and differentiate the construct from prior notions of identification from a social identity perspective.

GLOBAL ORIENTATIONS

Alongside the superordinate global identities, researchers have proposed orientations, worldviews, and attitudes over the years that are global in nature. These constructs do not fall under the conceptual umbrella of identity, but rather focus on values and desires that indicate a global orientation. We start the current section with a discussion of cosmopolitanism. Since, with one exception that we are aware of (Reysen, Pierce, Spencer, & Katzarska-Miller, 2013), most researchers measure cosmopolitanism as a set of characteristics and/or attitudes rather than identification with the category, we see it as fitting in this section. A discussion of several measures assessing global mindsets and orientations follow.

Cosmopolitanism

Cosmopolitanism has been approached from different theoretical and disciplinary lenses. For example, while some view the construct as focusing on social justice issues, morality, or as awareness and understanding (Lilley, Barker, & Harris, 2015), Saran and Kalliny (2012) suggest that cosmopolitanism is a desire to learn about other cultures. Various theorists have suggested different types of cosmopolitanism (Ngcoya, 2015). Erskine (2002) proposes an embedded cosmopolitanism where individuals possess ethical concerns that go beyond borders. Thin cosmopolitanism (Linklater, 1998) encompasses a broader concern for humanity but with weak ties, while thick cosmopolitanism (Dobson, 2006) suggests a strong moral obligation to others. Critical cosmopolitanism, a combination of concern for human rights and global citizenship, emphasizes greater attention to local customs and history rather than global hegemony (Mignolo, 2000). Similarly, indigenous cosmopolitanism combines local and global visions (Goodale, 2006). Radical cosmopolitanism also suggests an ethical recognition of all people's equality (Brincat, 2009). In emancipatory cosmopolitanism political and social forces can challenge the dominance of corporate power and globalization (Pieterse, 2006). Still others have employed terms such as "liberal", "neoliberal", and "economic cosmopolitanism" (Peters, 2014).

The construct of cosmopolitanism is mostly discussed absent of empirical research, with few exceptions. Cleveland et al. (2012) describe cosmopolitans as people who are knowledgeable about and open to other cultures. In their research examining the associations between Schwartz's (1992) 10 universal values and a measure of cosmopolitanism (e.g., "I am interested in learning more about people who live in other countries," "I like to learn about other ways of life"), the results showed that cosmopolitanism was positively correlated with values of benevolence, universality, self-direction, stimulation, and negatively with conformity, tradition, power, and security. In subsequent research, Cleveland, Laroche, Takahashi, and Erdoğan (2014) conceptualize cosmopolitanism "as a general dispositional orientation reflecting an affinity for cultural diversity and the proclivity to master it" (p. 268). The researchers administered a revised version of their cosmopolitanism measure along with a short measure regarding international travel (e.g., "I prefer spending my vacations outside of the country that I live in") to a nationally diverse sample of participants. A cluster analysis resulted in four clusters: (1) high on cosmopolitanism and travel, (2) low on cosmopolitanism and moderate on travel, (3) high on cosmopolitanism and moderate on travel, (4) and low on both. The researchers note that the first cluster matches what they argue is the stereotypical view of cosmopolitans: individuals who travel around the world. Women tended to fall disproportionately into the first and third cluster (i.e., high cosmopolitanism). Furthermore, more Canadians and fewer Turkish citizens were classified in the first and second than the third and fourth clusters, while Japanese and Lebanese individuals fell evenly across the clusters. Thus, the clusters show some proportion differences for gender and nationality indicating the contextual influence on endorsement of cosmopolitan values. Further research from this team veers into the business and consumer realms and therefore is discussed in more detail in Chapter 7. The main point in this line of research is that cosmopolitanism is thought to be a desire to learn and immerse the self in other cultures.

Building on the theory of thick cosmopolitanism, which argues that ingroup members realization of harm to an outgroup leads to collective guilt and increases desire to rectify the harm through helping, Faulkner (2017) examined U.S. participants' help endorsement after a reminder of the ingroup's harm (individuals in developed countries such as the United States) to an outgroup (workers in developing countries). In Study 1, participants read an article about harsh working conditions in developing countries that either mentioned the ingroup's responsibility for those conditions or not. Participants rated their degree of collective guilt, asked how much time they would be willing to work for an organization that attempted to mitigate injustices, and felt responsibility for the harm to distant workers. Although participants indicated greater responsibility when reminded of the ingroup's harm to the outgroup, no differences were observed for willingness to volunteer or felt collective guilt. In a second study, participants expressed greater collective guilt when ingroup responsibility was highlighted in the fictitious article (vs. not), however, participants also rated dehumanization of the outgroup higher in this condition. Highlighting responsibility only showed an indirect relationship to helping, therefore only partially supporting the notion of thick cosmopolitanism. Rather, the results suggest moral distancing and dehumanization of outgroup members deviating from the claims of thick cosmopolitanism.

In two studies, Sevincer, Varnum, and Kitayama (2017) examined U.S. participants' associations with a measure of a city's degree of cosmopolitanism. The measure (e.g., "is tolerant toward minority groups," "is an open-minded city") reflected the notion of diversity and creativity, components viewed by the researchers as defining of cosmopolitanism. In Study 1, positive associations between the degree of perceived cosmopolitanism of the city was positively correlated with indicators such as residents' income level, proportion of minority and foreign-born residents, number of patents generated (indicator of creativity), education level, and number of museums. In Study 2, participants listed and rated the degree of cosmopolitanism of three cities they wished to move to in the future. Participants' ratings of independent self-construal, individualism, extraversion, openness to experience, liberal political orientation, and sociability were positively correlated with desire to live in cosmopolitan cities.

From the limited empirical research on cosmopolitanism to date, the construct has moved from its philosophical moral and duty-based roots to a general notion of openness to, and interest in, other cultures. Although theorists, much like those adding to the discussion of global citizenship, have opined about different definitions and types, the end result in empirical research shows cosmopolitanism as thin. In other words, individuals are aware of their connection to the world and desire to immerse the self in other cultures, but do not act or feel obligated to work for the betterment of the world.

Other Global Orientation Measures

Early examples of a global orientation include Lentz's (1950) attitudinal measure of world citizenship (e.g., "I prefer to be a citizen of the world rather than a citizen of one country"). The measure contained world-mindedness, intergroup tolerance, and political values subscales. Sampson and Smith (1957) followed with a measure of individuals' degree of world-mindedness (e.g., "It would be better to be a citizen of the world than of any particular country"), positioning world-mindedness as an orientation rather than knowledge. Der-Karabetian (1992) later proposed a revised measure of world-mindedness orientation that was positively correlated with anti-nuclear activism, as well as with pro-environmental behaviors (Der-Karabetian, Cao, & Alfaro, 2014; Der-Karabetian, Stephenson, & Poggi, 1996) and a positive view of globalization (Der-Karabetian & Alfaro, 2015).

In perhaps the most utilized measure of a global orientation, Hett (1993) assessed U.S. individuals' degree of global-mindedness, defined as view of oneself as a member of the world community and felt responsibility to others. The measure contained five dimensions: (1) responsibility for people in the world, (2) cultural pluralism and appreciation of diversity, (3) efficacy that one's actions can make a difference, (4) globalcentrism, and (5) interconnectedness of humanity. Global-mindedness is associated with a liberal political orientation, grade point average, number of languages spoken (Kirkwood-Tucker, Morris, & Lieberman, 2010), and competence with a non-native culture or language (Cui, 2016). Students studying abroad (vs. comparison sample) have tended to score higher on global-mindedness (Clark, Flaherty, Wright, & McMillen, 2009; Golay, 2006). Building upon Hett's (1993) measure, Shadowen, Chieffo, and Guerra (2015) constructed a global engagement scale. Their dimension of global engagement, termed global-mindedness, was positively related to pluralism, interconnectedness, and openness to diversity.

Departing from mindset measures, Salgado and Oceja (2011) proposed Quixoteism, a motivation purported to reflect a desire to improve the world. Using Schwartz's (1992) 10 values measure, the researchers suggest that Quixoteism is a combination of stimulation (e.g., daring, exciting life), universalism (e.g., social justice, unity with nature, world at peace), and aspects of self-direction (e.g., freedom of action and thought). In other words, endorsing this combined set of values reflects a motivation toward transcendental change of the world. Quixoteism was positively associated with a desire to help others (Oceja & Salgado, 2013; Saldago & Oceja, 2011).

Lastly, two measures have been recently proposed to assess global orientations. First, Leung, Koh, and Tam (2015) developed a cosmopolitan orientation measure containing three factors: cultural openness (e.g., "I am willing to study or work abroad in another culture"), global prosociality (e.g., "I would serve the world community by helping human beings"), and cultural diversity (e.g., "I respect cultural differences"). The overall measure was positively correlated to variables related to global citizenship, global identity, multicultural personality, openness to experience, universalism, environmental sustainability, and negatively related to social dominance orientation. Second, Chen and colleagues (2016) proposed a global orientation measure assessing individuals' responses to globalization. The scale contains two dimensions reflecting approach—multicultural acquisition (e.g., "I am curious about traditions of other cultures")—and avoidance—ethnic protection (e.g., "I find living in a multicultural environment very stressful")—orientations toward globalization. The multicultural acquisition subscale was positively related to variables such as openness, language usage, multicultural ideology, promotion regulatory focus, holistic thinking, and cross-cultural efficacy. The ethnic protection subscale also showed a variety of negative associations with variables such as language usage, cross-cultural efficacy, multicultural ideology, interdependent self-construal, openness, and bicultural identity integration. Thus, the multicultural acquisition subscale captures the global, while the ethnic protection the anti-global component of this measure.

To summarize, cosmopolitanism and global orientation measures assess attitudes and values regarding one's perception of the world. Although they do not follow a social identity approach, the results across studies show they are related to prosocial values and behaviors similar to global superordinate identity measures. These positive associations may reflect the measurement of group content of global identities. In other words, individuals scoring high on these orientations are likely to also indicate self-categorization with a global superordinate identity and express the same values that are assessed with these measures. Further research using a longitudinal method is needed to observe a possible causal relationship between identification and values.

SIMILARITIES AND DIFFERENCES IN
CONSTRUCTS AND MEASURES

The foremost similarity across all of the reviewed identities and orientations is that nearly all of the research concerns salience or degree of connection to the world in some manner. Although there are some deviations such as cosmopolitanism, which focuses on interest and desire to learn and engage with other cultures, and Quixoteism, which focuses on values, the majority of research follows a social identity approach, even if not explicitly framed as such by the researchers. The second most striking similarity is the tendency of superordinate global identities and orientations to be associated with pro-social outcomes. The values can vary from desire to help others, mitigate global problems, donate to charities, to environmental sustainability and openness to diverse cultures. Theories, developed based on a social identity approach, may aid in explaining the latter similarity. In particular, we will discuss the common ingroup identity and crossed categorization models.

The common ingroup identity model (Gaertner, Dovidio, Anastasio, Bachman, & Rust, 1993) posits that categorization of the self with a more inclusive group reduces intergroup bias and conflict. Rather than viewing groups as "us" (ingroup) and "them" (outgroup), recategorizing with a super-ordinate group leads to the previously "them" becoming part of the ingroup. Making a superordinate identity salient results in greater empathetic concern, positive thoughts, cooperation, and helping of the previously outgroup members (Gaertner & Dovidio, 2008). For example, in a study of UK football fans, Levine, Prosser, Evans, and Reicher (2005) asked participants to rate their degree of identification with their favorite football team, thus, making the identity of fan of the ingroup team salient. For the next part of the study participants were asked to move to a different building. While walking to the other building, participants observed a confederate fall and hurt himself. The researchers found that participants were more likely to help the confederate wearing the ingroup, rather than outgroup or neutral, shirt. In the second study, instead of priming the ingroup team, the researchers made football fan in general salient. With this more inclusive category salient, participants were equally likely to help the confederate wearing the ingroup and outgroup team shirts than they were to help the person wearing the neutral shirt. In effect, making the superordinate identity of football fan turned a previously outgroup (i.e., rival team fan) into an ingroup member resulting in greater helping behavior. Similarly, making a superordinate group salient, such as global or world citizen, should lead to better intragroup relations (e.g., empathy, helping) because outgroups are now part of the ingroup. However, focusing on a single superordinate group may threaten subgroup distinctiveness (Hornsey & Hogg, 2002) and serve advantaged groups by avoiding intergroup inequality to maintain a status quo (Dovidio, Saguy, Gaertner, & Thomas, 2012). The crossed categorization model is posited to avoid these downsides.

The crossed categorization model (Crisp & Hewstone, 1999, 2007) posits that simultaneously making both a subgroup and a shared superordinate group salient results in reduced intergroup bias. Similar to the common ingroup identity model, a superordinate identity is made salient; however, an additional subgroup is also made salient. In theory, making the subgroup identity also salient should avoid the possible threat to subgroup distinctiveness. For example, if only thinking of the self as a social psychologist may result in bias toward economists, when crossing social psychologist with university professor (i.e., superordinate identity) less bias toward economists may result. Although there is continuing research in this area, the crossed categorization model may be more helpful in reducing intergroup bias in some contexts than the common ingroup (Crisp, Turner, & Hewstone, 2010). Both common ingroup and crossed categorization models may explain why global superordinate identities are associated with prosocial values and behaviors. Just as categorizing with a more inclusive identity results in less prejudice and greater empathy, helping, and cooperation, identifying with a superordinate global identity should result in similar prosocial outcomes. Thus, we may observe prosocial outcomes such as empathy, helping, concern for the planet, and valuing diversity (e.g., prejudice reduction) because the prior outgroups becomes part of the ingroup. The difference between the two models is whether or not a subgroup identity is also salient along with the superordinate group; however, the proposed outcomes would be the same (i.e., more favorable view of previously outgroup members).

While the above models may explain why global superordinate identities are associated with prosocial values, they do not explain why global orientations are related to similar prosocial constructs. A potential explanation is that the measures used to assess global orientations are closely tied to a cluster of values that are associated with global identities. For example, the group content of global citizenship is posited to include values such as valuing diversity and environmental sustainability (Reysen & Katzarska-Miller, 2013a). These two values are positively correlated with one another. A measure of cosmopolitanism that assesses one's desire to learn about other cultures should, in theory, be positively related to valuing diversity. And as valuing diversity is related to environmental sustainability, we would expect cosmopolitanism to also be related to environmental sustainability. In other words, the global orientations are tapping into a set of interrelated values that are also part of the group content of global superordinate identities. Another potential explanation is that global orientation measures are indirectly assessing global identities. The difference in measurement is that identities tend to use ingroup identification while the global orientations use values that reflect the identities.

Although there are similarities in the identities and orientations reviewed in this chapter, there are also differences. One of the main differences, already discussed, is the variety of ways the superordinate identities/orientations have been conceptualized and operationalized. Another potential difference may lie in the associations between particular identities and prosocial values. To examine whether different identities predict different attitudes and behaviors, Reysen, Pierce, et al. (2013) asked U.S. participants to rate their degree of ingroup identification with global citizens, cosmopolitans, world citizens, international citizens, and humans. The results showed that identification with global citizens uniquely predicted, above and beyond the other identities, accepting cultural differences, valuing diversity, environmental sustainability beliefs, endorsement of equality of nations, openness to new experiences, intergroup helping, and a felt responsibility to act for the betterment of the world. Identification with cosmopolitans was positively related to environmental sustainability and identification with world citizens to valuing diversity, but identification with other identities did not significantly predict prosocial values beyond global citizenship. In a subsequent study examining identification with global citizens, humans, Americans, Texans, and students, global citizenship identification, but not identification with the other identities, predicted endorsement of behaviors such as sponsoring a child in another country, giving to charity, micro-investing (e.g., Kiva.org), doing community service, civic engagement, protesting unethical corporations, seeking cultural experiences, and using the internet to learn more about other cultures. These studies show that global citizenship differs from other identities (e.g., human) in terms of the ability to predict both attitudes and intended behaviors. In other words, although theorists and researchers may sometimes use cosmopolitanism as a synonym for global citizenship, individuals' ratings of identification with the different identity labels show different results when predicting attitudes and behaviors.

   In another set of empirical studies, Reysen and Katzarska-Miller (2017a) examined the associations between global citizenship, human, and American identification with attitudes toward peace and conflict. After rating their degree of identification with the three identity labels, participants rated various indicators of attitudes toward peace and war. Global citizenship identification (as compared to human identification) was negatively associated with the belief that conflicts are intractable or inevitable, and was positively associated with concern for human rights, felt responsibility, support for diplomacy, and positive attitudes toward peace. Similar to the above research, global citizen identity was different from human identity in the associations with attitudes regarding peace. In other words, global citizen is not the same as viewing the self as a human. However, greater research comparing the various measures described above, beyond human identity, is needed.

   There are several reasons why there may exist differences between the global superordinate identities. First, the content of the identities may differ. This is most apparent when considering human compared to global citizenship in the above research. As will be shown in the next chapter, when participants are asked to define global citizenship, they tend to report similar values and behaviors such as feeling an obligation to act for the betterment of the world. However, when asked to define humans, the responses can be more varied and include themes reflecting having morals, goals, emotions, decision making ability, and learning from one's mistakes (Katzarska-Miller & Reysen, 2018a). Thus, prosocial themes are not inherently tied to the category prototypes. If an identity is less defined, participants are likely to project values onto the identity. This notion is also bolstered by the ease with which researchers can manipulate the perception of humans as benevolent or hostile. In this case, the researchers are projecting values onto the identity, which is then accepted by the participants. Another possible reason for the dissimilarity is the potential outgroups for global citizen compared to human. The outgroup for global citizens is non-global citizens, while the outgroups for humans can vary (e.g., robots, non-human animals: Haslam & Loughnan, 2014). What outgroup is salient when an identity is cognitively activated can change the salience of group prototypes (Chadborn & Reysen, in press). For example, for human identity, if robots are the salient outgroup then emotions may be a prototype of humans, but when non-human animals are salient, decision-making ability and intelligence may be prototypes. Lastly, there may be sociocultural or contextual reasons for understanding or conceptualizing global superordinate identities differently. As will be discussed in the next chapter, how individuals define global citizenship differs depending on the cultural context in which participants are embedded. Participants are likely drawing upon their life experiences and knowledge to explain or define an identity. Cultural context is thus likely to have an impact on their explanation, which is also likely to influence what participants think identities are associated with. For example, if a participant lives in a part of the world that is economically deprived and they do not have the financial means to travel, they may define global citizenship in terms of traveling.

Cultural context may also explain the mixed results regarding the association between global and national identity. The relationship between the two remains a contested topic within the area of superordinate identities (Türken & Rudmin, 2013). Buchan et al. (2011) found a positive correlation between national identity and identification with the world as a whole. McFarland and colleagues' (2012) measure of identification with all humanity (combining both subscales) was positively related to the same items tapping identification with all Americans. Reysen and Katzarska-Miller (2017a) note that global citizenship is sometimes positively related and other times non-significantly related to identification with Americans. Ariely (2018) examined correlations between identification with world citizens and one's nationality across 49 countries to find a general negative correlation between world citizen and nation. However, there were differences in the direction and degree of the association depending on country and the degree of globalization within the country. We contest that global and national identity are not necessarily at odds. In other words, individuals can be highly identified, or low identified, with both groups. Future research may explore the association between these two variables further, especially the interaction between the two and potential outcomes. For example, perhaps individuals who are high on both constructs, arguably perceived as bicultural (see Arnett, 2002), are more open than individuals high on global but low on national identification. Resolving the mixed results in research examining this association is likely dependent on the context, as shown by Ariely (2018), yet more research in this area is needed.

CONCLUSION

Occurring simultaneously with the growth of global citizen research is the increased examination of psychological connection to other superordinate identities. In the present chapter we reviewed work on identification with world citizens, identification with the world as a whole, global identity, identification with the world community, identification with all humanity, human identity, psychological sense of global community, cosmopolitanism, and other world-view/orientation lines of research. There are similarities across these research lines with the main finding being an association between psychological connection with a superordinate/global group and prosocial values and behaviors. However, not all identity labels appear to tap into the same construct and have identical associations with prosocial values. Research comparing measures and their ability to predict attitudes and behaviors will aid in distinguishing between the concepts. Academics, often-times, tend to overthink or dissect concepts to such an extent that jargon becomes an inherent component of these concepts. Therefore, we will also review how laypersons view global citizenship. In the next chapter, we explore understandings of global citizenship from a lay perspective.

NOTE

1. Although Reese et al. (2015) term their interpretation of McFarland et al.'s (2012) dimensions (i.e., global self-definition, global self-investment) based on factors identified by Leach et al. (2008), McFarland et al. explicitly state that "none of the Leach et al. items or factors assess the proactive care and concern for others that are critical to identification in the sense of Adler and Maslow or that were exemplified by the rescuers during the Holocaust" (p. 831). Thus, McFarland et al. are explicitly stating that social identity is not a theoretical framework for the measure and that terms or items used by Leach et al. (2008) do not apply.

Chapter Three

Lay Perceptions of Global Citizenship

In the present chapter we turn to lay conceptualizations of global citizenship and related concepts. We begin by emphasizing the importance of lay beliefs and their relevance to social identities. Next, we review and describe qualitative work examining how students, teachers, individuals in higher education, and community members describe and define global citizenship. In this we highlight the common themes that emerge when asking non-academics to describe the concept. Additionally, we discuss the contextual influence on individuals' understandings of global citizenship. Similar to the previous chapter we also review lay understandings of concepts that are related to global citizenship (e.g., global awareness, global education) by noting the themes that are prevalent when describing these related concepts.

PROTOTYPICAL GROUP CONTENT

There is a long history of lay theories research in psychology. Although different labels have been used (e.g., common sense psychology, naïve psychology, implicit theories), they all reflect people's beliefs and theories about the world (Hong, Levy, & Chiu, 2001). Lay beliefs are important for psychology because they can aid in developing social scientific theories, but also can impact individuals' everyday actions (Cargile, Bradac, & Cole, 2006). Lay theories aid individuals by instilling a sense of understanding and predictability in the world, thus facilitating interpersonal interactions (Hong et al., 2001; Plaks, Levey, & Dweck, 2009). Beyond providing a sense of control, they can also promote social relationships, bolster endorsement of values, and justify individuals' prejudice and societal inequalities (Levy, West, & Ramirez, 2005). Similar to scientific theories, lay theories are structured systems of beliefs, but differ in that they are usually untested by individuals who endorse them, are less explicit and rigorously formulated, and tend to be self-serving (Levy, Chiu, & Hong, 2006). They are culturally dependent (Uchida, Townsend, Markus, & Bergsieker, 2009) such as between and within cultures, the theories may differ in content, the degree that they are highlighted by individuals in a particular culture, and the degree of connection between belief and everyday actions (Levy et al., 2005).

Stereotypes—beliefs regarding a group or category of people—are one example of a lay theory (Hong et al., 2001) and also a key component of a social identity approach to group content. A variety of other terms have been used to describe the prototypical content of the group, such as "normative content", "attributes", "stereotypical group characteristics" (Turner et al., 1987), "category attributes" (Hogg & Smith, 2007), "meaning or content" (Livingstone & Haslam, 2008), "group properties" (Oakes, Haslam, & Turner, 1998), "group norms" (Hogg & McGarty, 1990), or "group-defining characteristics" (Hogg & Abrams, 1988). Prototypes are fuzzy inter-related sets of characteristics that highlight intragroup similarities and intergroup differences specific to social categories (Hogg & Smith, 2007). Similar to stereotypes, group prototypes tend to be consensually shared among both ingroup and outgroup members (Turner et al., 1987). Since being a global citizen is an identity, we need to examine the content of the category. One method to accomplish this is to examine how lay people describe and conceptualize global citizenship (Ashmore, Deaux, & McLaughlin-Volpe, 2004). This method is akin to examining lay beliefs in psychology. Thus, by examining what non-academics think global citizenship is we can gain a better understanding and inform academic research about the stereotypes, prototypes, content of groups that people associate with the category global citizen.

LAY PERSPECTIVES OF GLOBAL CITIZENSHIP

In the present section we present a review of research examining lay perceptions of global citizenship. In the 31 samples (29 studies) researchers asked lay participants about their understanding of global citizenship. The questions asked pertaining to the definition of global citizenship varied (e.g., define global citizenship, what does it mean to be a global citizen, what are the characteristics of global citizens, what are your understandings or conceptualizations of global citizenship), but all converged on the notion of what people think global citizenship is or how they would describe global citizens. For convenience, we provide a table of the studies, sample size, population, country of sample, whether or not certain characteristics (e.g., empathy, social justice) were mentioned, and a list of other less frequent characteristics noted by participants (see Table 3.1). The research presented in the table is in ascending order by participants' age. The characteristic columns were chosen based on the main components of the global citizenship identification model that will be described in the next chapter. These characteristics, with the exception of normative environment, are also the most frequently and consistently mentioned aspects of global citizenship found in the lay descriptions. We review respondents' usage of these characteristics, in descending order of frequency mentioned.

Global Awareness

The most commonly stated component of global citizenship in lay descriptions of the term was global awareness. This awareness was comprised of two parts—interconnectedness with others in the world and knowledge about other cultures. Regardless of whether they were mentioned together or separately, in all of the studies global citizens were described as aware. In most studies participants mentioned knowledge and interconnectedness explicitly. However, participants in other studies used synonymous terms that we interpreted as global awareness. For example, individuals described global citizens as people who know about global issues (Jaberi, 2014), understand the world, share things in common with others, interact with the world (Pasha, 2015), pursue learning to be aware of the world (Hendershot, 2010), and knowledge of other cultures (McDougall, 2005). Similarly, the interconnectedness aspect was described as an awareness of interdependence of ecosystems (Niens & Reilly, 2012), being impacted by the actions of others in the world (Myers, 2010), understanding of interconnectedness (Massey, 2013), acknowledging interconnectedness of all people (Hendershot, 2010), inclusive view of others in the world (Streitwieser & Light, 2016), and thinking globally and taking a larger perspective (Günel & Pehlivan, 2016). Thus, although different terminology was used to describe a sense of knowledge and interconnectedness, all studies mentioned this characteristic in some manner.

Table 3.1. Lay Characteristics of Global Citizenship

Researchers	N	Population	Country	NE	GA	IE	DV	SJ	ES
Balbağ and Türkcan (2017)	30	4th grade students	Turkey		X	X	X	X	X
Niens and Reilly (2012)	ns	8–9 and 12–13 yr. students	Northern Ireland		X	X	X	X	X
Jaberi (2014)	22	12–13 yr. students	Canada		X	X	X	X	X
Pasha (2015)	6	15 yr. students	Pakistan		X				X
Myers (2010)	77	Secondary students in international studies program	USA		X			X	
Massey (2013)	7	Grade 12 students who completed world issues class	Canada		X	X		X	

Researchers	N	Population	Country	NE	GA	IE	DV	SJ	ES
Thier (2016)	8	11–12th grade students at leadership conference	Various		X	X	X	X	X
Hendershot (2010)	65	Undergraduate college students	USA		X		X		
Roddick (2008)	15	Post-secondary students in seminar program in West Africa	Canada		X	X	X	X	X
Perdue (2014)	15	African American undergradua	USA		X	X			X

Researchers	N	Population	Country	NE	GA	IE	DV	SJ	ES
		te college students							
McDougall (2005)	38	Undergraduate college students in international leadership programs	Various		X		X		X
Song (2016)	25	Undergraduate student volunteers at Olympic Games	China		X	X	X	X	X
Streitwieser and Light (2016)	29	Undergraduate students who completed study abroad	USA	X	X		X		
Günel and Pehlivan (2016)	10	Pre-service teachers	Turkey		X	X	X	X	X
Byker (2016)	136	Pre-service teachers	USA		X	X	X	X	X

Researchers	N	Population	Country	NE	GA	IE	DV	SJ	ES
Wang (2017)	8	Graduates of transnational Communication degree program	China and Canada		X	X	X	X	X
Harshman and Augustine (2013)	126	International baccalaureate teachers	Various		X	X	X	X	X
Balbağ and Türkcan (2017)	15	4th grade social studies teachers	Turkey		X	X	X		
Pasha (2015)	5	Teachers who had participated in a global citizenship program	Pakistan		X				

Researchers	N	Population	Country	NE	GA	IE	DV	SJ	ES
Leduc (2013)	29	Grade six social studies teachers	Canada		X	X	X	X	
Rapoport (2010)	6	Secondary school teachers	USA		X		X	X	X
Goren and Yemini (2016)	7	Secondary school teachers	Israel		X		X	X	X
Lilley, Barker, and Harris (2015)	26	Individuals working in higher education	Australia and European Union		X		X		X
Lilley, Barker, and Harris (2017)	26	Individuals working in higher education	Various		X		X		
Al Sarhan, Abbadneh, and Abu-Nair (2015)	162	Individuals working in education	Jordan		X		X	X	X
Kuleta-Hulboj (2016)	12	NGO workers in education system	Poland		X	X	X	X	X

Researchers	N	Population	Country	NE	GA	IE	DV	SJ	ES
Thanosawan and Laws (2013)	ns	Individuals working in higher education and students	Thailand		X			X	X
Lindahl (2013)	7	Young adults	India and Nepal		X		X	X	X
Katzarska-Miller et al. (2012)	357	Students and community members	USA, Bulgaria, India		X	X	X		
Schattle (2005)	126	Self-identified global citizens	Various		X				
Schattle (2008)	157	Self-identified global citizens	Various		X	X	X	X	X

Note. N = sample size, ns = sample size not stated, NE = normative environment, GA = global awarenes
diversity, SJ = social justice, ES = environmental sustainability, IH = intergroup helping, RA =
noted by participants.

We offer three possible explanations for why awareness was mentioned consistently throughout this research. First, all, in some form, rely on participants conceptualizing global citizens based on their own prior experiences and exposure to the term "global citizen," but also breaking down the term and relating it to similar concepts. This is a consistent theme for most of the components of global citizenship in the present chapter. Participants often appear to take "global" and "citizen" and form a definition based on what these terms mean individually and when connected together. Thus, participants state that human beings are born on earth (at least at present), and are therefore global citizens by default (Streitwieser & Light, 2016). In this manner, participants are connecting the notion of being a citizen of a nation with birth in that nation and extending it to a global level—we are all global citizens because we are born on this globe. This is associated with awareness because individuals need to be cognitively aware of this connection (i.e., be cognitively salient that we are all born on the same planet). A similar notion is included in social identity theory (i.e., individuals must categorize the self as part of a group to identify with the group) and part of Schattle's (2008) model of global citizenship (i.e., individuals must first recognize that they are global citizens before becoming global citizens).

A second possible reason is the association between global citizenship and globalization. Globalization is tied to the notion of interconnectedness of the world in various domains (e.g., economic, cultural). Participants may be connecting the "global" in global citizenship with the interconnectedness component of globalization (Rapoport, 2010). In other words, there may exist an implicit association between global and interconnectedness with others that is salient when asked to think about a global citizen. Reysen, Pierce, et al. (2014) presented U.S. college student participants with frequently used words derived from lay definitions of global citizenship and asked the participants to categorize the words as either "global citizen" or "other" in a reaction time task. "Globalization" was quickly and frequently categorized as global citizen, thus, showing a strong implicit association between globalization and global citizenship. Additionally, the word "connected" was frequently categorized with the label "global citizen" (vs. "other"), suggesting that connectedness is cognitively associated with global citizens.

The third possible explanation is that the image of a global citizen contains the perception of an individual who is knowledgeable about the world. To be aware of one's interconnectedness individuals must also be knowledgeable (Kuleta-Hulboj, 2016). These two concepts go hand in hand for many participants. We should note that in the reaction time study mentioned above, "educated" was also a word closely associated with global citizen. Together, the results place a heavy importance on awareness as knowledgeable and interconnected as either a component or precursor to global citizenship.

Responsibility to Act

The second-most frequently mentioned characteristic of global citizenship was a felt responsibility to act for the betterment of the world. Indeed, participants in all samples, but two, noted this. Thus, this concept of action is conceivably just as important to global citizenship as awareness. Most researchers found individuals explicitly describing this felt responsibility, but a few noted usages of synonymous terms. For example, students viewed global citizens as individuals who act to make the world a better place (Jaberi, 2014), a moral commitment to improve the world (Myers, 2010), a commitment to action (Massey, 2013), and serving the world (Günel & Pehlivan, 2016). Although we recognize that a semantic argument can be made about the difference between responsibility and commitment or action compared to serving the world, we argue that these descriptions are tapping a felt responsibility to act.

Similar to the first explanation concerning global awareness, Rapoport (2010) noted that teachers who indicated not knowing what global citizenship was broke down the term to describe "citizenship," but with reference to the world rather than to one's local community or nation. For example, a pre-service teacher stated that citizenship when applied to the world means standing up when there is cruelty or harm to the environment (Günel & Pehlivan, 2016). These participants are thinking about what it means to be a citizen of one's nation and then expanding it to apply to the world. To be a citizen means to have rights and responsibilities (Banks, 2008), therefore, to be a global citizen indicates certain responsibilities; in this case to other people and the natural environment.

Valuing Diversity

The third-most mentioned characteristic of global citizens was valuing diversity. We conceptualize "valuing diversity" as interest in and appreciation for diverse cultures.[1] Beyond explicitly mentioning diversity, participants used terms such as "respect" (Balbağ & Türkcan, 2017; Lilley, Barker, & Harris, 2017; McDougall, 2005) and "tolerance" (Byker, 2016; Günel & Pehlivan, 2016; Wang, 2017) when talking about others who differ from the self. They also described taking the perspective of others and showing a curiosity about other cultures (Niens & Reilly, 2012). Furthermore, they used phrases such as "inclusion of others" (Jaberi, 2014), "acceptance of diversity" (Hendershot, 2010), "dignity of difference" (Roddick, 2008), "cultural recognition" (Song, 2016), "interest and engagement with different cultural practices"

(Streitwieser & Light, 2016), "regarding people as unique individuals" (Harshman & Augustine, 2013), "understanding of others" (Leduc, 2013), and "interacting with people from different backgrounds" (Goren & Yemini, 2016). All of these statements capture aspects of valuing diversity.

A possible reason for the frequent mention of diversity is that if everyone is part of the same ingroup, then acceptance, tolerance, regard, and respect is needed for the group to interact harmoniously. In other words, as global citizenship is a superordinate category there exists an expectation that members of various subgroups will be part of the category. As noted in the previous chapter, both common ingroup identity (Gaertner et al., 1993) and crossed categorization (Crisp & Hewstone, 1999) models propose that viewing the self as part of an inclusive group results in reduced intergroup bias. The participants in these studies may be expressing a lay theory of the characteristics needed to work and live as part of a global community.

An image of global citizens as world travelers may also inform the association between valuing diversity and global citizenship. When we first began global citizenship as a line of research we conducted focus group interviews with individuals in the United States. One participant's response has stuck with us over the years. When asked to describe a popular or famous person who they would consider a global citizen, they mentioned the Dos Equis guy. For those who have not seen the commercials for the beer brand, they center around the purportedly most interesting man in the world. The commercials feature this person traveling around the world, interacting with people, and participating in various feats (e.g., wrestling a bear). The image of the Dos Equis guy fits that of the global citizen as a world traveler. In the portrayal he is interacting with individuals from diverse cultural backgrounds comfortably and effectively. His motivation to travel reflects an appreciation and desire to experience the world and its diverse cultures. Although fictional, the image painted in these commercials is that valuing diversity is linked with being a person who effortlessly traverses boundaries while enjoying the experience. Alternatively, as we will also suggest for the remaining characteristics mentioned, valuing diversity is simply a stereotypical or prototypical component of global citizenship. Indeed, the word diversity is quickly categorized as related to "global citizen" rather than "other" in the reaction time research mentioned earlier (Reysen, Pierce, et al., 2014).

Environmental Sustainability

The fourth-most frequently mentioned characteristic of global citizenship was environmental sustainability or concern for the natural environment. Most often this reference was straightforward in participants' responses; however, there were some phrases used that we interpreted as capturing the environmental sustainability component. For example, global citizens were described as people who work for environmental causes such as helping wildlife (Jaberi, 2014), as concerned about the well-being of the environment (Perdue, 2014), connected by the environment (McDougall, 2005), play a role in sustainable development (Song, 2016), are sensitive to the environment (Günel & Pehlivan, 2016), and act to preserve the environment (Harshman & Augustine, 2013). All of the above reflect either concern or action related to environmental sustainability.

A possible reason for the association between environmental sustainability and global citizenship is that part of being a responsible citizen is caring for and acting for one's local community or nation. If participants are breaking down the term "global citizen," then participants may be extrapolating care for one's local community to care for the earth on a global level. Another possible explanation for the close connection between environmentalism and global citizenship is that environmental issues are increasingly discussed in the media across numerous countries in recent decades (Schäfer, Ivanova, & Schmidt, 2014). Greater coverage of climate change in the media is strongly linked with the general concern shown by those in the public (Carmichael & Brulle, 2017; Lee, 2011). Indeed, one of the most pressing problems that everyone on earth faces is the possibly detrimental outcomes of climate change. This global issue may be highly salient when thinking about what affects all individuals on earth and therefore is one topic that connects us all.

Social Justice

The fifth-most mentioned component of global citizenship was concern for social justice. We conceive of social justice as attitudes related to human rights and equitable and fair treatment of all humans (Reysen & Katzarska-Miller, 2013a). Although not all participants noted social justice explicitly, they used terms such as "fairness" (Song, 2016), "equality" (Lindahl, 2013; Roddick, 2008), and "human rights" (Leduc, 2013; Roddick, 2008; Thanosawan & Laws, 2013). Some participants noted specific issues, which fall under the umbrella of social justice such as knowledge about genocides, health epidemics, and human trafficking (Myers, 2010). Other participants suggested that global citizens make consumer choices related to fair trade to mitigate sweatshop labor abuses (Massey, 2013) and promote fair practices in international trade (Harshman & Augustine, 2013). Global citizens were thought to be non-discriminatory and sensitive to the social problems in the world (Günel & Pehlivan, 2016), act to prevent discrimination (Balbağ & Türkcan, 2017), understand privilege and power relations (Wang, 2017), promote equality (Jaberi, 2014), and have favorable attitudes regarding the redistribution of wealth (Niens & Reilly, 2012).

We suggest three possible reasons why social justice is associated with global citizens. First, as noted earlier, a felt responsibility to act for the betterment of the world is strongly connected to the identity global citizen. Participants may conceive of concern for social justice issues as a way of acting for the betterment of the world. Social justice revolves around mitigating or reversing harm to oppressed groups. Helping underprivileged or harmed groups is one way to improve the world. Second, there may exist an image of a global citizen as an activist. The values and activities of social activists are similar to those of a global citizen (see Reysen & Hackett, 2017). Activists work to make the world a better place, similar to the felt responsibility to act component of global citizenship. Activists, and the social movements which they support, may be another prototypical or stereotypical image of a global citizen given the close match in values and activities. Third, social justice is related to other components that are often mentioned when describing global citizenship such as valuing diversity (Reysen & Katzarska-Miller, 2013a). If an individual values diversity they are also likely to support social justice causes.

Intergroup Empathy

The sixth-most frequently mentioned characteristic of global citizenship was empathy. We prefer to use the term intergroup empathy as participants imply that the felt empathy is a connection or concern for people that are outside one's ingroup. In other words, they are not describing empathy for a family member or close friend, but rather someone that people would not consider as part of one's everyday ingroup. Most of the time participants explicitly mentioned empathy. When they did not they used words such as "love" (Balbağ & Türkcan, 2017), "caring" (Massey, 2013; Roddick, 2008), "being concerned about the well-being of others" (Günel & Pehlivan, 2016; Perdue, 2014), and "embracing others" (Song, 2016).

When describing participants' understanding of global awareness earlier in this chapter, we noted that many of them framed global citizenship as one large ingroup in which all humans are connected. To shift the degree of inclusiveness from all people in one's nation to all people on earth means that empathy for others in one's ingroup also needs to shift to all people on earth. Past research shows that viewing others as part of the same ingroup is related to felt empathy for previous outgroup members (Capozza et al., 2010). Extending this line of reasoning would imply that viewing others as global citizens would mean feeling a sense of empathy for people who may have previously been outgroup members. Another reason may be the close connection between empathy and the other components of global citizenship. Taking the perspective of others is the cognitive component of empathy (Andrighetto et al., 2012). Perspective taking should also be closely associated with other outcomes of global citizenship such as caring about diversity and social justice. To value diversity and social justice implies the ability to take the perspective of minority and victimized others. Empathy is also connected to the next component—intergroup helping.

Intergroup Helping

The seventh-most often mentioned characteristic of global citizenship was intergroup helping. We define intergroup helping as any aid given to others outside one's ingroup. Intergroup helping spans from donating to charity to active volunteering. Although not stated explicitly in all of the reviewed research, participants noted that global citizens are people who perform selfless acts of kindness (Jaberi, 2014), are willing to help others (Roddick, 2008), and feel a responsibility to help others (Perdue, 2014). Furthermore, participants described global citizens as helping others through charities and fundraising (Niens & Reilly, 2012; Song, 2016), activism (Hendershot, 2010), volunteering (Lilley et al., 2015), and standing up to cruelty or destruction of nature (Günel & Pehlivan, 2016). Similar to prior components of global citizenship we posit two possible explanations of why this is spontaneously mentioned by participants when describing a global citizen: being a good citizen means helping others, and helping is likely part of a cluster of similar prosocial constructs such as empathy, valuing diversity, responsibility to act, and concern for social justice.

Normative Environment

One of the least frequently mentioned aspects of global citizenship was the notion that one's normative environment is pro-global. Indeed, the idea, although not explicit, was only mentioned in one study in which participants described being born into a family with international connections as a characteristic of global citizens (Streitwieser & Light, 2016). However, the idea that individuals live in sociocultural settings that can engender (or hinder) a global citizen identity was implied in participants' responses when describing the sources of global citizenship. Students mentioned developing their knowledge of global citizenship through school classes, internet, family and friends (Balbağ & Türkcan, 2017), work, and personal reading (Roddick, 2008). Pre-service teachers indicated that they learned about global citizenship through sources such as media, NGOs, classes, social media, and friends (Günel & Pehlivan, 2016). Jaberi (2014) found that students who were descendants of multiple ethnic groups and identified themselves as citizens of the world noted that through their upbringing they were exposed to different cultures, languages, music, food, and media in general. Furthermore, when asked what aspects of life influenced their understanding of global citizenship, the students mentioned clubs in school, media, and family (e.g., travel, family who speak multiple languages, media consumed by family members). Thus, although an often invisible concept for lay participants, one's normative environment is mentioned when asked to describe how people become global citizens. Furthermore, we view the normative environment as an essential component for understanding how individuals come to identify with global citizens, a point elaborated upon in the next chapter.

Other Components

Beyond the most often mentioned components as indicated in Table 3.1, various other concepts were stated, just at a less frequent rate. These include travel to other countries, being fluent in multiple languages, being open-minded, using technology (e.g., internet, social media platforms), intercultural communication, peace, being flexible, and critical thinking. For example, Harshman and Augustine's (2013) participants wondered if travel is necessary to be a global citizen. As noted by participants, on one hand, travel exposes individuals to different perspectives and ways of being, while on the other hand, individuals can be exposed to diverse beliefs through interacting with others without travel. Travel can also be supplemented by technology which offers individuals the ability to vicariously travel and interact with diverse others. For a young girl in Pakistan the inability to travel and talk about her country and religion with others meant she could not be a global citizen (Pasha, 2015). Other students noted that speaking the language is important for intercultural communication (Balbağ & Türkcan, 2017). And when asked what sources influence their understanding of global citizenship, they reported use of social media as exposing them to the outside world (Jaberi, 2014). Technology was also linked to social justice in that individuals should have equal access to technology and information (Lindahl, 2013). These concepts may be connected due to the participants' position (e.g., teacher wishing for students to learn languages) or sociocultural setting (e.g., desire to travel but unable due to political or economic position). In other words, infrequently mentioned characteristics of global citizens are likely related to participants' role, context of research, and sociocultural settings.

Unknown and Unsubscribed

In a portion of the studies, the researchers noted that participants appeared to be describing global citizenship for the first time (e.g., Goren & Yemini, 2016; Rapoport, 2010; Roddick, 2008), without clear understanding of what the concept is. For example, Pasha (2015) who interviewed six 15-year-old grade nine students in the Saddar district of Karachi, Pakistan, regarding their understanding of global citizenship. Although the researcher noted that students appeared to lack a clear understanding of what a citizen was in addition to lack of a clear understanding of a global citizen, the students provided reasonable descriptions. The responses mentioned being a citizen of multiple countries, understanding of the world and being part of the world, shared characteristics or traits with others in other countries, and having a universal education. The students also proposed that knowledge of the world is not enough to consider oneself a global citizen, but rather some action is needed. Pasha also interviewed teachers at the same school and they echoed the students with respect to the need for action to consider the self a global citizen. Thus, even without a clear understanding of global citizenship, students still provided reasonable guesses that tended to match those of the above studies.

Additionally, in some of the studies, participants explicitly stated that they do not consider themselves global citizens (e.g., Roddick, 2008). For example, Perdue (2014) interviewed African American students regarding their understanding of global citizenship. The major themes that emerged included interconnectedness with others, helping others for the greater good, civic engagement and serving as role models for others, and global awareness. While the students mentioned the theme of interconnectedness, their responses alluded to the notion that they do not feel connected to the larger world, but are rather focused on family an immediate contexts. In addition, students expressed their lack of global competency, but recognized its importance for global citizenship. Together, the responses tended to reflect a lack of connection to the larger world due to immediate concerns (e.g., discrimination, systemic oppression) that supersede thoughts of global citizenship. This result may provide a unique starting point for greater examination of oppression or threat in students' environments hindering identification with global citizens. Similar to Pasha (2015), despite the apparent rejection of the identity, students' perceptions of global citizenship tended to match those in other studies reviewed here. Taken together, lay participants may not agree or know what a global citizen is, but when pressed they describe stereotypes that are consensually shared with many others of varied age groups and living in different parts of the world.

Cultural Context

In this chapter so far we have highlighted consistent themes in descriptions of global citizenship across a variety of cultural spaces. However, we need to impress the importance of cultural context for a fuller appreciation of why certain characteristics of global citizens were or were not mentioned. Some of the researchers explained differences in lay descriptions of global citizenship based on participation in college class, global citizen workshop, or study abroad program (e.g., Byker, 2016; Hendershot, 2010; Massey, 2013;

McDougall, 2005; Wang, 2017). Justifiably, in these studies, participants' understandings of global citizenship changed based on some educational interventions. However, the majority of participants, who did not have a prior conceptualization of global citizenship, drew upon the component words of the term or past life experiences to define the concept (Goren & Yemini, 2016; Rapoport, 2010). In drawing upon understandings of the words in the term and one's prior experiences there will inevitably be cultural influences that are expressed through participant responses. Some researchers noted these cultural influences in defining a global citizen.

Goren and Yemini (2016) interviewed three teachers at an Israeli public school and four teachers at an international school in Tel Aviv regarding global citizenship. The researchers noted three themes in the responses including: inclusion and exclusion (boundaries of global citizenship), practical aspects of education (benefits and purpose of inclusion and balance with curriculum), and the Israeli context (teaching in a conflict-ridden state). Importantly, this study was conducted in a context, as noted by the researchers, in a nationalistic, conservative, and conflict-ridden society that promotes national identity in their educational curriculum. The Israeli teachers (vs. international school teachers) did not mention more of the active political elements of global citizenship (e.g., being a "citizen" of the world). They suggested that this omission is perhaps an effort to avoid appearing unpatriotic or the notion that the concept hinders students' national identification. Furthermore, the Israeli teachers noted national issues of difficulty in travel, militaristic society, and threat (without mentioning the Israel-Palestine conflict) as hindering global citizenship, because survival was more salient. In effect, the Israeli teachers appeared to avoid global citizenship as it may weaken national identity, while international teachers were open to inclusion to foster a global identity alongside a national identity. Even within the same nation, these teachers at different schools reported varying definitions that appeared to reflect both personal experiences, but also understandings of the national context in which they were embedded (i.e., the need to engender national identity and values). In their examination of kids' understanding of global citizenship in Northern Ireland, Niens and Reilly (2012) also noted a lack of discussion or connection between conflict in other parts of the world and the sectarian conflict in one's own community. For Goren and Yemini, Israeli teachers were reluctant to include global citizenship as a way of mitigating local ongoing conflicts. Teachers' silence on the topic may be inadvertently passed on to students. Omission by teachers may lead to a reproduction of silence as observed by Niens and Reilly. In effect, the national context can color teachers' attitudes and understanding of global citizenship and inadvertently color students' beliefs.

The responses from students in Pakistan suggest that living in an environment where nationalism is high hinders global citizenship identification. In research with students in China, participants were found to shy away from connecting global citizenship to political issues (Song, 2016). Given the nationalistic environment in which these students where embedded, national pride came before connection to the world. Thanosawan and Laws (2013) found somewhat similar outcomes in their research at two universities in Thailand. The researchers interviewed administrators, lecturers, and students regarding their understanding of global citizenship and how it applies to higher education at an international college and a national university. The researchers noted that the two universities differed with respect to the student population. One contained mainly Thai students while the other had a majority international students. The majority Thai university focused more on national identity, while the latter focused on human rights. The results, again, show that nationalistic atmosphere hindered faculty at the Thai university from teaching for global citizenship.

For young 15-year-old students in Pakistan, the history of the nation, separation from India, represented a need to maintain strong nationalistic values that obviated the need to engage with the world as global citizens (Pasha, 2015). In this context, the problems of the nation at present superseded the problems of the world. Responses from young students highlight the influence of threat at a subgroup level to identification with a superordinate group as part of the context in which global citizenship is understood. Indeed, as discussed later (chapter 5), empirical research shows that a threat to the nation hinders identification with global citizens. The students in this highly nationalistic environment approached global citizenship as a concept highlighting aspects that could advantage themselves (e.g., travel) or advance their nation. While the notion of global citizenship is positive, it is unattainable given the present circumstances in which the students find themselves. Even within the United States, African American college students also noted a lack of caring about global citizenship (Perdue, 2014). Again, the immediate local needs were perceived by students as more important than global problems.

Katzarska-Miller, Reysen, Kamble, and Vithoji (2012) asked participants in the United States, Bulgaria, and India to define global citizenship. The definitions were then coded for common themes which included (1) tolerance and acceptance of other people and cultures, (2) interconnectedness with others, (3) knowledge of places, people, and cultures, (4) engaging in actions for the betterment of the world, (5) travel to other countries, (6) concern for other people and the world, (7) rejection of the nation state, and (8) freedom to travel and work anywhere in the world. Some cross-national differences were found. For example, Bulgarians were more likely than expected to define global citizenship in terms of travel and freedom to work in other parts of the world than either U.S. or Indian participants. U.S. participants were more likely than Bulgarian and Indian participants to define global citizenship in terms of knowledge of the world. The authors posit that the observed differences in definitions are likely due to the importance of these issues for the participants. For example, Bulgarians, due to low economic wealth, are likely unable to afford traveling to other countries. Thus, when asked about global citizenship they highlight a feature that is not afforded to them. Although the participants did mention the other components, travel was mentioned more by Bulgarians than those in the other two countries. The results highlight both similarities and differences of the definition depending on the cultural context in which one is embedded.

Summary

In the above sections we reviewed conceptualizations of global citizenship from students, teachers, individuals in higher education, and individuals in the general population. The most frequently referenced characteristics or prototypes of global citizenship across samples in descending order included awareness of the world and interconnection with others, felt responsibility to act for the betterment of the world, valuing diversity, environmental sustainability, social justice concerns, empathy, and helping others. Given the lay perspective of global citizenship combined with prior academic theorizing we adopt the definition of global citizenship as "global awareness, caring, embracing cultural diversity, promoting social justice and sustainability, and a sense of responsibility to act" (Reysen et al., 2012, p. 29). This definition reflects lay perceptions of global citizenship outside of academia. This definition also contains components mentioned by academics in previous discussions of global citizenship (Reysen, Pierce, et al., 2013), although fragmented at times due to disciplinary silos that highlight one or another component over others. In other words, rather than highlighting one or two specific components (e.g., responsibility, social justice) the present definition encompasses the most referenced ones across both academic and lay populations. We should also note that this definition does not contain our conceptualization of one's normative environment. Although important, it tends to be an invisible component with both academics and lay persons not referencing it. However, it is an essential component when considering what predicts individuals to describe themself as a global citizen. In chapter 2 we reviewed prior research of constructs that were similar to global citizenship such as cosmopolitanism, global identity, and identification with the world. In the following section we review lay conceptualizations of constructs (e.g., global education) that are similar to global citizenship in an effort to highlight commonality between global citizenship and comparable constructs.

LAY PERCEPTIONS OF RELATED CONSTRUCTS

Cosmopolitanism

To examine conceptions of self as cosmopolitan citizens, Jaffee, Watson, and Knight (2014) conducted interviews with 20 West African immigrants in the United States. Of the 20 interviewed, the researchers determined that six expressed ideas that were complementary to the notion of enacted cosmopolitan citizenship (orientation toward the world rooted in everyday experiences, including various perspectives, and showing a commitment to act for the betterment of the world). The larger themes expressed, and reflective of enacted cosmopolitan citizenship, were that of a felt attachment with the global community and action within the world. Participants expressed feeling both a loyalty to their national identity, but also to all of humanity. In terms of action, participants expressed working in various political movements for issues broadly related to social justice (e.g., poverty issues) as a key component of cosmopolitanism. In general, the participants viewed cosmopolitanism as being a global citizen and working for the betterment of all people.

Using the term "cosmopolitanism", Braun, Behr, and Medrano (in press) asked participants to rate the degree to which they viewed themselves as citizens of the world. The follow-up prompt asked participants why they felt that they are a citizen of the world. Participants ($N = 1,883$) included individuals sampled in Spain, Denmark, Hungary, Germany, Canada, and the United States. The researchers organized the responses around probable reasons for either high or low scores on the measure of citizenship with the world. With respect to the reasons for a high score on the measure of identification as a world citizen, the researchers noted three main groupings of response. The first, they termed "banal cosmopolitanism" reflected responses such as geographical references (we are all born on this planet), facilitated border crossing (traveling when opportunity arises), and technology (online information and interactions). The second, "behavioral cosmopolitanism", included transnational experience (travel or living in multicultural places), ancestry (relatives, past or present, living in other countries), and friends (friends with diverse cultural backgrounds). The third, "attitudinal cosmopolitanism", included tolerance (respect for culturally diverse others), globalization (felt responsibility for the world), and common sharings (tendency to see similarities rather than differences in other people/cultures). Two main themes emerged in the data concerning low scoring responses. The first, termed "behavioral non-cosmopolitanism", included themes regarding an absence of transnational experiences (lack of travel), no ancestry, and no friends in other parts of the world. The second theme, "attitudinal non-cosmopolitanism", included non-globalization (lacking perceived interconnectedness) and differences (highlighting differences between cultures rather than similarities). In essence, individuals who felt a connection to others, either through technology or relationships and travel, and those who valued diversity and shared understandings rated themselves as citizens of the world, while an absence of these characteristics were related to low ratings of world citizenship. Together, both of the above studies share similarities with the attributes of global citizenship, namely awareness, concern for social justice, and a felt obligation to act.

Global Identity

In an effort to understand what students' conceptualizations of global identity are, Türken and Rudmin (2013) emailed university student organizations in 24 countries and asked students to write about what they thought a global identity was. The responses included themes such as interest in other cultures, respect/tolerance, international travel, non-nationalism, openness, living in other countries, anti-racism, language usage, global consciousness or perspective, caring for diverse others, being a citizen of the world, identifying with a world community, and knowledge of other cultures. When asked to describe a cosmopolitan person, similar themes emerged.

Mansoory (2012) interviewed 12 university students in Sweden about their understandings of the terms "global identity" and "world citizenship". Global identity was described as feeling a sense of belonging to humanity. World citizenship, similarly, was connected to belongingness; however, students also frequently mentioned a sense of responsibility to work for the betterment of the world. Other topics that were described included environmental sustainability, respect for human rights, empathy, social justice, and concern for global issues. The students described gaining a global identity through education and through socialization by parents, school, and institutions. Again, the attributes described by students are similar to those used when providing understandings of global citizenship.

Global Awareness

As it is apparent from the characteristics used to describe global citizens, global awareness and a felt connection to others in the world is one of the most cited themes. To examine how teachers understand the notion of global awareness, Jing (2013) conducted interviews and discussion groups with 17 English language teachers in Henan province of China. The main themes emerging from the interviews centered on global awareness as knowledge, skills, and attitudes. For teachers, the knowledge component included understanding of globalization, cultures, languages, and global issues. With respect to culture, the discussions included both a knowledge of and respect for others' cultures, as well as of one's own culture, and how that influences one's perspective of the world. The skills component included students' skills in critical thinking, language and communication, and ability to learn. Lastly, the teachers emphasized attitudes such as responsibility for themselves and society, tolerance of others' views and cultural backgrounds, openness, and social justice. In general, the themes focused on openness to others without prejudice or judgment. The teachers believed that their role in encouraging global awareness was to help their students to be become global citizens for both personal and career development. In effect, for teachers to engender global citizenship in their students, they sought to include global awareness in their instruction, which included characteristics similar to those observed when describing global citizens.

Global Education

Although not an identity, global citizenship is often discussed in relation to global education. Teachers hold a strong belief that global education for students' global citizenship is important. Robbins, Francis, and Elliott (2003) surveyed 187 pre-service teachers at the University of Wales to find that teachers believe that global citizenship and promoting a global perspective is important for students. To examine teachers' understanding of global education, McLean, Cook, and Crowe (2008) surveyed 120 pre-service teachers in a teacher-education program in Canada. Although the responses varied in how the teachers explained their conceptualization of global education, the common themes that emerged included social justice and human rights, empathy, respect and tolerance of diversity, as well as a felt responsibility as global citizens. Reimer and McLean (2009) also surveyed 58 Canadian pre-service teachers regarding global education. The themes that emerged were (in order of frequency of mentions): global interdependence (e.g., global awareness), intercultural communication, cooperation, human rights, with fewer participants mentioning environmental sustainability awareness and critical pedagogy.

Horseley, Newell, and Stubbs (2005) surveyed 16 pre-service history teachers studying at the University of Sydney about their conceptualization of global education. History teachers' responses included notions of interconnectedness and relationships between people across countries, working for others and social justice, globalization, and environmental sustainability. Ten students studying teaching in the domain of geography and social sciences, on the other hand, mentioned globalization and the impact on individuals, global citizenship and global awareness, and lastly global issues that impact everyone in the world. The researchers suggest that the difference in disciplines is likely the reason for differences in conceptualizations of global education.

Lastly, Moizumi (2010) interviewed two Canadian elementary-intermediate teachers about their understanding of global citizenship education. One emphasized the interdependence of the world, social justice issues, and the need to act. The other teacher emphasized global awareness and the need to think critically. Similar to teachers' understandings of global awareness and inclusion in their instruction, the teachers in the above studies appear to take the characteristics similar to global citizens and describe global education as containing those components. In other words, starting with the attributes of a global citizen, teachers then describe those components as integral to global education. These results also raise the question about whether there is a difference between global education and global citizenship education. Given the apparent, and large, overlap in conceptualizations we suggest there may be very little difference.

Globalization

Globalization is often cited as a reason for a greater emphasis on global education and the affordance of a global citizen identity. To understand students' views regarding globalization, Chang (2015) interviewed Taiwanese English major university students enrolled in a freshman English class. The university in which the students were situated promoted a global worldview and the specific class included discussions regarding world affairs. At the end of the class, six participants volunteered to have their discussion posts analyzed and participate in one-on-one interviews with the researcher. Of interest for the present chapter are students' view of globalization, as well as their perception of their position in the world. Themes regarding globalization centered on (1) the understanding and definition (e.g., Westernization, influence of globalization on thoughts, students' access to information about the world), (2) degree of familiarity or lack thereof of globalization (e.g., how often and where students are exposed to global information, relevance of globalization for one's self, the vagueness of the concept), (3) the negative aspects of globalization (e.g., Americanization of the world, loss of local customs and traditions), (4) positive aspects of globalization (e.g., access to information), and (5) the influence of Taiwan on the world. With respect to students' position in the world, they mainly focused on their current position as college undergraduates. However, issues related to their language competence, respect for others as part of the world, and a concern of their legitimacy as second language speakers when interacting with others in the world were also recorded. Thus, students shared nuanced understandings of globalization and their place in the world. Although they viewed the positives such as cultural understanding of others and the need to share their culture with others to reach that understanding, they also perceived the negative spread of Western culture that may obviate local cultures. The students also viewed themselves as world citizens and active participants in the global culture. Thus, for these students, when describing globalization, the notion of being a global citizen as an active participant in the world became salient, lending credence to the notion that globalization as a concept is tied to global citizenship.

Summary

In the above research, students and teachers were asked about their conceptualization of constructs (cosmopolitanism, global identity, global awareness, global education) that are related to global citizenship. Similar to the prototypical characteristics associated with a global citizen category label, the respondents in the above diverse samples mentioned themes regarding global awareness and interconnectedness with others, social justice, valuing diversity, responsibility or obligation to act, empathy, environmental sustainability, and helping others. The similar responses point to a number of possible connections between participants' understandings regarding global citizenship and cosmopolitan and global identities, as well as teachers' understandings of what global awareness and global education is and how to teach for engendering global citizenship in students.

CONCLUSION

As noted at the beginning of the present chapter, understanding the lay beliefs and prototypical content associated with category labels is important for informing research. In the present chapter we reviewed lay conceptions of global citizenship from individuals of different ages, nationalities, and roles in society. A common set of themes was observed that matched those theorized by various academics. The frequency of themes across studies suggests that there exists a relatively wide and consensually shared understanding of what a global citizen is. Even when people did not self-categorize as a global citizen or did not know what a global citizen was, they tended to provide definitions that highlighted similar concepts. We suspect that individuals are breaking down the words "global" and "citizen" to construct a definition of global citizenship. However, there also exist context-situated components of global citizenship, such as omission of critical or political aspects in places that emphasize loyalty to the nation. Furthermore, in the present chapter we noted the similarities in concepts related to global citizenship (e.g., global education, global identity). The similarities again highlight the association between global citizenship and these constructs. The results suggest a constellation of topics and concepts that include global citizenship, even if not surrounding it.

NOTE

1. The term "diversity" has been criticized in recent years for becoming a broad and vague term that leads to issues of race and gender to be ignored (e.g., Embrick, 2011) in the U.S. context. Furthermore, because diversity is associated with groups that are "different" from the norm, it establishes Whiteness, maleness, and heterosexuality, as being the norm. We agree with the various criticisms of the term, but chose to keep the mainstream terminology that is utilized in the literature and empirical studies.

Chapter Four

A Model of Antecedents and Outcomes of Global Citizenship Identification

As discussed in the proceeding chapters, the conceptualization and development of global citizenship on both theoretical and lay levels has resulted in multiple commonalities and differences. However, one of the remaining questions is how the different elements of global citizenship relate to each other. What leads some people to experience themselves as global citizens, while others do not? And for those that do experience themselves as global citizens, what are the consequences of that experience? In the current chapter we try to answer the above questions through an empirical model of global citizenship identification (Reysen & Katzarska-Miller, 2013a). Prior to the explanation of the model we review examples of current models of global citizenship, and discuss some of the issues related to the measurement of the concept. Next, we review the theoretical and empirical support for antecedents, identification, and outcomes of global citizenship.

EXAMPLES OF CURRENT MODELS OF GLOBAL CITIZENSHIP

Schattle (2008) conducted interviews with over 150 self-described global citizens of various nationalities. Based on participants' responses to questions such as "what informed your thinking in using 'global citizenship' that didn't necessarily show up in print" (p. 5), Schattle proposed three primary concepts of global citizenship: (1) awareness of self and the outside world, (2) responsibility to all life on the planet, and (3) participation in local and global community. For Schattle there is a suggested temporal order, and while not always adhered to, the general pathway to global citizenship starts with awareness (consciousness of self and the outside world), followed by felt responsibility (shared moral obligation to others in the world), and leading to participation (involvement in different activities such as community, politics, activism to influence government). Schattle also proposed three secondary components of global citizenship, including (1) intergroup empathy, (2) achievement motivation (an aspiration to do some public good such as a teacher engendering global citizenship in students or working to improve human rights), and (3) international travel. The secondary themes were not central to respondents' experience of global citizenship, yet are suggested to provide a fuller view of the concept.

Breitkreuz and Songer (2015) proposed what they termed the "emerging 360 degree model for educating socially responsible global citizens" for U.S. students in STEM disciplines participating in study abroad service-learning programs. Slightly tweaking Schattle's (2008) order of global citizen socialization, the researchers suggest that students must first gain global awareness, then participate in the international community, and lastly, take responsibility (a responsibility to others beyond local loyalties). Through this process of international service learning students are purported to become socially responsible global citizens. The educational experience begins at students' home university through classroom discussions regarding the meaning of the above concepts. By working with partners in another country, a specific need for that country is identified. The students, still at their home university, work with other students (who are from different academic disciplines) to construct solutions to the problem. Once abroad the students work to complete the project with team leader responsibility rotating daily. Back at their home university, students are expected to reflect on the experience, give a presentation, and generally think about how they can be responsible global citizens. Thus, awareness is gained prior to travel, participation occurs while abroad, and responsibility is gained upon reflection of the experience. Assessing opinions regarding the experience indicate participants' high levels of global awareness and desire to continue learning.

Based on interviews of Australian and European academic staff and students, Lilley et al. (2015) proposed a process of global citizen learning. The first step to becoming a global citizen is students "getting out of their comfort zone," during which time they engage in interpersonal encounters with others who are culturally different. Interpersonal interaction with diverse others exposes individuals to alternative viewpoints, and allows for the development of interpersonal relationships. A third aspect of becoming a global citizen is having a cosmopolitan role model (an individual who modeled openness to other cultures and led students to think differently). For Lilley and colleagues this process allows students to develop a global mindset and become global citizens.

Although the above models propose a path to becoming a global citizen in and outside of the classroom, they lack empirical backing and fully developed theoretical frameworks. For example, despite measuring student attitudes at the end of the program, Breitkreuz and Songer (2015) do not measure each component of their model and show the change over time. Although Schattle (2008) provides a great deal of qualitative data to back his model, empirical measures should also be developed to complement and demonstrate the components. The above models do rely on past theorizing; however a broader overarching framework is needed to capture the process of adoption and performance of a global citizen identity. Additionally, although all models note positive aspects of global citizenship, they lack detail in terms of the outcomes of global citizenship. In an effort to reduce the confusion and clutter in the global citizen literature, Reysen and Katzarska-Miller (2013a) proposed and empirically tested a model of antecedents and outcomes of global citizenship identification, which is supported by a growing body of empirical research. The model is based on widely accepted theories, and it has explicit constructs to tap antecedents and outcomes of identifying as a global citizen.

The model contains two antecedents—normative environment and global awareness—which predict global citizenship identification, and global citizenship identification then predicts six clusters of prosocial values (see Figure 4.1). Because of the fluid and dynamic nature of identity adoption, the model of global citizenship identification is positioned both within the notion of intentional worlds (Shweder, 1990), as well as social identity perspective (Tajfel & Turner, 1979; Turner et al., 1987). Intentional worlds posits that individuals inhabit sociocultural spaces constructed by prior generations of actors that influence those embedded in the spaces, while simultaneously those inhabiting them also influence the spaces. Valued others (friends, family) prescribing a global citizen identity and one's degree of global awareness (perceived knowledge and felt interconnectedness with others) predict identification (psychological connection) with global citizens. If one's intentional world does not afford the identity, or if the identity is not viewed as important by valued others, or there is a lack of educational opportunities or access to information, then one is less likely to adopt a global citizen identity. Thus, the left side of the model in Figure 4.1 is explained through the concept of intentional worlds. A social identity perspective governs the right side of the model—global citizenship identification predicting prosocial values. From a social identity approach, when an identity is salient, greater identification predicts greater adherence to the group content (e.g., norms, values, emotions, personality). In other words, if a global citizen identity is salient, greater identification predicts greater endorsement of prosocial values and beliefs. Three main differences between this model and those described above include: (1) the inclusion of normative environment to account for one's sociocultural setting, (2) explicit notion of global citizen as an identity, and (3) outcomes above and beyond responsibility to act.

MEASURING GLOBAL CITIZENSHIP

Another issue, as complex and fragmented as the prior theorizing on global citizenship, pertains to the question of how to measure such an abstract concept. One problem emerges from the vast array of terms used to construct measures around. For example, while Türken and Rudmin (2013) published a measure of global identity and McFarland et al. (2012) a measure assessing identification with all humanity, Salgado and Oceja (2011) published a measure of Quixoteism, and Braskamp (2008) a measure of global perspectives. The first two measures are conceptualized around an identity (arguably), while Quixoteism is defined as a social motive, and global perspectives is a six-factor measure including cognitive knowledge and knowing, intrapersonal identity and affect, and interpersonal social interaction and responsibility. [1] Based on the theoretical and lay conceptualizations of global citizen, we see the concept as identity related. As already discussed in Chapter 1, global

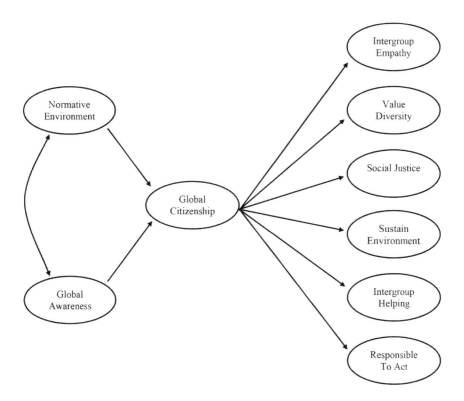

Figure 4.1. Model of antecedents and outcomes of global citizenship identification.

citizen is a psychological category (i.e., identity) that one can attribute to oneself. Because of this, as well as the multiplicity of different terms around which measures are constructed, in the present chapter we only discuss those that specifically mention global citizenship (for general review of related concepts, see chapter 2). We discuss the two major approaches (content and identification) in which global citizen identity has been measured, and identify some of problems related to these approaches.

Measuring Content

A social identity approach suggests that different groups have content (e.g., norms, values, beliefs) that aid in distinguishing one group from another. The studies that approached measuring global citizen identity content had varied in terms of the number of factors that they include, as well as the specificity of the attitudes and behaviors associated with the identity. However, it appears that three-factor scales tend to be favored by researchers. For example, as part of a measure assessing students' "graduateness," Coetzee (2014b) included a dimension termed "global and moral citizenship". Global and moral citizenship is defined as graduates' attitude toward the world and their communities, implicit in which is the importance of aspiring to work for the betterment of the world. To assess the global and moral citizenship dimension, in a sample of South African undergraduate students, Coetzee utilized a measure containing three subscales: *ethical and responsible behavior* (an individual upholding ethics and taking responsibility for one's actions), *presenting and applying information skills* (clear presentation of one's ideas to convince one's audience), and *interactive skills* (effective use of language when communicating with diverse others).

Similarly to Coetzee (2014b), Chui and Leung (2014) examined a three-factor measure assessing individuals' attitude toward global citizenship in a sample of undergraduate students in Hong Kong. The first dimension—*ethnocentric tendency*—reflects desire to work with others from diverse backgrounds. The second dimension—*interest in foreign affairs*—contains items reflecting consumption, discussion, and interest in foreign news. The third dimension—*orientation towards international volunteer activities*—assesses interest to volunteer abroad. Presumably, higher scores on these three indicators reflect a positive attitude toward global citizenship.

Morais and Ogden (2011) developed a three-factor scale of global citizenship in samples of U.S. undergraduate students. In their conceptualization the core components that constituted an individual's degree of global citizenship are social responsibility, global competence, and global civic engagement. *Social responsibility* comprises interdependence with others including a concern for others, as well as concern for society in general and the natural environment. As part of the social responsibility dimension, is students' attention to social issues and concern for social justice. *Global competence* is described as openness to others' cultures and the use of cultural knowledge to interact with others and work outside one's environment. *Global civic engagement* comprises a desire, or actual actions, to participate in improving the lives of others at any level (i.e., local or global). This component of global citizenship includes activities such as political organizing, volunteering, or other forms of participation around one's community. According to the researchers, all three components need to be embodied by individuals for one to be considered a global citizen.

Cho and Chi (2015) proposed and tested a seven-factor measure of global citizenship with undergraduate Korean students. The seven factors include *social responsibility* (importance of social justice, obeying rules, and living conscientiously), *trust* (trust in government and the media), *national identity* (pride in one's country and history), *multicultural awareness* (openness toward people from other cultures and countries), *global awareness* (concern for global problems), *equality* (importance of social and gender equality), and *social participation* (responsibility and importance to work in one's community).

Van Gent, Carabain, De Goede, Boonstoppel, and Hogeling (2013) constructed a measure assessing global citizenship in Dutch adolescents (ages 12 to 17). The researchers defined global citizenship as "behavior that does justice to the principles of mutual dependency in the world, the equality of human beings, and the shared responsibility for solving global issues" (p. 72). Thus, global citizenship is primarily defined and operationalized as engaging in behaviors. Their measure is unidimensional and composed of various behaviors related to energy conservation, recycling, responsible consumption, expressing values related to global citizenship (e.g., talking about poverty to others), donating to charity, and volunteering. In addition, the researchers provided measures for the three proposed principles that are thought to underlie the global citizenship construct, including international equality, international dependency, and shared responsibility.

Although there are similarities in some of the factors tested by the researchers in these various studies, there are differences as well. This points to one of the issues related to measuring an identity via its content. The reviewed measures suggest that if one endorses the associated dimensions then they are a global citizen. If one does not score high on these components then they are not. The problem with this conceptualization of identity is that measuring an identity via its content does not account for its fluidity and potential for change as a function of the cultural and social context.

For example, let us say a researcher wants to create a scale to measure American-ism. One could posit that a core theme of being an American is freedom of speech. Perhaps a second core dimension is consumerism and endorsement of capitalism. Maybe a third is a love for guns. If one approaches the construction of a measure in terms of these dimensions, it will mean that to be an American you must have all of the three present. Scoring high on the three will indicate being American. One must espouse the greatness of free speech, love buying things, and own at least five guns. Although this is an extreme example, we are using it to make the point that these dimensions are trying to pin down something that is constantly shifting. What it means to be an American today is different from what it meant to be an American 100 years ago or what it will mean to be an American 10 years, or even 10 minutes, from now. Similarly, the above measures regarding global citizenship specify particular beliefs, attitudes, and behaviors. Another complication is that since there may be 1,000 different things an American may do, it is impossible to capture all of them on a measure. Indeed, as seen from the above review, many components across various measures differ from one another.

As already demonstrated in Chapter 3, and argued above that measuring the content of an identity can be heavily influenced by context, the most likely explanation for the differences in factors in the above measures is the cultural context of the participants. For example, Cho and Chi (2015) participants were Korean university students, who were receiving higher education either in Korea or in the United States. Although the seven-factor model held for both groups, U.S.-educated Koreans scored higher on trust and national identity, while the Korean-educated ones scored higher on social responsibility and participation. Similarly, while Chui and Leung (2014) participants were Hong Kong university students, Van Gent et al. (2013) participants were Dutch people from various ages and educational backgrounds. Morais and Ogden (2011) participants were students (although not explicitly stated in the paper, we assume American students) enrolled in faculty-led education abroad programs and undergraduate programs that had a relatively brief international experience. What it means to be a global citizen can differ depending on the context. To say that measuring this group content is measuring one's degree of global citizenship is far from ideal as those aspects of the group can change.

Measuring Identification

Instead of trying to capture the content of an identity (measuring endorsement or adherence to a list of characteristics), another way, well known and widely practiced among social identity researchers, is to measure one's psychological connection to that identity (i.e., ingroup identification). Tajfel (1978) defines social identity as "that part of an individual's self-concept which derives from his [sic] knowledge of his [sic] membership of a social group together with the value and emotional significance attached to that membership" (p. 63). Although this definition implies three components of identification with a group (i.e., categorization within group, valuation of group, and emotional connection), over the years a variety of dimensions of ingroup identification have been proposed (Ashmore et al., 2004). Similarly, researchers have constructed measures to capture all of these components; however, the debate of which components are best is ongoing. Thus, the psychological literature is rife with measures of ingroup identification. This can present a difficulty in terms of figuring out which measure to use. For example, a relatively recent scale from Leach and colleagues (2008) proposes five dimensions of ingroup identification: felt solidarity with other group members, satisfaction with the group, centrality of the group for the self, self-stereotyping, and perceiving the group as homogeneous. However, when you move past the variety of proposed dimensions and multitude of measures of ingroup identification, it comes down to one's psychological connection to the group/identity. Indeed, you can measure ingroup identification with a single Likert-type item—I strongly identify with [*insert group*] (Postmes, Haslam, & Jans, 2013; Reysen, Katzarska-Miller, Nesbit, & Pierce, 2013)—from *strongly disagree* to *strongly agree*. We argue that measuring a connection to the group avoids the tedious, and oftentimes impossible, task of measuring the content of an identity. Researchers do not have to place boundaries on characteristics or behaviors, but rather measure how much one feels connected to the identity.

Having answered the question of how to measure an identity, or rather one's level of identification with identity, we turn to the question of what predicts viewing the self as a global citizen. In the remainder of this chapter we review the research of the antecedents to global citizenship identification and the outcomes of that psychological connection. The larger theoretical frameworks that we use—intentional worlds and social identity perspective—are also briefly discussed. Here we apply the theories to understand when individuals identify with global citizens, and what outcomes to expect from highly identified global citizens. The model of antecedents and outcomes of global citizenship identification is depicted in Figure 4.1. On the left side are the antecedents to global citizenship, normative environment and global awareness. These predict global citizenship identification, and global citizenship identification predicts six clusters of prosocial values that represent the group content. In the remainder of the chapter we discuss each of the variables in turn.

ANTECEDENTS TO GLOBAL CITIZENSHIP

The identities that humans have are a way of making sense of the world. Surprisingly, little research has examined the process in which individuals come to identify with different identities/groups (Ashforth, Harrison, & Corley, 2008). One line of research (van Veelen, Eisenbeiss, & Otten, 2016) suggests that attraction to others within the group predicts growing identification over time. Social identity theory (Tajfel & Turner, 1979) suggests that individuals strive to gain or maintain positively distinct group memberships. For example, we want our favorite sport team to be the best because we, as fans, feel a part of the winning team. The group is therefore positive and distinct because the team is objectively better on a relevant dimension than the other comparable teams. Optimal distinctiveness theory (Brewer, 1991) emphasizes affiliation/belongingness and differentiation/distinctiveness as key predictors of choice of group memberships. For example, furry fans— fans of anthropomorphic art and cartoons—who perceive the group as distinct from other fan groups and gain a sense of belonging with other furries by being a fan report a high degree of identification with the fan community (Reysen et al., 2016). However, motivations for joining and engaging with a group differ depending on the group (Schroy et al., 2016). Thus, we may identify strongly with one group because it provides interpersonal distinctiveness, while we may identify with another group because it provides affiliation with similar others. Thus, the answer to how individuals come to strongly identify with groups does not have a straightforward answer.

There are suggestions in the literature about what leads people to identify as global citizens. As mentioned previously, Breitkreuz and Songer (2015) and Schattle (2008) suggest awareness, responsibility, and participation in community activities. Lilley and colleagues (2015) suggest getting out of one's comfort zone, interpersonal interactions with culturally diverse others, and having a cosmopolitan role model. The largest collection of theorizing regarding engendering global citizenship concerns global education (Hicks, 2003). Theorists in this academic arena tend to highlight skills, knowledge, and values to nudge students toward global citizenship. Others suggest greater training for teachers (McLean et al., 2008), or specific programs or activities for global citizenship, such as simulating a model United Nations (Gaudelli & Fernekes, 2004). A growing body of research shows increase in global citizenship after studying abroad (e.g., Chickering & Braskamp, 2009). Others promote the benefits of service learning (e.g., Lilley et al., 2015). Thus, there exist a variety of propositions from theorists for how to induce global citizenship. Most of these suggestions could conceivably fall under the antecedents in the global citizenship identification model.

The two antecedents in the model include one's normative environment and one's degree of global awareness. Normative environment is measured as the perception that valued others (friends, family) promote and support oneself to be a global citizen (i.e., an injunctive norm: Cialdini & Goldstein, 2004). However, the broader conceptualization of normative environment in regard to global citizenship contains a variety of people (e.g., teachers, work supervisors, local government), artifacts (e.g., globe, billboards, community spaces), and cultural patterns (e.g., beliefs and behaviors that promote inter-cultural interaction, notion of helping others in need, social justice beliefs) that can influence one's view of self as a global citizen. Global awareness is defined as knowledge of and felt connectedness with others in the world. Both normative environment and global awareness are closely related to one another. For example, a person who is knowledgeable about the world is more likely to have friends and family who are informed and model the importance and desire of such information. The two antecedents fall under the umbrella of intentional worlds, as an individual enters this constructed environment that is premade to influence, direct, and shape the person toward a particular end (i.e., be a global citizen). One's normative environment as pro-global and global awareness depend on the intentional worlds in which one is embedded. In the following sections we review conceptualizations of these constructs as related to global citizenship as well as empirical research showing that these two variables predict identification with global citizens.

Normative Environment

In educational contexts, students' normative environment is often assumed but rarely specifically mentioned in theorizing on global citizenship, where a greater attention is focused on global awareness, mindset, or competencies. This is most likely due to awareness and knowledge as highly salient themes for educators, while the fluid and often-unconscious aspects of one's environment are not. However, mentions of components that suggest a focus on changing the normative environment to bolster students' educational world to promote global citizenship exist in the literature. Some examples include increasing the number of international students on campus (Blondin, 2015) to improve the diversity of university community (Killick, 2012, 2013), using faculty as mentors or role models (Chickering & Braskamp, 2009), or availability of a greater number of international volunteering opportunities (Bourn & Shiel, 2009). Thus, although not all education theorists ignore students' environment, indeed Young and Commins (2002) suggest the entirety of students' daily environments (i.e., schools, parents, friends, and community members) should model global citizen values and behaviors, there is more emphasis on students' awareness than environment.

Following an intentional worlds perspective (Shweder, 1990), educators and university administrators may *consciously* shape the environmental context for students by changing a mission statement or increase the money afforded to study abroad programs. Teachers may consciously infuse global components into their classrooms with an eye on engendering global citizenship. Parents may intentionally place children in service (e.g., volunteering) or diverse contexts (e.g., travel) or expose them to diverse beliefs (e.g., media such as documentaries). Although students may not be consciously aware of these intentional attempts to influence them, they do have an impact. On the other hand, people (e.g., administrators, teachers, parents) may also *unconsciously* promote global citizenship. For example, one's parents or friends may be interested in other cultures and thus afford opportunities to learn about them. However, to measure each and every aspect of one's normative environment that leads individuals to become global citizens is impossible, although our worlds are filled with people, media, settings, and artifacts that may contribute to global citizenship identification. To simplify measurement, we chose to focus primarily on valued others—most notably friends and family—as targets for tapping the degree that one's normative environment influence their degree of global citizenship identification. Friends and family are proximal influencers on many individuals' lives (vs. more distal influence such as billboard marketing). Similar to trying to measure an identity that has numerous possible characteristics, one's normative environment has a multitude of possible artifacts, media, people that could influence global citizenship. Indeed, we suspect that many people are oftentimes unconscious of the elements in their environment that could promote global citizenship or the degree of influence those elements have on them. For example, one may not be aware that a passion for watching documentaries may have subtly shaped their opinions of others in the world. In other words, the normative environment seems natural, as if it just is, or is taken as a given.

In a study on the cross-national similarities and differences of conceptualization and degree of global citizenship identification, Katzarska-Miller et al. (2012) asked participants in Bulgaria, India, and the United States to rate the perception of their normative environment and global citizenship identification. Both Bulgarian and Indian participants rated themselves significantly higher on both normative environment (belief that friends and family value being a global citizen) and global citizenship identification. Mediation analyses showed that comparison of the samples (Bulgaria vs. United States, India vs. United States) predicted global citizenship identification through the perception of their normative environment as prescribing the global citizen identity. In other words, a possible reason why Bulgarians and Indians report greater global citizenship identification than U.S. participants is because they perceive valued others as placing importance on the identity.

To delve deeper into the results, Reysen and Katzarska-Miller (2017b) conducted a series of studies to both examine a potential explanation of the cross-national differences and to experimentally manipulate normative environment. One component of the normative environment is media. First, the researchers examined media (i.e., newspapers and magazines) popular in both countries. Stories in Bulgaria and the United States were coded for whether they focused on a domestic or global issue. When the story focused on an issue outside one's nation (i.e., global story), it was also coded for whether it related the event back to one's nation. In other words, although the news story may mention an event that occurred in another part of the world (e.g., Russia) it can also focus on whether that event related to one's own nation (e.g., Russia threatening the United States, or Russia withdrawing support for Bulgaria). In both newspapers and magazines, Bulgaria (vs. United States) had more global than domestic stories. Furthermore, when the stories were global, Bulgarian media tended to focus solely on the story while the U.S. media tended to relate the event back to the United States. In other words, the media in Bulgaria focused more on global events and was less likely to place the ingroup in that narrative. The news media's global stories influenced Bulgarians' global citizenship identification.

In a second study, Bulgarians rated how frequently they watched news on television and read newspapers and magazines, as well as their perception of their normative environment and global citizenship identification. News consumption predicted both their perception of their normative environment as prescribing a global citizen identity and their degree of identification. Importantly, participants' ratings of their normative environment mediated the relationship between news consumption and global citizenship identification. In other words, exposure to news containing global stories predicts viewing the self as a global citizen partly because participants thought that valued others place an importance on the identity. Since news is just one aspect of the everyday worlds in which people reside and the study was correlational, the researchers conducted a third study, experimentally manipulating normative environment.

In the third study, U.S. college students were asked to list three ways in which their friends and family exemplify or do not exemplify being global citizens, or did not write about their valued others (i.e., control condition). Participants who wrote about how their friends and family do not exemplify global citizens rated their normative environment and their degree of global citizenship identification significantly lower than participants who wrote about how their valued others do exemplify global citizens. Furthermore, a path model showed that the manipulation of the perception of friends and family influenced the model of antecedents and outcomes of global citizenship identification. Specifically, the manipulation predicted global citizenship identification through ratings of participants' normative environment. The manipulation also influenced ratings of the outcomes (i.e., prosocial values) through the antecedents and global citizenship identification.

The above studies are a few examples of the research demonstrating how one's normative environment affects global citizenship identification. In a qualitative study, Carano (2013) examined self-identified globally minded teachers. In the interviews they suggested that the key contributors to their global mindedness were one's family, exposure to diversity, mentors, and classes with global components. Again, this shows the wide variety of aspects of one's everyday settings that can lead one to global citizenship. We are sure future research will continue to highlight other cultural patterns and components to engender global citizenship. We will also cover other variables that influence the model in the next chapter. However, at this point we turn to the other antecedent to global citizenship identification—global awareness.

Global Awareness

Although global citizen theorists often neglect one's normative environment, they certainly do not miss giving attention to global awareness. As noted in the models mentioned at the beginning of this chapter (Breitkreuz & Songer, 2015; Lilley et al., 2015; Schattle, 2008), they all contain a concept related to global awareness. Indeed, a look through global education literature finds global awareness in nearly every description of global citizenship. And as with the prior models, the researchers and theorists tend to place global awareness as preceding viewing the self as a global citizen. For example, Hanvey (1976) proposed a five stage model of awareness that leads to taking a global perspective (perspective consciousness, awareness of the state of the planet, cross-cultural awareness, knowledge of global dynamics, and awareness of human choices). Banks (2001) argues that teachers must first become aware of their global identification before helping students. Braskamp (2008) highlights students' global perspective as an indicator of global citizenship. Larsen (2014) splits awareness into different dimensions, such as self-awareness and responsibility awareness. Needless to say, although many notions of global citizenship are contested and debated in various academic circles, nearly everyone agrees that global awareness is important for global citizenship. This is also true for the present model.

We define global awareness as individuals' knowledge of the world and felt interconnectedness with others. Similar to one's normative environment, individuals' degree of global awareness is likely shaped by the intentional worlds in which they are embedded. A person may be afforded greater education with a global focus due to privileges of affluence of one's family. Or, through friendships with people from diverse groups, one may feel a stronger connection to some cultural groups than others. An important note is that empirical evidence shows that global awareness is perceived, rather than reflective of actual knowledge about the world. A person may know a lot of facts about the world but that will not necessarily translate into feeling knowledgeable or connected to others. Conversely, one may lack world information but view themselves as knowledgeable and connected. We expect that some educators will not be pleased by this notion (including one of us), as they may believe that teaching factual knowledge will transform students into global citizens; however, research suggests that perceptions are more important than actual knowledge. This is not to say that the two are not connected; people who know a lot will be more likely to perceive themselves as knowledgeable, although that will not always be the case.

To start, factual knowledge is related to global citizenship identification. To examine the association between global awareness and global citizenship identification, Reysen, Katzarska-Miller, Gibson, and Hobson (2013) administered a test of factual world knowledge prior to rating model related items. U.S. college students completed multiple-choice questions such as "Where is Argentina located?" and "What country produces the most carbon dioxide emissions annually?" The number of correct answers was correlated with students' degree of global citizenship identification. However, as we assert, perception of one's global awareness is more important than factual knowledge. Due to the correlational nature of this study, in a second one the researchers manipulated students' perception of their knowledge.

In a second study, students were brought into the laboratory for individual testing sessions. Students were informed that the researchers were examining a new test of world knowledge that predicts their interconnectedness with the rest of the world. Participants then completed the same multiple-choice test as Study 1. After finishing the test on a computer the experimenter left to an adjoining room while the participant waited for the results. Within earshot, but out of eyesight, of the participant, the experimenter printed a blank sheet of paper and shuffled papers around. Upon returning to the room, the experimenter handed the participant a manila folder with the purported results of the test. In actuality, the experimenter had randomly selected the folder from a stack containing the manipulation. The results given to the student either said that the student had performed poorly, the student had received a high score, or a statement was given that the test was still undergoing validation and no results could be presented at that time (control condition). The experimenter, blind to the participants' feedback, then instructed the student to complete a questionnaire and left the room. Students completed a survey of the antecedents and outcomes of global citizenship identification.

The manipulation of students' perceived knowledge showed that students who were informed they scored high on the test rated their perceived global awareness significantly higher than participants who were informed they scored low or were in the control condition. Students who were told they scored high on the test also reported higher global citizenship identification than those who scored low on the test. A path model showed the influence of the manipulation on students' ratings of the model. The manipulation influenced global citizenship identification through both perceived normative environment and global awareness. The manipulation also influenced prosocial values through the antecedents and global citizenship identification. The results provide experimental evidence of the role of perception of one's global awareness on global citizenship identification. Regardless of the students' actual scores on the test, their perceptions of doing well or poorly caused their global citizenship identification to fluctuate accordingly.

Students, and people in general, may have an illusion or perception that they know more about the world than they actually do. The concept of an illusion of explanatory depth (Wilson & Keil, 1998) posits that individuals fail to realize how little they actually know about various topics. People perceive themselves to be knowledgeable until they are asked to describe their knowledge in detail. In a study of this illusion on global awareness and global citizenship identification, Parkerson and Reysen (2015) had U.S. undergraduate students first rate their perceived knowledge of global issues, normative environment, global awareness, and global citizenship identification. Participants then answered a short multiple-choice test regarding a global issue (e.g., environmental sustainability) before rating the measures again. Participants were then informed of the correct answers and then rated the same measures again. This procedure then repeated itself two more times regarding other global issues. At each time point of measurement ratings of knowledge, normative environment, global awareness, and global citizenship identification decreased. In other words, when asked to show their knowledge, students' illusion was chipped away and they felt less globally aware and less identified with global citizens. The drop in perceived knowledge of global issues (from first rating compared to last rating) predicted the drop in global citizenship identification through the decrease in students' perception of their global awareness. The results again support the influence of perceived knowledge and awareness on global citizenship identification.

GLOBAL CITIZENSHIP IDENTIFICATION AND PROSOCIAL OUTCOMES

Up to this point we discussed the left side of the model, where normative environment and global awareness are antecedents that predict individuals' degree of global citizenship identification. Now we are turning our attention to the right side of the model (i.e., the outcomes of global citizenship identification). Following a social identity perspective, when a global citizen identity is salient, greater identification predicts greater adherence to the group content (e.g., norms, values, behaviors, personality). The model posits six clusters of prosocial values that represent the outcomes or the group content of global citizen identity. As noted previously, there are a multitude of measures, unidimensional and multidimensional, to assess individuals' degree of ingroup identification (see Reysen, Katzarska-Miller, Nesbit, & Pierce, 2013). The measure often used in research examining the model is best described as a measure of self-categorization, which captures the extent to which one categorizes themselves as a global citizen. Another way of thinking about global citizenship identification is the degree of one's psychological connection to the identity.

In a series of studies, Reysen, Pierce, et al. (2013) sought to examine variables that may be part of the content of global citizen identity. Furthermore, they explored whether identification with global citizens was different than identification with synonymous terms (e.g., cosmopolitans). The results suggested that global citizenship identification uniquely predicted various prosocial values (e.g., environmental sustainability) above and beyond identification with other identities (e.g., cosmopolitan, world citizen). For example, identification with global citizens, but not identification with humans, predicted variables such as intention to sponsor a child, intention to give to a charity and micro-financing, and intention to act in environmentally sustainable ways. In other words, the content of global citizen identity differs from the content of other group labels. The results of this research also tended to show that identification with global citizens consistently predicted endorsement of the six clusters of prosocial values, which also were often mentioned by lay participants as components of global citizenship, to be discussed next.

Across multiple studies, researchers have examined the association between global citizenship identification and various other concepts. As shown in Table 4.1, global citizenship identification is positively correlated with other identities, dimensions of big five personality, values related to valuing diversity, environmental sustainability, social justice, and variables related to peace, just to name a few. However, the variables that most closely associated with global citizenship identification across multiple studies tended to revolve around six clusters of prosocial values. These six prosocial outcomes include: (1) intergroup empathy, (2) valuing diversity, (3) social justice, (4) environmental sustainability, (5) intergroup helping, and (6) a felt responsibility to act for the betterment of the world. Following a social identity perspective, greater identification with global citizens should predict higher endorsement of these prosocial outcomes if they are components of the group content. Each of these prosocial values is briefly discussed below.

Intergroup empathy is a felt connection and concern for people outside one's ingroup. This concept is often mentioned in prior theorizing concerning global citizens. For example, Schattle (2008) suggests that awareness of interconnectedness with others, regardless of subgroup memberships, leads to greater empathetic concern. Golmohamad (2008) suggests that empathy results from identifying as a global citizen, and further proposes that empathy will lead to altruistic acts to help others. Empathetic concern is also related to valuing others regardless of their geographical, cultural, ethnic, or religious backgrounds. In other words, intergroup empathy is a felt connection and concern for others regardless of what group they belong to. *Valuing diversity* represents an interest and appreciation for the multitude of cultures in the world. Following prior theorizing, global citizens respect diversity in per-

Table 4.1. Correlations with Global Citizenship Identification

Variable	Correlation	Paper
Human Identification	.21**	A
American Identification	.12**	A
Texan Identification	.12**	A
Student Identification	.22**	A
Extraversion	.04	A
Agreeableness	.16**	A
Conscientiousness	.14**	A
Emotional Stability	.11*	A
Intellectualism/Openness	.20**	A
Exposure to Global Information	.18**	B
National Equality	.23**	B
Concern for Global Warming	.28**	B
Factual Knowledge of World	.30**	C
Intentional Worlds view of Culture	.27**	D
Desire to Attend Cultural Events	.57**	E
Desire to Learn about other Cultures	.61**	E
Environmental Human Interference	.49**	E
Environmental Equity in Development	.46**	E
Environmental Duties to Nonhumans	.55**	E
Consumerism	.02	E
Economic Individualism	.01	E
Economic Equity	-.09	E
Normative Environment	.75**	F
Global Awareness	.53**	F
Intergroup Empathy	.42**	F
Valuing Diversity	.51**	F
Social Justice Beliefs	.41**	F
Environmental Sustainability	.38**	F
Intergroup Helping	.39**	F
Responsibility to Act for World	.56**	F
Positive Emotions	.35**	G
Academic Motivation	.56**	G
Protesting Unethical Corporations	.47**	G

Variable	Correlation	Paper
Pro-Gay Attitudes	.14*	H
National Attachment	.20**	H
National Glorification	.10	H
World Peace	.23**	H
Ethnocentrism	.06	H
Multiculturalism	.12*	H
Liberal Political Orientation	.17*	H
Religiosity	.07*	H
Intrinsic Religious Motivation	.10*	H
Extrinsic Religious Motivation	.17*	H
Quest Religious Motivation	.17*	H
University Normative Environment	.47**	I
Attitude toward Technology	.16**	J
Social Network Usage	.12**	J
Grade-point Average	.05**	J
Intergroup Forgiveness	.25**	K
Concern for Human Rights	.44**	K
Support for Diplomacy	.36**	K
Attitude toward Peace	.35**	K
Support for the War on Terror	-.14*	K
Nationalism	-.08	K
Patriotism	.03	K
Internationalism	.39**	K

Note. $* p < .05$, $** p < .01$. A = Jenkins, Reysen, & Katzarska-Miller, 2012; B = Katzarska-Miller, Reysen, Kamble, & Vithoji, 2012; C = Reysen, Katzarska-Miller, Gibson, & Hobson, 2013; D = Reysen & Katzarska-Miller, 2013b; E = Reysen, Pierce, et al., 2013; F = Reysen & Katzarska-Miller, 2013a; G = Snider, Reysen, & Katzarska-Miller, 2013; H = Katzarska-Miller, Barnsley, & Reysen, 2014; I = Blake, Pierce, Gibson, Reysen, & Katzarska-Miller, 2015; J = Lee, Baring, Sta Maria, & Reysen, 2017; K = Reysen & Katzarska-Miller, 2017a.

spectives (Morais & Ogden, 2011) and beliefs and practices of others (Dower, 2002a, 2002b; O'Byrne, 2003). *Social justice* includes attitudes concerning human rights and equitable treatment of all humans. Global citizen theorists often link global citizenship with the notion of respecting and protecting human rights (Dower, 2002a, 2002b; Heater, 2000; O'Byrne, 2003; Pitty et al., 2008).

Environmental beliefs are a set of values related to protecting the natural environment and acting in an environmentally sustainable manner. Global citizens are posited to feel a duty to the planet (O'Byrne, 2003), responsibility to future generations to protect the environment from pollution (Heater, 2000), express concern for environmental issues, and display a commitment for sustainable development (Gibson et al., 2008). *Intergroup helping* is defined as behaviors that aid outgroup members. This can be locally (e.g., community service), but also globally (e.g., helping by volunteering or giving to charities that work across national borders). Thus, global citizens contribute to or assist global organizations, advance prosocial global agendas (Morais & Ogden, 2011), and identify and work to reduce global problems (Arcaro, 2009). A *responsibility to act* is reflected in an acceptance of a moral duty or obligation to act for the betterment of the world. This felt responsibility can manifest itself in a variety of actions such as trying to solve global problems (Osler & Vincent, 2002), feeling an obligation to help marginalized peoples (Dower, 2008), a felt commitment to civic action to improve the world (Banks, 2001), engagement with democratic political processes (Ibrahim, 2005), or service in the community (Golmohamad, 2008).

CONCLUSION

Across a wide variety of studies (e.g., Katzarska-Miller, Barnsley, & Reysen, 2014; Blake, Pierce, Gibson, Reysen, & Katzarska-Miller, 2015), greater identification with global citizens predicts these six clusters of prosocial values. We use short two-item measures to assess each of these constructs to reduce possible fatigue on the part of participants. However, research with longer measures show the constructs are related to global citizenship identification. Despite the use of short measures, future researchers may one day construct a longer scale to tap into dimensions within the six clusters of values and behaviors (e.g., break down responsibility into different dimensions). Also, we should reiterate that identification and the content of global citizenship are separate constructs. Researchers should not combine identification and values in the same construct when assessing these variables. What should also become apparent from prior theorizing (see Chapter 1) and lay perceptions (see Chapter 3) of global citizenship is that the six clusters of prosocial values match both theoretical and lay conceptualizations. The prosocial values are also similar to the dimensions of global citizenship found in prior measures reviewed in this chapter. In other words, academics' and lay persons' perceptions of global citizenship map onto those dimensions that empirical evidence also suggest are related to global citizenship. The main difference between the present model and those proposed before is a clearer theoretical framework and a wealth of evidence to support it. This is not to say that all possible dimensions are included in the present model. Other variables may be identified in future research and included. Indeed, as we touted earlier the advantage of measuring identification rather than specific dimensions of global citizenship is that the dimensions can be fluid depending on historical, situational, and cultural context. At present these six clusters of prosocial values and behaviors appear to represent the content of global citizen identity; however, that may change in the future. Regardless, the current state of research points to the present model as consistent and inclusive of the various conceptualizations of global citizenship. The next step is to explore what influences the model, as will be described in the next chapter.

NOTE

1. Braskamp (2008) discusses the Global Perspectives Inventory (GPI) as including an item "I see myself as a global citizen" under the intrapersonal affect factor. The GPI has undergone changes resulting in an updated version from 2014 (Braskamp, Braskamp & Engberg, 2014). The "I see myself as a global citizen" item is no longer part of the inventory.

Chapter Five

Predictors of the Global Citizenship Identification Model

In the last chapter we detailed the theory and measurement of a model of antecedents and outcomes of global citizenship identification. In the present chapter we review research examining factors that influence the model. We begin by noting the influence of taking classes with a global focus or containing global topics, as well as the relationship between grade point average and global citizenship identification. Stepping back more broadly, we review how the educational environment itself may influence global citizenship. This focus on global citizenship in education is understandable as schools are one place that we as a society have control in shaping students for desired outcomes, but also because research shows that education is the best predictor of viewing the self as a citizen of the world (Smith et al., 2016). Following education, we review research related to culture and self-construal as predictors of the model, followed by research suggesting that technology and the media consumed by individuals affects global citizenship. Culture and technology are omnipresent factors in our lives and often mentioned when discussing globalization. The spread of culture and use of technology are essential for understanding others in the world. Next, we review research on individual characteristics of political orientation and religiosity and religious motivation, and discuss research related to the self and global citizenship. Politics and religion, while two conversational topics to avoid at dinner parties, deeply influence peoples' lives and perception of the world. Lastly, we highlight intentional worlds and the aspects of everyday environments as affording and promoting a global citizen identity. Together, the chapter provides a review of factors in an exploration of how aspects of our lives influences antecedents and outcomes of global citizenship identification.

EDUCATIONAL CONTENT

As noted in Chapter 1, many nations have incorporated global education into their national educational policies, with more explicitly beginning to reference global citizenship as an outcome for students. Furthermore, the bulk of theorizing and research on global citizenship revolves around education. Given this predominance of education in the area of global citizenship we felt it appropriate to start this chapter examining education, both content and environment, as predictors of the model of antecedents and outcomes of global citizenship identification. Although we delve deeper into global citizenship in education in the next chapter, presently we focus on aspects of education that influence the model.

In an early study examining predictors of the model of antecedents and outcomes of global citizenship identification, Reysen and colleagues (2012) administered measures of the model to students in 30 different classes, predominantly U.S. participants, at the beginning and end of a college semester. The key predictor was the number of words contained in class syllabi related to global citizenship. First, to arrive at a global citizen–related word list, the researchers collected over 500 definitions of global citizenship provided by students. Then, in the laboratory, participants were presented with the most frequently used words in the definitions and asked to categorize them as either related to "global citizen" or "other" in a reaction time task. Words that were categorized as related to global citizen the most quickly comprised the word list (for evidence of validity of the global citizen word list see Reysen, Pierce, et al., 2014). Each class syllabi was analyzed counting the number of words related to global citizenship with the assumption that syllabi with more global citizen–related words would indicate greater coverage of global topics and issues.

A structural equation model was conducted with the number of words predicting the antecedents, the antecedents predicting global citizenship identification, and identification predicting the six clusters of prosocial values assessed at the end of the semester (controlling for ratings at the beginning of the semester). The number of global citizen–related words in the syllabi predicted global awareness. Both global awareness and normative environment predicted global citizenship identification, and identification, in turn, predicted the prosocial values. The number of words in the syllabi also indirectly predicted prosocial values through the antecedents and identification. In effect, enrollment in a class with a greater number of global citizenship–related words predicted greater global citizenship identification and endorsement of the prosocial values at the end of the semester (while controlling for ratings at the beginning of the semester). Since we did not assess whether students perceived the class as containing global components, the results provided only indirect support for the importance of education on global citizenship identification.

In an effort to directly measure students' perception of their class as global, Blake and colleagues (2015) assessed measures of the model at the beginning and end of a college semester. At the end of the semester, students, predominantly U.S., also rated the extent to which the class contained information regarding economic, social, cultural, technological, and environmental global issues. The items were combined to form a measure of the global components of the class. Viewing the class as global predicted both normative environment and global awareness at the end of the semester. The antecedents predicted identification, and identification predicted prosocial values all while controlling for ratings at the beginning of the semester. As with the prior study, perception of one's class predicted greater global citizenship identification at the end of the semester through the antecedents, and greater endorsement of prosocial values through the antecedents and identification. In effect, perceiving one's college class as global influences antecedents, identification, and outcomes of global citizenship. However, although this study provides a direct measure of students' perception of the class as containing global elements in the curriculum, the study does not measure actual (factual) knowledge. Does students' actual knowledge relate to global citizenship identification?

As noted in the prior chapter, the global awareness component of global citizenship is operationalized as the perception of knowledge and one's felt interconnectedness with others in the world. As also noted, perception of global awareness or knowledge is a better predictor of global citizenship identification than factual knowledge (Reysen, Katzarska-Miller, Gibson, et al., 2013). When students' awareness of their factual knowledge is chipped away, their perception decreases along with their identification with global citizens (Parkerson & Reysen, 2015). However, as shown in the above studies, taking a class with global components predicts students viewing themselves as globally knowledgeable. Thus, perception of knowledge is a strong predictor of identification. However, factual knowledge is still important, as learning factual information is likely to also increase students' perceived knowledge. Another measure of knowledge that is universally recognized, although often debated with respect to validity (Richardson, Abraham, & Bond, 2012), is students' grade point average.

College students' grade point average has been shown to predict greater awareness, knowledge, and engagement with cultural diversity (Engberg, Davidson, Manderino, & Jourian, 2016), world-mindedness (Kirkwood-Tucker et al., 2010), as well as willingness to become a global citizen (Zhang, Hsu, & Wang, 2010). In a study examining the influence of students' grade point average on the model, Lee et al. (2017) assessed measures of the model in a large sample of students at a university in the Philippines. Students' grade point average directly predicted normative environment and global awareness, which in turn, directly predicted identification, and identification the prosocial outcomes. Students' grade point average indirectly predicted global citizenship through the antecedents, and prosocial values through the antecedents and identification. Thus, greater grade point average influences the model through both of the antecedents.

To summarize, the present research shows that classes with global content influence the model of antecedents and outcomes of global citizenship identification. This was shown with an indirect measure of words related to global citizenship in the syllabi, as well as students' ratings of the extent to which the class contained global topics. Although education influences the model, we note that the measures regard perceived knowledge. Factual knowledge is related to global citizenship identification, but perception of knowledge is a better predictor. Lastly, another measure of students' knowledge—grade point average—is also found to predict the model. Across the studies, participation and better grades in school are related to viewing the self as a global citizen.

EDUCATIONAL ENVIRONMENT

Following the notion of intentional worlds (Shweder, 1990), individuals are influenced by, and influence, the everyday environments in which they are embedded. Beyond the specific classes that students take, which may include global components, students walk out of the class into the campus environment. The model of antecedents and outcomes of global citizenship identification takes into account that various aspects of our everyday worlds (e.g., media, people, places, artifacts) can influence our sense of self. Although normative environment is operationalized as valued others (friends, family) prescribing a global citizen identity in the model measures, other aspects of one's normative environment can indirectly influence global citizenship identification. For example, universities have faculty, administrators, organizations, programs, students, as well as artifacts (e.g., wall displays) which can prime and condition a global citizen identity as well as impressing upon students more generally that global citizenship is a valued construct of the organization. As such, researchers have also examined students' perception of their university environment as influencing the model.

Blake and colleagues (2015) directly measured students' perception of the university environment as a predictor of the model. U.S. college students rated a single item "The university encourages me to be a global citizen" along with the model measures. Students' perception of the university as prescribing a global citizen identity predicted both normative environment and global awareness. The antecedents predicted identification, and identification predicted prosocial outcomes. The perception of the university as prescribing a global identity indirectly influenced global citizenship identification through the antecedents, and prosocial values through the antecedents and identification. In a similar study examining U.S. students' perception of the university as ethically responsible (i.e., environmentally responsible and fair treatment of employees and students), Assis, Reysen, Gibson, and Hendricks (2018) found university perception again influencing the model. Viewing the university as modeling ethical behavior predicted the antecedents, antecedents predicted identification, and identification predicted the outcomes. The results of these studies support the assertion that the university itself is part of the normative environment, can be perceived by students as prescribing an identity, and can influence students' sense of self.

Beyond these broad perceptions of the university as prescriptive of an identity and modeling ethical behaviors, the university is filled with faculty and administrators who can impact students. For example, one of the authors of this book attended a freshman orientation at their university. On stage, in front of the hundreds of undergraduate students, a university administrator brought up Thomas Friedman's (2005) book, *The World is Flat*. The administrator spoke about the world as shrinking and the job market that the students will eventually enter as globally competitive. Presumably, the speech was meant to encourage students to work hard in college to be competitive after they graduate and enter that global job market. Bringing this example back to the laboratory, Snider and colleagues (2013) presented U.S. college students with either a message about the job market becoming globally competitive, jobs becoming culturally diverse, or no information presented (i.e., control condition). After reading the message claimed to be from an administrator of the university, students rated various measures including global citizenship identification. The results showed that students reported significantly lower global citizenship identification when presented with the competitive job market speech than the culturally diverse job market speech, alongside students' academic motivation. In effect, a speech meant to bolster students to work hard by emphasizing global competition had the opposite effect when tested experimentally with students reporting lower academic motivation and global citizenship identification.

Although the above study shows how a school administrator can unintentionally decrease students' motivation and identification with global citizens, students spend more time in college interacting with faculty than administrators. Gibson and Reysen (2013) conducted two studies examining faculty perceptions of global citizenship and the impact of these perceptions on students. In Study 1, U.S. university faculty defined globalization, diversity, culture, and global citizenship, as well as rated the model measures (i.e., antecedents, identification, prosocial outcomes). Most of the faculty mentioned themes revolving around global citizenship and global awareness.

However, a small portion of the faculty also wrote comments reflecting unfavorable attitudes about global citizenship (e.g., politically correct jargon, more a religion than science). The researchers compared ratings on the model measures for faculty who answered the definition question and those who wrote that they did not know the definition of global citizenship. The faculty who provided a definition (vs. those who responded that they did not know the definition) reported higher normative environment, greater global awareness, and were more identified with global citizens. Thus, in this first study, faculty showed varied responses to the definition questions that tended to either be positive (global awareness) or negative. Knowledge or attempt at a definition was related to higher ratings of viewing the self as a global citizen.

In a second study the researchers presented U.S. undergraduate students with the faculty-generated definitions from Study 1 as part of a lecture from a university instructor. The lectures either focused on global awareness (e.g., "Global citizenship relates to the individual's awareness of other cultures, countries, races, traditions, and resources"), negative connotations (e.g., "This sounds like politically correct jargon to me and more a religion than a science"), or information about how a thermometer works (i.e., control condition). After the manipulation, participants rated the model measures. Participants in the negative connotations condition (vs. globally aware) rated normative environment, awareness, and global citizenship identification significantly lower. In other words, hearing a faculty member speak discouragingly about global citizenship directly impacted students' view of themselves as global citizens. Using the conditions as a predictor of the model, the manipulation predicted normative environment, the antecedents predicted identification, and identification predicted the prosocial outcomes. Thus, how a faculty member presents their opinion of global citizenship has a significant impact on students' view of themselves. The results once again highlight that important people in individuals' everyday environment, in this case university faculty, influence students' attitudes and identification.

To summarize, students are influenced by more than the books, articles, and lectures in the classroom. Students' perceptions of the university as prescribing a global citizen identity, as modeling ethical behavior, and administrators and faculty influence students' global citizenship identification and have a downstream effect on endorsement of prosocial values and behaviors. Given the amount of time students spend at school as part of their daily lives, greater attention to the aspects of the school normative environment as pro-global is warranted. This is discussed further in the next chapter on education.

CULTURE

Prior measures of cultural intelligence tend to assess one's knowledge and ability to adapt and work effectively in international contexts (Ng, Van Dyne, & Ang, 2012). However, such measures do not necessarily address individuals' perceptions of culture. Building upon Shweder's (1990) notion of intentional worlds, Reysen and Katzarska-Miller (2013b) examined U.S. college students' belief in an intentional worlds view of culture as a predictor of antecedents and outcomes of global citizenship identification. Intentional worlds, the theoretical basis for the antecedent side of the model, can be boiled down to four main points: (1) intentional worlds are filled with meaningful cultural patterns from prior generations, (2) everyday worlds are experienced by those in them as reality, (3) intentional worlds shape behavior and human experience, and (4) people can facilitate propagation of those patterns, reject them, or transform them. In this view culture is presented as dynamic (people shape culture and culture shapes people) and fluid (cultural patterns rather than traits inherent in people and change over time). After participants rated their perception of culture as intentional worlds, they completed the model measures. Endorsement of an intentional worlds view of culture predicted the antecedents, the antecedents predicted identification, and identification predicted the prosocial measures. Endorsement of intentional worlds showed indirect effects on global citizenship identification and prosocial values. The results show that individuals' view of culture, in this instance as dynamic and fluid, predicts viewing the self as a global citizen. A possible explanation is that viewing culture as dynamic reflects a more holistic perception of the world. Global education proponents (Pike, 2008; Selby, 1999; Young, 2010) often highlight the importance of dynamic interconnectedness as a way to induce global citizenship. Viewing culture as intentional worlds is similar to this view of the world.

Researchers within psychology have long studied and measured indicators of cultural patterns. A popular distinction between independent and interdependent self-construal is often assessed cross-culturally (Oyserman, 2017). An independent self-construal reflects individuality, uniqueness, self-assertion, promotion of personal goals, and a focus on one's internal states, while an interdependent self-construal reflects connectedness with others, social relationships, belonging, promotion of others' goals, and a focus on others' behaviors and emotions in relation to the self (Markus & Kitayama, 1991). Interdependent self-construal is related to interpersonal connectedness, cooperation, environmental concern (Arnocky, Stroink, & DeCicco, 2007), perception of common humanity (Neff, Pisitsungkagarn, & Hsieh, 2008), community participation (Xin, Yang, & Ling, 2017), empathy (Miyahara et al., 2018), and helping others (Pavey, Greitemeyer, & Sparks, 2011). One can hypothesize that interdependent construal will be related to global citizenship identification to a higher degree than independent self-construal. One reason is that interdependent self-construal reflects an interconnectedness with others. Interconnectedness is also part of the global awareness antecedent to global citizenship identification. A second possible reason is the overlapping associations between interdependent self-construal and outcomes of global citizenship such as viewing the self as connected to others in the world, intergroup empathy and helping, and environmental sustainability.

To test the above hypothesis Gibson, Reysen, and Katzarska-Miller (2014) asked U.S. and Chinese college students to write about meaningful personal characteristics (independent self-construal prime), meaningful personal relationships (interdependent self-construal prime), or no prime (i.e., control condition) prior to rating the model measures. Collapsed across samples, participants in the interdependent condition (vs. control) rated their normative environment and global citizenship identification significantly higher. The manipulation of self-construal predicted normative environment, the antecedents predicted identification, and identification predicted the prosocial outcomes. The manipulation (control and independent vs. interdependent), similar to prior studies, had a downstream effect on identification and prosocial values. Thus, priming one's meaningful personal relationships (i.e., interdependent self-construal) highlighted valued others who were then rated as prescribing a global identity. Together, the results of this research show that different conceptualizations of culture have distinctive relationship with global citizenship. A belief in culture as fluid and dynamic, and priming an indicator of a cultural pattern—interdependence—predicts the global citizenship identification model.

MEDIA AND TECHNOLOGY

Media and technology are ubiquitous aspects of individuals' everyday environment. In other words, they are part of the intentional worlds in which we are embedded. The spread of technology has spurred the advance of globalization and afforded individuals the ability to connect with others across the world. Social network sites offer individuals the opportunity to make and maintain friendships, and feel connected to others more broadly (Bonds-Raacke & Raacke, 2010). Beyond connecting with others, the internet also allows the spread of news and information nearly instantaneously. As noted in Chapter 3, technology and communication through technology was a theme (although not a frequent one) that participants mentioned when describing a global citizen. Furthermore, information and technology usage allows individuals to learn about other parts of the world and stay up-to-date on events, including global problems. In a sample of college students in the Philippines, Lee and colleagues (2017) assessed the number of social network sites (e.g., Facebook, Twitter) that students used along with attitude toward technology as predictors of the model. Both the number of social network sites used and a positive attitude toward technology predicted normative environment and global awareness. The antecedents predicted global citizenship identification, and identification predicted the prosocial outcomes. Connecting to others on more social network sites and a favorable view of technology also showed indirect effects on global citizenship identification and prosocial values. However, this study did not assess frequency or type of usage of social network sites or how technology is used, prompting the need for future research in this area. As technology advances, greater research will aid in understanding how increased usage influences individuals' sense of self and the connection with others in the world.

Fan communities have long been associated with particular forms of media such as science fiction (e.g., *Star Trek*) (Reysen & Lloyd, 2012). Fans are ardent and enthusiastic supporters of an interest (Reysen & Branscombe, 2010). Although fan interests can be diverse (e.g., collecting stamps or Barbie dolls) most interests are connected in some manner with media (e.g., music, television show, books/authors, movie or genre of movies). For example, sport fans tend to watch sport on television and follow news of teams and players on the internet. Even when individuals are not part of organized fan groups or clubs, they still feel that they are part of a community of like-minded others who also enjoy that interest (Reysen & Branscombe, 2010). Although some academics may not view fan communities as impactful on individuals' daily life (see Jenkins, 1992), research suggests otherwise. Indeed, fans have been found to rate their connection to fan groups stronger than their connection to traditional communities such as one's neighborhood (Chadborn, Edwards, & Reysen, in press). Some artists and fan communities are associated with prosocial causes (e.g., global poverty, gay rights) or linked with charitable organizations (Bird & Maher, 2017; Jung, 2012; Pareles, 2012; Schulman & Godard, 2010). Thus, fans in these fandoms are encouraged to join or contribute toward mitigating global problems. Fandoms that encourage prosocial values and behaviors may also encourage viewing the self as a global citizen. Given the strong importance placed on fans' interests and the fandoms that surround them, we sought to examine whether fan communities influence individuals' global citizenship.

To explore the possible influence of fan communities to promote a global citizen identity, Plante, Roberts, Reysen, and Gerbasi (2014) conducted two studies including measures of the model. In Study 1, the researchers administered the model measures to furries—fans of art and stories featuring anthropomorphized animal characters (Plante, Reysen, Roberts, & Gerbasi, 2016)—and a sample of U.S. community members from Amazon's Mechanical Turk. Although the furry community is most well-known for dressing in mascot-like costumes (only a minority of furries own or wear such a costume), the fan community has norms of acceptance and tolerance of diverse others, environmentally sustainable beliefs and behaviors, and donations to animal welfare charities. These latter characteristics are similar to those endorsed by highly identified global citizens. Furries (vs. community members) reported greater normative environment, global awareness, and importantly higher global citizenship identification. The sample comparison predicted the antecedents, antecedents predicted identification, and identification predicted prosocial values. Furries (vs. community members not primed with a fan identity) showed indirect effects on global citizenship and prosocial values. In other words, membership and engagement with the furry community (vs. non-furry) is related to global citizenship identification. However, this study examined a specific fan group which may be unique with respect to its association with global citizenship, therefore a second study was conducted to examine fans in general.

In the second study, the researchers surveyed participants from a variety of different fan interests. Fans completed a single item regarding the injunctive norm of being a global citizen ("Other fans of this interest think that being a global citizen is desirable") along with the model measures. Fans' perception that other fans prescribe a global citizen identity predicted the antecedents, antecedents predicted identification, and identification predicted prosocial values. Similar to the above studies examining predictors of the model, the perception of one's fan group as endorsing global citizenship had downstream effects on identification and prosocial values. In other words, one's fan community is part of one's normative environment and can influence individuals' attitudes and identity. The above research shows that self-categorizing as part of an ingroup that contains global citizen related values (e.g., environmentalism) can predict greater identification. Additionally, engagement with a fandom that is perceived to encourage global citizenship can engender the identity in fans of that interest. Together, the results suggest that fan interest and activities are impactful for members of those communities. Being a fan of certain interests can have an influence on one's identity and attitudes. In effect, rather than simple hobbies or leisure activities, engaging with pro-global fan communities can influence how individuals see themselves and the world.

As noted in the previous chapter, Reysen and Katzarska-Miller (2017b) found that Bulgarian (vs. U.S.) news contains more global (vs. domestic) stories, and greater consumption of news by Bulgarians predicts global citizenship identification. However, U.S. news often frames events and stories as problematic and threatening (Altheide, 1997). Indeed, a discourse of fear is pervasive in U.S. news media (Altheide & Michalowski, 1999), and research shows that greater exposure to U.S. news predicts more perceived threat of global issues such as war, global warming, and religious fanaticism (Ridout, Grosse, & Appleton, 2008). To examine the impact of a threat to one's nation on global citizenship identification, Reysen, Katzarska-Miller, Salter, and Hirko (2014) conducted two studies with U.S. college students. In Study 1, participants rated their degree of identification with global citizens at the beginning of the semester as part of a larger prescreen. Later in the semester participants read about a threat to the United States from China or no threat was mentioned. Participants in the threat condition reported significantly lower global citizenship identification compared to identification rated at the beginning of the semester, while those in the control condition showed no change in global citizenship identification. In Study 2, participants read about a threat to the United States or no threat was mentioned prior to rating the model measures. Participants in the threat (vs. no threat) condition reported lower normative environment and global citizenship identification. The manipulation predicted normative environment, the antecedents predicted global citizenship identification, and identification predicted the prosocial values. The manipulation of threat versus no threat showed indirect effects on global citizenship identification and prosocial values. In effect, a threat to a subgroup reduced participants' identification with the superordinate global citizen group. The researchers hypothesized the reduction of global citizenship is due to the perception that under threat friends and family would not support global citizenship or prescribe it as a valued identity. Survival of one's group supersedes thought of superordinate identity (Goren & Yemini, 2016). However, greater research is needed to examine whether this outcome is unique to a threat to one's nation or if a threat to any subgroup hinders identification with global citizens.

To summarize, media and technology impacts global citizenship; however, the results are tentative. While greater social network usage and favorable attitudes toward technology influence the model, further research is required examining how that technology is used. For example, the number of friends, and nationality, that one is connected with through social media sites may impact global citizenship identification. Additionally, while being part of a fan group with norms of tolerance and environmental sustainability, or groups where a global identity is valued, is associated with global citizenship identification, research concerning aspects of the group that promote such values is needed. For example, if a content creator promotes a global citizen identity is this the same as other members prescribing the identity? Lastly, although news consumption is associated with global citizenship in Bulgaria, the same result may not occur in other cultural spaces, particularly if the framing and content of the media is interpreted by viewers as threatening to a subgroup.

POLITICS AND RELIGION

Numerous studies have demonstrated that political and religious orientation are related, with conservative individuals reporting greater religious identification (e.g., Onraet, Van Assche, Roets, Haesevoets, & Van Hiel, 2017). Prior research shows that endorsing a liberal political orientation is associated with global identities and orientations. A liberal political orientation is positively related to a psychological sense of global community (Hackett, 2014), global-mindedness (Kirkwood-Tucker et al., 2010), identification with all humanity (Iyer et al., 2012), and the desire to live in cosmopolitan cities (Sevincer et al., 2017). Liberal (vs. conservative) individuals tend to advocate for change, social justice, and the rejection of inequality, and report greater empathy and openness to experiences (Hackett, 2014; Iyer et al., 2012). Such openness, empathy, and social justice orientation should be positively related to global citizenship identification. Beyond a study showing a positive correlation between spiritual beliefs and identification with all humanity (Jack et al., 2016) and a negative correlation between political conservatism and psychological sense of global community (Hackett, 2014), much less research has examined the association between religiosity and religious orientation and identification with a superordinate identity such as global citizen. There is a reason to suspect that religiosity should be related to global citizenship as it is related to prosocial behaviors such as membership in charitable organizations (Stavrova & Siegers, 2014). Yet, this prosocial helping tends to be restricted to the ingroup and not extended to outgroups (Johnson, Rowatt, & LaBouff, 2012). For example, identification with a religious group is consistently positively correlated with racial prejudice (Hall, Matz, & Wood, 2010). Thus, with respect to an association between religiosity and global citizenship, based on the norms and messages promoted by religious institutions (Farrell et al., 2018) there should be a positive relationship; however, based on prior research showing exclusion of outgroup members (e.g., Hall et al., 2010) there may also be a negative relationship.

To examine the associations between political orientation, religiosity, and global citizenship, among other variables, Katzarska-Miller and colleagues (2014) conducted four studies with predominantly U.S. college students and community samples. In Study 1, global citizenship identification was positively related to a liberal political orientation and pro-gay attitudes, while nonsignificantly related to religiosity. Religiosity was negatively related to pro-gay attitudes, while a liberal orientation was positively related. In Study 2, global citizenship identification was positively related to a liberal political orientation, endorsement of world peace, and social justice concerns, but nonsignificantly related to religiosity. Religiosity was positively related to endorsement to restrict outgroups, national glorification, and endorsement of non-cooperation with other countries. A liberal political orientation was positively related to world peace and social justice, and negatively related to restricting outgroups and non-cooperation. Although one may suspect that religiosity given the prosocial messages and purported prosocial norms within the group would closely match, the nonsignificant relationships with global citizenship identification suggests a more complex association. In the remaining studies, the researchers added measures regarding individuals' religious orientation.

Prior research shows that individuals tend to endorse one of three types of religious orientation or motivation, including intrinsic religious motivation (e.g., a true belief in religious teachings), extrinsic motivation (e.g., belong to the group to gain or maintain social connections), and quest motivation (e.g., view of religion as a search for the meaning of life) (Batson, Schoenrade, & Ventis, 1993). A large body of research within social sciences focuses on the relationship between religious orientation and prejudice toward outgroups. In a large meta-analysis, Hall and colleagues (2010) found that extrinsic was positively, and intrinsic and quest negatively, related to racism. In a U.S. community sample, Goplen and Plant (2015) found that intrinsic, but not extrinsic, religious orientation was related to prejudice toward atheists. In a sample of U.S. undergraduate students at an evangelical Christian university, Mather (2015) found intrinsic, but not extrinsic or quest, orientation was positively related to anti-gay prejudice. Van Droogenbroeck, Spruyt, Siongers, and Keppens (2016) sampled youth (ages 14–23) in Belgium to find that quest orientation was negatively related to sexual prejudice for Christian and Muslim participants. Across this wide swath of research, of which we are only providing some examples, whether intrinsic or extrinsic orientation predicts prejudice tends to depend on the group the prejudice is directed toward (Van Camp, Barden, & Sloan, 2016). However, of the three orientations, quest appears to be most consistently related to non-prejudicial judgments (Hall et al., 2010; Whitley, 2009). Other research with a U.S. community sample shows intrinsic and extrinsic, but not quest, orientations are predicted by participants' voting conservative in elections (Larson & Heimrich, 2015). Quest orientation is also positively associated with principled moral reasoning (James, Fine, & Lester, 2015) and an analytic thinking style (Bahçekapili & Yilmaz, 2017), and negatively related to fundamentalism and dogmatism (Vonk & Pitzen, 2017). Together, these results point to quest motivation being related to rejecting dogmatic tradition, morals, and more complex thinking. In two studies with U.S. undergraduate students, Sparks and Gore (2017) assessed students' religious orientations along with identification with all humanity (although they did not separate the two dimensions; see Chapter 2 for a discussion). The results were mixed across the two studies. In Study 1, intrinsic was positively related, extrinsic negatively related, and a nonsignificant relationship was found between quest orientation and identification with all humanity. In Study 2, intrinsic and quest were positively related, but extrinsic nonsignificantly related, with identification with all humanity. The mixed results are odd, and further confusing as identification with all humanity was also positively related to social dominance orientation. Despite this, the results across multiple studies suggest that quest orientation should be positively related to global citizenship given that past research shows the variable is associated with non-prejudicial judgments, unrelated to conservatism, moral reasoning, rejection of dogmatic thought, and positively related to identification with all humanity.

In Study 3, Katzarska-Miller and colleagues (2014) found that global citizenship identification was again positively related to a liberal political orientation and nonsignificantly related to religiosity. However, global citizenship identification was positively related to both extrinsic and quest religious motivations. Similar to past research intrinsic and extrinsic motivations were related to attitudes related to exclusion (e.g., ethnocentrism), while quest motivation was positively related to inclusion (e.g., favorable view of Muslims). The positive association between global citizenship identification and extrinsic religious motivation was odd. The researchers posited that individuals with an extrinsic motivation are likely to attend to and adhere to prevailing societal values (e.g., friends, family) rather than religious group norms.

In Study 4, the researchers examined political orientation, religiosity, and the three religious motivations as predictors of the model. Political orientation predicted normative environment and global awareness, and showed the same downstream indirect effects on identification and prosocial values as in prior studies described above. Religiosity did not predict the antecedents. Quest religious motivation predicted both antecedents, and showed downstream influence. Intrinsic motivation predicted global awareness, while extrinsic motivation predicted normative environment. However, both did not influence global citizenship identification through these variables. The results show that, in general, religiosity is not closely associated with global citizenship identification. Yet, a quest motivation to be religious is associated and more strongly than either intrinsic or extrinsic religious motivations. The notion of seeking answers rather than participating in religious groups because of a strong belief in doctrine or wanting to please others is a better predictor of viewing the self as a global citizen.

There are various indicators in past research to suggest that a global identity, such as global citizenship, will be associated with activism and social movements (Fattori, Pozzi, Marzana, & Mannarini, 2015). A liberal political orientation is often associated with social movements and activism (Curtin, Steward, & Duncan, 2010). Compared to individuals who had not participated in activism, social activists tend to be more liberally politically oriented (Giugni, 2008). As noted above, a liberal political orientation is also related to global citizenship identification. Activists often work to mitigate or correct social injustices, environmental degradation, and oppression of marginalized peoples. These social movements are typically related to values we propose are outcomes of global citizenship identification. Furthermore, past research shows global identity is related to environmental activism (Renger & Reese, 2017), and global citizenship identification is associated with protesting unethical corporations (Reysen, Katzarska-Miller, Gibson, Mohebpour, & Flanagan, 2017; Snider et al., 2013). Although most research examines what predicts and sustains social movements, there is reason to believe that participation in social movements can promote an identity (Smith, Thomas, & McGarty, 2015; Thomas et al., 2015) such as global citizen. The perception that one's friends and family are supportive of collective action predicts one's intention to engage in activism (Fielding, McDonald, & Louis, 2008). Once in a movement, the environment of the movement tends to socialize individuals toward commitment in related social movements beyond the initial topic for which the individual joined (see Berstein, 2005). As social movements are increasingly globally oriented with respect to topics and membership, we suggest that participation in activist movements orient members to take a global perspective of social injustices and highlight the interconnectedness with others for the collective good. In effect, participation in activist movements should engender a global citizen identity.

To examine this notion, Reysen and Hackett (2017) examined past activism as a predictor of the model. Participants (undergraduate U.S. college students and a sample of community members) rated the degree of participation in activist movements related to poverty, women's issues, peace issues, civil rights issues, and human rights prior to rating the model measures. In both samples, participants' prior activism predicted both antecedents, the antecedents predicted global citizenship identification, and identification predicted prosocial values. Prior activism showed indirect effects on identification and prosocial values. The results highlight that a potential outcome of participation in activist movements is associated with viewing the self as a global citizen. However, it is important to note that the movements included in the study revolved around relatively liberal political issues. Future research may examine whether activist movements per se are associated with global citizenship identification (e.g., pro-life, pro-guns) or if only stereotypically left-leaning movements induce global citizenship.

Together, the above studies point to the failure of religiosity alone as a predictor of global citizenship. However, quest religious orientation, as well as a liberal political orientation, are associated with global citizenship identification. Individuals who endorsed the quest religious motivation and a liberal political orientation are likely to be associated with others who value global citizenship and discuss international events. We argue, as throughout this chapter, that engagement in such intentional worlds where activism and liberal values are discussed and encouraged can promote a global citizen identity and subsequent endorsement of prosocial values.

PERCEPTION OF THE SELF

The language people use reflects a variety of psychological functions that are related to relationships, personality, cognitive patterns, and beliefs (Tausczik & Pennebaker, 2010). The language used when describing the self may also give cues to one's degree of global citizenship identification. Following a social identity approach, one's degree of ingroup identification reflects the degree of psychological connection to the self (Coats, Smith, Claypool, & Banner, 2000). Stated differently, identification indicates the degree to which the group is part of the self. To examine whether the language used when describing oneself predicts global citizenship identification, Reysen, Pierce, et al. (2014) analyzed the number of global citizen–related words used when U.S. college students wrote about their values, beliefs, goals, and important things to teach the next generation. After writing about themselves, participants completed the model measures. The number of global citizen–related words used by participants when describing themselves predicted both normative environment and global awareness, the antecedents predicted identification, and identification predicted prosocial values. The number of words used showed indirect effects on identification and prosocial values. The results highlight that the language used to describe the self can be an indicator of one's degree of global citizenship. This study also highlights the connection between identification and use of words related to global citizenship as an indicator of inclusion of the identity in the self.

Beyond thinking of the present self's values and beliefs, individuals are able to image themselves in the future. Possible selves (Markus & Nurius, 1986) represent how individuals view themselves in the future and are typically categorized as hoped-for (or what one wishes to become in the future) or feared-self (or a future self that one is afraid of becoming). To examine the influence of possible selves on the model of antecedents and outcomes of global citizenship identification, Blake and Reysen (2014) asked U.S. college students to write about themselves in the future as either an active global citizen (hoped-for self), inactive global citizen (feared self), or write about their typical day (i.e., control condition) prior to rating the model measures. The results showed that participants who wrote about themselves as inactive (vs. active) global citizens in the future rated their normative environment and global citizenship identification higher. The manipulation of focus of future self predicted the antecedents, the antecedents predicted identification, and identification predicted prosocial values. The manipulation also showed indirect effects on identification and prosocial values. Thus, when a feared self was made salient to participants they reacted by endorsing their friends and family as prescriptive of global citizenship and themselves as more identified as global citizens. The results show that being an inactive global citizen is an undesirable future. Furthermore, making this inactive global citizen salient is one method to motivate low identified global citizens to strive to improve and become global citizens.

The above studies show that global citizenship prototypical characteristics seep into the language used when describing the self. Additionally, it is possible to assess one's degree of psychological connection with global citizens by counting the words related to global citizenship used in descriptions of the self. Being an active global citizen is desired and the salience of being an inactive global citizen in the future is feared. A potential motivational intervention for greater identification with global citizens may be to remind individuals what an inactive global citizen is for the future self. Individuals may then move toward behaviors to reduce the discrepancy between the present self and future self to avoid being an inactive global citizen. From a social identity perspective, when an identity is salient, individuals take on aspects of the group into the self. These aspects can be seen in the language used to describe the self as well as motivate individuals to live up to the ideals of the ingroup through threatening the self as non-prototypical of the group. Together, the results show that global citizen as an identity is closely tied to the self and a desired self at that.

CONCLUSION

In this chapter we reviewed research examining variables that can act as predictors of the model of antecedents and outcomes of global citizenship identification. In all of the studies the model was replicated. In other words, the perception of one's normative environment as prescribing a global citizen identity and global awareness (perceived knowledge of the world and felt interconnectedness with others in the world) predicted global citizenship identification. In turn, global citizenship identification predicted the six clusters of prosocial values (i.e., intergroup empathy, valuing diversity, social justice, environmental sustainability, intergroup helping, and a felt responsibility to act). Although the majority of the research in this chapter was conducted with undergraduate students in the southern United States, there were some exceptions such as students from the Philippines and U.S. community members. Regardless, we should highlight this limitation and note the need for replication, especially in other cultural spaces.

This review, and the research within, shows a variety of factors that can influence global citizenship identification. The factors in this chapter represent the initial efforts to identify and measure aspects of individuals' environment as influencing global citizen identity. While in the last chapter we reviewed empirical evidence showing that normative environment and global awareness are direct predictors of global citizenship identification, the present research additionally shows factors that indirectly influence identification and prosocial values through the antecedents in the model.

We began this chapter exploring aspects of the educational environment that affect the model. Classes with global topics or a global focus were associated with global citizenship evidenced via both indirect (number of global words in syllabi) and direct (students' perception of classes) measures. How college administrators and faculty talked about globalization and global citizenship impacted students, and students' cumulative grade point average predicted identification. Students' endorsement of culture as fluid and dynamic, and priming an interdependent self-construal were related to greater identification. Holding a favorable view of technology and engaging with multiple social networks predicted global citizenship, along with viewing others in one's fan community as prescribing a global citizen identity. Individual characteristics such as a liberal political orientation and quest religious motivation predicted global citizenship identification along with past participation in social activist movements. The language one uses to describe the self reflected one's identification, and thinking of the self in the future as an inactive global citizen motivated greater connection to global citizens. Together, the research highlights aspects of one's everyday life that promote the identity such as the people (e.g., faculty, family), places (e.g., school), and things (e.g., technology, fan interests) that can shape and direct movement toward identifying with global citizens.

Chapter Six

Global Citizenship in Education

The vast majority of theory and research concerning global citizenship is within the domain of education. In the present chapter we review past suggestions by education theorists regarding the approaches, dimensions, and goals of global education. To highlight the current state of the research in global citizenship education we also review studies for particular methods of inclusion of global citizenship in educational institutions. Through this review we point to areas where research is lacking as well as those in which the results of multiple studies suggest that certain strategies are working. Although the model of antecedents and outcomes of global citizenship identification demonstrate that aspects of students' normative environment and perceived global awareness predict viewing the self as a global citizen, much of the educational research to date has not taken this approach. However, all strategies of inclusion proposed do relate to the model. As noted in the previous chapter, schools are part of students' normative environment and through education students gain global awareness. In the present chapter we highlight what empirical research has been done, what is still needed, and some future directions for global citizenship education.

GLOBAL CITIZENSHIP IN EDUCATION

Education Going Global

In part as a response to increasing globalization, universities are moving to internationalize through a variety of methods such as recruitment of international students, exchange programs, international partnerships, and curriculum changes (Maringe, 2010). Although the notion of global education and efforts to incorporate global components into education has been ongoing for decades (Hicks, 2003; Zhao et al., 2007), the movement has intensified in recent years, particularly with UNESCO's 2014 endorsement and promotion of global citizenship education (Toukan, 2018). For example, universities increasingly use the term "global citizen" in policy documents (Clifford & Montgomery, 2014). When asked, chief academic officers note the increased number of global courses and knowledge of the world as one of the most important learning outcomes for college students (Connell, 2016). When surveyed, students and alumni concur with this assessment, suggesting global education aids in understanding political issues, and helps in both students' preparedness for work outside of school, and their chances of employment (Bista & Saleh, 2014). Similar to the definition of global citizenship, there are currently no agreed-upon definitions of global citizenship education, or even more generally, global education (Sim, 2016). Although theorists have suggested that global education and global citizenship education are distinct, both reflect a movement toward greater inclusion of global components in the education process. For this reason, we use them interchangeably in the present chapter. The lack of shared definition has not precluded education theorists from speculating on approaches to global citizenship education.

Galinova (2015) suggests that currently there are two perspectives on global citizenship education. The first reflects moral cosmopolitanism that highlights helping others as a responsibility or ethical imperative. The second perspective reflects neoliberalism and the push to prepare students for a global workforce. The latter perspective is more closely in tune with higher institutions' policies, where universities advocate for the need to innovate and produce students for the growing competition in the workforce. However, the moral cosmopolitan perspective is suggested to more closely reflect the concept of global citizenship and is best practiced with a focus on integration throughout the university experience. Shultz (2007), on the other hand, suggests three approaches to global citizenship education. The first approach, the neoliberal global citizen, aims to increase students' knowledge and skills with respect to global mobility, cultural understanding, and language acquisition. In effect, the goal is to prepare students for a global marketplace. The second approach, the radical global citizen, focuses on global structures and their relationship to inequality. Students are encouraged to act against global institutions (e.g., banking system) to mitigate inequality and oppression. The third approach, the transformationalist global citizen, focuses on viewing globalization as more complex than commonly thought. Students embedded in this approach are encouraged to act for democratic community building and bridge local and global problems with respect to equality and oppression.

Instead of theorizing, Aktas, Pitts, Richards, and Silova (2017) took an empirical approach to global citizenship education. The researchers reviewed global citizenship programs from 24 U.S. universities examining what the current practices are in this domain. The researchers noted that six of the programs had departments dedicated to global citizenship, showing the maturation of the field. Based on this observation the researchers mused that in the future global citizenship may emerge as its own discipline. The programs tended to require longer than one year to obtain a certificate in global citizenship and the majority contained components regarding (1) international travel (encouraged, but not required in most), (2) language instruction, (3) service learning, and (4) classes in different content areas with a global focus. Since these four components are the most often mentioned in theory and research regarding global citizenship education, the research (in some instances limited research), supporting each of these practices is described in detail later in this chapter.

Regardless of the specific approach taken by universities, the trend toward global education is there and further evidenced by a shift in how universities market themselves. Clayton, Cavanagh, and Hettche (2013) collected and analyzed 110 public service announcements from schools in NCAA Division I classification system to examine how universities were branding themselves in television commercials that aired during football games. After coding for the rakings of the school (i.e., top tier vs. bottom tier) the researchers noticed a trend with top tier (vs. lower tiered) schools being more likely to include themes representing their international reach and study abroad. In a follow-up study, the researchers examined the top-tiered schools' commercials that included the international reach and study abroad themes. The results showed that universities included messages about changing the world (the university and students work to change the world), students around the world (students studying abroad), and global imagery (e.g., image of student looking at the Eiffel Tower) in the commercials. In essence, the results support the notion of a shift in marketing of higher prestige schools to brand themselves as global institutions advancing and teaching for global citizenship. Given this trend we expect in the foreseeable future lower-tiered schools to catch on and imitate this marketing strategy.

However, there are no published studies demonstrating that the above marketing strategy is successful in attracting students. To examine if marketing a university as global or not influences students' perception of the university, Reysen and Katzarska-Miller (2017c) conducted an experiment, in which participants (U.S. undergraduates) were randomly assigned to read a description of a fictitious university filled with descriptive terms reflecting a global school (e.g., global environment, awareness of interconnectedness, moral values, social justice, peace and conflict resolution, global understanding) or a description that omitted such phrases. Following the manipulation, participants rated their perception of the university on various dimensions. In general, no significant differences were found in perceptions between the two universities. Students did not show interest in attending the global university or perceive the university's reputation, brand, quality, programs, or environment as better than the university in the control condition (i.e., lacking any mention of global components). Thus, while universities are shifting their marketing strategy, at least this single study did not show any benefits to such a strategy.

Dimensions and Goals of Global (Citizen) Education

Education theorists have suggested a variety of dimensions of global education. For example, Long (2013) suggests three dimensions: (1) the epistemic dimension where students need to understand interconnectedness of global structures and institutions, (2) the psychological dimension where students need to learn to engage with the world and build an identity which includes the self in the world, and (3) the civic dimension where students need to foster global citizenship and act and feel responsible to mitigate world problems. Nguyen (2013), following a Buddhist orientation of global education, also suggests three dimensions: awareness of interdependence, compassion, and an awareness of intention to endure absence of ego-driven actions. Oxfam (1997), the most cited source of global citizenship education dimensions, suggests three components including knowledge and understanding of global problems, skills for critical thinking and problem resolution, and values and attitudes reflecting environmental sustainability, valuing diversity, and equality. Lastly, Gaudelli and Heilman (2009) identified six curricula clusters that could be categorized under the umbrella of global education including disciplinary global education (global spin on traditional education disciplines), human relations global education (social skills and focus on human universals), neoliberal global education (understand global to advance in world market), environmental education (focus on environmental issues), critical justice education (critically think about equality and oppression), and cosmopolitan global education (focus on inequality, responsibility, and human rights).

Just as theorists have proposed different dimensions of global citizenship education, theorists have also proposed various goals and student learning outcomes. Banks (2001) suggests that global education's biggest goals are to aid students in understanding global interdependence and interconnectedness, clarify attitudes toward other nations, and develop and reflect upon one's identification with the world community. Grudzinski-Hall (2007) surveyed administrators at universities that promoted global citizenship programs. The most frequently endorsed global competencies included knowledge of cultures and world events, skills related to effectively engaging with other cultures, and attitudes related to openness to other cultures. Pike and Selby (1988) proposed five goals of global education including system consciousness (holistic conception of systems within the world), perspective consciousness (understand subjective nature of perception of world), health of planet awareness (global awareness and understanding of human rights), involvement consciousness (awareness of consequences of actions with focus on future of the world), and process mindedness (personal development is a journey without a fixed end). Across these dimensions and goals are common themes revolving around awareness of interconnectedness, knowledge (e.g., world events, global problems), skills (e.g., critical thinking, intercultural communication), and attitudes and values.

The above dimensions and goals are positive, from our perspective, and reflect aspects of the model of antecedents and outcomes of global citizenship identification outlined in this book. However, there are critiques of global citizenship education that should be acknowledged. To date, there are no widely used assessment measures or strategies to ensure that these goals are met (Sperandio et al., 2010). Furthermore, when academics attempt to assess outcomes, a potential lack of reliability is oftentimes evidenced (Dzhuryak, 2013). Global education has also been criticized for approaching education from a top-down perspective that is dominated by economic and neoliberal beliefs that obviates local cultural issues (Toukan, 2018). Andreotti (2006) makes a distinction between "soft" and "critical" global citizenship education, which emerges consistently throughout the global education literature. For example, a goal of global citizenship education from a soft approach is to "empower individuals to act (or become active citizens) according to what has been defined for them as a good life or ideal world," while with a critical approach the goal is to "empower individuals to reflect critically on the legacies and processes of their cultures, to imagine different futures and to take responsibility for decisions and actions" (p. 48). From a soft approach the strategies for global citizenship education reflect "raising awareness of global issues and promoting campaigns," while from a critical approach the strategies would be "promoting engagement with global issues and perspectives and an ethical relationship to difference, addressing complexity and power relations" (p. 48). As noted by Andreotti, "the notions of power, voice and differences are central for critical citizenship education" (p. 49). Andreotti and Pashby (2013) argue that the current state of global education is soft and often overlooks or underplays current social injustices, and suggest that more critical examination within education is needed regarding the complexity of global issues (e.g., poverty). Indeed, within the research concerning global citizenship education there is a dominant theme of the need for more critical global citizenship (Goren & Yemini, 2017a). Additionally, as we will cover in the next chapter concerning businesses and messages of corporate social responsibility, what universities claim with respect to global education is not always the same as what is practiced.

Researchers examining curriculum and practices within schools find a lack of critical approach to global education. In a study of the curriculum changes in Poland, Leek (2016) notes that while there is a greater emphasis on global citizenship education over time, the emphasis is as much about engendering good national citizens as it is about global citizens. Alviar-Martin and Baildon (2016) analyzed curriculum in schools in Singapore and Hong Kong to find that global citizenship was focused on economic neoliberal understandings to encourage students to prepare for the global marketplace. Friedman (in press) examined practices at two high status and two low status universities in the UK. Although all of the schools emphasized the benefits of global citizenship, the opportunities afforded to the students in the higher status institutions and focus on cultural capital framing (nearing a neoliberal legitimization of the need for global citizenship) highlighted the disparities between elite and public education. In other words, although programs may purport to include critical coverage of social issues, what is actually taught may be more akin to soft global citizenship. For example, themes found in discussions of teachers and administrators about the trend to include global citizenship as a way to internationalize universities showed them questioning the applicability of global citizenship in capitalist societies, notions of light or superficial coverage rather than critical examinations of social justice issues, and the tendency to stick to the status quo and avoid change (Clifford & Montgomery, 2014).

To summarize, while there continues to be an ongoing push for schools, at all levels of education, to incorporate more global components, there remain ambiguous definitions and assessment strategies. Most theorists have suggested dimensions and goals that tend to reflect the need for a greater understanding of interconnectedness (between self and world and nation and world), skills (mainly regarding empathy, intercultural communication, perspective taking), and values/attitudes (e.g., human rights, environmental sustainability). The approaches that theorists have observed and the critiques of global citizenship education align with regard to an overemphasis on soft, neoliberal, global citizenship education being taught in schools despite those schools promoting a critical perspective. There appears to be a disconnect between what is promoted and what is taught in classrooms.

Teacher Training

As noted above, international organizations as well as governments have called for greater global education in school. However, also noted above, what is posited is not always followed. Bergen and McLean (2014) examined Canadian curriculum in required social studies courses to find that 24% focused on social justice issues and 19% on similarities and differences between peoples' worldviews. The curriculum, thus, concentrated mostly on human rights and tolerance of cultural diversity, while not fully encapsulating the other concepts of global education. Rock, Polly, and Handler (2016) examined U.S. pre-service elementary teachers' curriculum during a year of internship in which integration of global content was a requirement. Teachers mainly integrated aspects of global content that concerned different perspectives and awareness/knowledge components, while showing low or no integration of local or global affairs, inequality, cross-cultural awareness, or marginalized points of view. Rapoport (2013) observed U.S. high school social studies courses and interviewed teachers regarding pedagogical delivery of global citizenship related topics and issues in their classes. None of the teachers used the term "global citizen". While all of the teachers endorsed the need for global citizenship in schools and suggested that their curriculum encouraged informed citizens of the world, none included components of global citizenship education in their instruction. In other words, the coverage of global citizenship–related topics while endorsed are not being incorporated into the curriculum, or when they are they tend to be those related to soft and not critical global citizenship. This is, of course, if global citizenship and related concepts are mentioned at all in the classroom.

Several explanations have been proposed for why teachers may not be incorporating global citizenship in classes. For example, Andrzejewski and Alessio (1999) suggest that global citizenship is not part of the curriculum because (1) educators do not see global issues as immediate problems and distant from one's own nation, (2) the global issues are perceived as too large to tackle, (3) educators are attempting to avoid political issues in the classroom, and (4) educators lack the skills and confidence to teach about the issues. Most research supports the latter two propositions. Researchers have noted the reluctance on the part of teachers to start controversial discussions (e.g., racism, sexism, reproductive rights, power relations) as they may become political (Carr, Pluim, & Howard, 2014; Davies, 2006; Veugelers, 2011) and anger parents (Goren & Yemini, 2017b). Furthermore, lack of confidence and knowledge are often cited by teachers as reasons to avoid global citizenship (Clifford & Montgomery, 2014; Gibson & Reysen, 2013; Rock et al., 2016). For example, Robbins et al. (2003) surveyed pre-service teachers in the United States to find that while the majority thought that global citizenship education was important and should be prioritized in the curriculum, only a minority (35%) felt confident in their ability to contribute to global citizenship in their schools.

These findings suggest that greater attention to teacher training is needed for the implementation of global citizenship education in classrooms (Clifford & Montgomery, 2014). As noted by Banks (2001), global education needs to start with a focus on teachers. At least in the United States, teachers tend to be White, middle-class women who view themselves as non-cultural and are colorblind to race (Banks, 2001). Thus, effort needs to be afforded to expand teachers' own perspectives before asking them to teach for global citizenship (Carano, 2013). Selected work has been made toward this end.

For example, Byker (2016) constructed and conducted a workshop in two universities with U.S. elementary pre-service teachers. Participants completed pre and post surveys regarding perceptions of global and cultural awareness. Increases were found for survey items regarding understanding of current world events, knowledge of technology to communicate ideas, ability to find resources to help students learn about the world, and willingness to take action for social justice. However, the data analysis and reporting in this research is limited (e.g., did not provide statistical analysis of pre and post mean ratings from participants). Camilleri (2016) also interviewed four teachers from France participating in a workshop about an online website that offers teachers and students a place to conduct projects and collaborate with distant others (e.g., making a recipe book with participants from different countries contributing). The teachers indicated that the activities provided students with greater cross-national awareness and learned more about their own culture in addition to other cultures. Thus, workshops may aid in preparing teachers for global citizenship instruction.

Other researchers have noted the benefits of travel abroad for teachers. Kaowiwattanakul (2016) interviewed Thai university lecturers who had spent time abroad. Themes from the interviews showed that teachers felt they had gained intercultural communication skills and a more global perspective. The teachers appeared willing and driven to bring their experiences into the classroom to aid students in developing respect for diversity and global awareness. Larsen and Searle (2017) examined Canadian pre-service teachers' attitudes 3–12 months after participating in a service-learning trip (either in Texas, United States helping build homes on the U.S.-Mexico border or in Lima, Peru, doing community service). The teachers reported greater self-awareness of responsibility to help others, appreciation of different perspectives, and global awareness concerning inequality. However, while the results seem promising in the small sample of participants, the responses tended to reflect soft rather than critical global citizenship.

Other suggestions to aid teachers for global citizenship instruction include ways to help teachers spot areas in which they may need further training. McLean and Cook (2016) developed guiding questions for new and pre-service teachers (e.g., appropriateness of activity for different ages, use of visual materials, does the activity highlight an inequality?, is the activity inclusive with respect to gender, race, culture, class, sexual orientation?, etc.) to assist in preparation of materials for global citizenship education. The researchers conducted interviews and reported generally favorable impressions (e.g., aided in identifying assumptions or omissions from activities) from teachers who used the resource to evaluate their teaching activities. Kerkhoff (2017) constructed a teaching for global readiness scale to assess secondary school teachers' preparedness to include global components in their instruction. The final scale contained four factors. The first factor, termed "situated practice", reflects the extent to which teachers ensure that the instruction is relevant to students (e.g., consider students' perspective and background). The second factor, "integrated global learning", reflects the extent that teachers connect local issues to global issues. The third factor, "critical literacy", reflects teachers' encouragement of engaging in discussion and analyzing sources, perspectives, and agendas in content. The fourth factor, termed "transactional experiences", reflects teachers' encouragement of collaboration via technology and use of diverse outside speakers. In both of these studies, the benefit for teachers is the ability to assess one's own curriculum to identify areas for improvement. Although ideal goals, we suspect that in practice, teachers will not use or know that these scales/resources exist.

The research, thus far, shows that global citizenship is not being taught in a manner that reflects the dimensions and goals outlined by education theorists. Furthermore, when teachers do try to incorporate global citizen related concepts in their instruction it tends to be soft components rather than critical. The two main reasons for this lack of integration include avoidance of controversy and lack of confidence to teach global citizenship. Researchers have suggested and examined workshops, travel, and guides/scales to pinpoint areas for training; however, there is little research with respect to teacher training. In other words, there is adequate research to say that teachers need more training, but to date, there is little research on how to train them. Although teacher training is lacking, researchers have examined areas in which global citizenship and related values are being incorporated into education. The evidence for these approaches is detailed next.

STRATEGIES FOR GREATER INCLUSION

Curriculum

Perhaps the least costly change for schools in revising their programs is the inclusion of more extensive coverage of global topics in the curriculum. One can argue that this change will need to be started by teachers as textbooks are lagging behind with respect to inclusion of global citizenship. Buckner and Russell (2013) examined usage of the terms "globalization" and "global citizenship" in 559 secondary school social studies and history textbooks from 76 countries published between 1970–2008. In general, both terms appeared predominantly when international events were mentioned. The usage of globalization increased greatly over time, mostly in relation to economic issues. Global citizenship also saw a rise in usage in the 1990s, but leveled off after (in 2005 40% of texts mentioned global citizenship). The term was commonly used in mostly social studies textbooks when mentioning human rights or when contrasting the term with national citizenship.

Although we see this as an optimistic trend, greater inclusion is warranted. The impact of globalization should be examined beyond the economic realm. Similarly, global citizenship can be applied to more areas beyond human rights.

In the prior chapter we reported two studies that showed indirect and direct assessments of classes as containing global content predicted global citizenship identification (Blake et al., 2015; Reysen et al., 2012). Other researchers have also noted positive outcomes by students after completing a class with global components. Tuazon and Claveria (2016) assessed secondary school students' (Batangas City, Philippines) perception of their social studies class as containing global education components and students' ratings of the global perspective inventory (Braskamp, 2008). The global perspective inventory assesses intrapersonal (identity formation and purpose in life, affective ability to handle ambiguity), interpersonal (social responsibility to act for others, social interaction with diverse others), and cognitive dimensions (knowing how to take multiple perspectives, knowledge or global awareness). Students' perception that their class contained topics related to interdependence of nations, world problems, environmental concerns, and global citizenship was positively related to all of the global perspective inventory dimensions. In effect, if students perceived the class curriculum as containing global content, they reported more global values and attitudes. Schutte, Kamans, Wolfensberger, and Veugelers (2017) examined Netherlands undergraduate students' attitudes before and after taking an honors course focusing on global social justice. The course covered topics regarding historical causes of injustice, intercultural sensitivity acknowledging one's mainstream perspective, intercultural communication, and civic engagement. Students showed increased efficacy in preventing social bias, taking the perspectives of, and empathizing with others. Furthermore, students reported greater global competency and civic engagement. These studies support the notion that for students, greater inclusion of global content in a class predicts global citizenship and related values at the end of the specific class.

If one class can result in prosocial values and greater identification, then it stands to reason that taking multiple classes with global components will produce similar outcomes, or even multiply the effect. Martin (2014) administered Morais and Ogden's (2011) measure of global citizenship to three groups of U.S. students at the beginning and end of an academic year; (1) students in a high school global cultures program, as well as (2) students on a waitlist for the program and (3) students who did not apply for the program. The cultures program included various classes (e.g., English, history) that had a focus on world issues and interconnectedness of cultures. For all of the groups, no changes were found on ratings of altruism and empathy, global interconnectedness and personal responsibility, self-awareness, intercultural communication, or civic involvement. The only significant change was that students in the program showed greater increase in global knowledge and political voice compared to the waitlisted students. Contrary to the results of the studies addressed above, the current study suggests that changes observed for those students in the program (vs. not) were those that were directly addressed in the program. In other words, the results did not generalize to beliefs and attitudes beyond the knowledge and engagement components included in the program.

Despite the mixed results for the program mentioned above, which is only one study and may not replicate in different programs, there were changes observed that were not seen in the control samples. In general, the evidence detailed above tends to suggest that curriculum changes work. When teachers do include global content in classes there are measurable changes in students' degree of global citizenship identification and related prosocial values.

Language

As noted earlier one method that global citizenship programs promote is the acquisition of a second language (Aktas et al., 2017). Ahn (2015) examined English language programs in South Korea and their purported missions to encourage global citizenship. Ahn examined the teacher recruitment materials of four language programs and promotional materials of 52 immersion camps. All camps focused on communication competence and the majority promised development of global citizenship or global leadership through learning English (e.g., change one's way of thinking, embracing different cultures). However, the descriptions often lacked details on the means through which they cultivate global citizenship. Together, the programs were being advertised preparing for international and workplace leadership, but offering few details of how intercultural knowledge would be taught in the program. Similar to the promotion materials of schools, for these language-learning programs global citizenship is a selling point, but there is little evidence of it in curriculum or outcomes.

Although research shows that a greater number of languages spoken by participants is associated with higher ratings of global identity (Türken & Rudmin, 2013), global-mindedness (Kirkwood-Tucker et al., 2010), and multicultural acquisition (Chen et al., 2016), further research is needed to evidence that language instruction leads to global citizenship identification.

One study suggests that students may link the desire to learn another language with a desire to be a global citizen. Gonzales and Lopez (2016) developed a measure of motivations to learn a foreign language. One of the six dimensions of the measure was termed "desire to become a global citizen," and was the second highest ranked motivation behind desire to communicate with foreigners. This illustrates the motivation students in language learning classes have to be global citizens. However, the eight items that comprised this subscale referenced a desire to understand other cultures (e.g., "Learning a foreign language is one way of learning another culture") and did not mention global citizenship in any way. Thus, it is unclear whether the researchers' interpretation of the construct matched the students' understanding.

Language programs claim an association between language acquisition and global citizenship. Students may be motivated to take language classes to become global citizens. There is clearly evidence that knowing more than one language is associated with identification with a global identity and related values. However, this field of inquiry into the inclusion of language programs for global education is sorely lacking evidence. Longitudinal, or at least pre/post, research is desperately needed to examine the potential increase of global citizenship identification when learning another language.

Travel Abroad

Researchers have given study and travel abroad the greatest amount of attention compared to other ways of internationalizing and including global components in education. Following interviews with students who had studied abroad, Killick (2012) highlighted the notion of being a global citizen through interactions with others. The idea is that to know one's self and gain a sense of self in the world, one needs to compare themselves and learn from others. A sense of global identity emerges through the interactions with members of diverse groups, facilitated by experiences such as travel abroad or living in diverse communities. For Killick (2013), such experiences personalize the 'other,' highlight intercultural perspectives, lessen egoistic tendencies, and promote intercultural communication practices and self-efficacy. Schmiers (2017) interviewed 18 individuals who traveled on the Interrail in Europe regarding their experience and possible connection to global citizenship. Themes emerged in the interviews regarding intercultural communication, awareness of privilege, cultural diversity, felt global perspective, empathy, and felt interconnectedness with others. Based on these qualitative studies, travel appears to have beneficial outcomes as related to global citizenship.

Other researchers also noted positive outcomes in students who had traveled abroad. Angwenyi (2014) interviewed 11 New Jersey high school students regarding their experience during a short-term travel abroad program. Students reported gaining greater global awareness through interacting and understanding a different culture, greater openness and respect for other cultures, cultural sensitivity, and feeling better prepared for college. Allan and Charles (2015) interviewed 25 adolescents at two private schools in the UK regarding foreign travel. Both schools promoted developing global citizens for the world of tomorrow in their promotional materials. Both schools contained artifacts from multiple cultures, promoted travel for students (e.g., one school held assemblies regarding the importance of travel for understanding other cultures), and held charity weeks to raise money for travel. The students interviewed spoke of life-changing experiences while traveling. The focus on international travel by the school appeared to have changed students' focus on the importance of understanding other cultures and living in a globalized society.

A variety of quantitative studies have also found that travel abroad has implications for students. In general, students who do study abroad report greater endorsement of seeing oneself as a world citizen (Miller, 2014), global-mindedness, intercultural communication skills, openness to diversity (Clarke et al., 2009), intellectual engagement with diversity and engagement with diverse peers (Hanson, 2017), and identification with all humanity (Belt, 2016). In a study of Taiwanese students who had participated in a study abroad program while in college, Chang (2016) found that students' perception of their experiences impacted their worldview, understanding of global politics, economics, and cultures was positively correlated with global citizenship identification, global awareness, intergroup empathy, and felt responsibility to act for the betterment of the world. Thus, students who have traveled abroad, compared to those who did not, report greater global identification, intercultural interactions, and prosocial values. These positive outcomes of travel and study abroad are also observed for dimensions of the global perspective inventory.

In research utilizing the global perspective inventory, Chickering and Braskamp (2009) surveyed 500 students before and after studying abroad. In addition to the cognitive, intrapersonal, and interpersonal domains, the measure contains dimensions related to well-being (although beyond an item about purpose in life the items tapping this dimension are unlike traditional well-being measures) and global citizenship (identification and endorsement of behaviors reflecting valuing cultural diversity and acting for the welfare of others). Students reported higher ratings (comparing pre and post measurement) on all of the dimensions, with the greatest gains in knowledge. Other researchers have mostly replicated these results with the global perspective inventory to find increases on all of the dimensions from pre and post study abroad in samples of U.S. college students (Engberg, 2013; Ferrari & Fine, 2016). Thus, again, study abroad is found to result in greater global identification and related values.

The above research focused mainly on study abroad programs. However, other researchers have suggested that the benefits of traveling abroad may be enhanced when coupled with classroom instruction. Tarrant, Rubin, and Stoner (2014) conducted pre and post tests of U.S. undergraduate students that were enrolled in a class that either (1) was focused on environmental sustainability and had a travel abroad component, (2) was focused on environmental sustainability but did not have a travel abroad component, (3) was not focused on the environment but did have a travel abroad component, and (4) no travel and not focused on sustainability. Students rated endorsed behaviors (e.g., give money to an environmental group), policies (e.g., pay higher taxes to protect the environment), and consumer behaviors (e.g., buy high-efficiency light bulbs). The results showed a general trend of students in the sustainability classes showing greater increases on the measures than those students in the non-sustainability classes. However, for two of the three measures, post-test scores were higher for those students in the sustainability classes that had a study abroad (vs. no travel) component. Similar results have been observed in other research using the same measures (Tarrant et al., 2013). We should note that the researchers use the term "global citizenship", but are measuring environmental sustainability. The researchers suggest that the travel component enhanced students' global citizenship as students placed greater importance on learning than they normally would in traditional classroom instruction. In other words, being outside one's everyday learning experience opens the self to more profound learning.

In research that more directly assessed global citizenship, Ogden (2010) measured U.S. college students' global citizenship (early version of Morais & Ogden's (2011) measure) before and after returning from an embedded program (class that includes a short-term abroad component, but the majority of the class is taught in the United States), as well as students in similar courses that did not contain a travel component. Overall, the level of global citizenship significantly increased for participants in the control classes, but not for students in the embedded program. When examining the pre and post change by dimension, only global civic engagement (not social responsibility or global competence) increased for students in the embedded program classes. The evidence from this large sample suggests that adding a travel component to an already globally oriented class did little to increase global citizenship as measured. The results highlight the need for caution when making generalizing statements such as all study abroad travel will increase students' global citizenship. There are likely a variety of factors that impact students' degree of global citizenship change when studying abroad that may be difficult to capture.

The majority of studies above assess travel soon after returning home. To examine the potential long-term outcomes of study abroad, Murphy, Sahakyan, Yong-Yi, and Magnan (2014) surveyed U.S. university alumni who had either participated in a study abroad program while a college student (either semester or year-long study abroad) or had not. Participants who had studied abroad (vs. not) showed higher civic engagement, voluntary simplicity (leading a modest, simple lifestyle), and international leisure activities (engaging with global individuals and activities such as watching foreign films and reading international news). With respect to philanthropic activities (volunteering or donations to international causes), the study abroad alumni had greater involvement with issues related to international development, environment, and social justice, while those who did not study abroad showed greater participation in youth and religious organizations. There were no significant differences between the two groups with respect to engagement with knowledge production (sharing ideas through media) or social entrepreneurship (creating a new organization that aims to aid the world). Thus, the findings were mixed and dependent on the type of philanthropic activity. Hence, there did appear to be a variety of long-term outcomes of study abroad in terms of the activities alumni chose to participate in after college. In general, those who did study abroad did tend, compared to students who did not participate in a program, to engage in various activities related to international engagement and consumption. Although both groups engaged in philanthropy, it was the study abroad alumni who tended to focus on activities that were international in nature. However, which is often the case in this research, students in the study abroad sample may be different with respect to these outcomes and self-selected into the study abroad program.

Less research has examined the notion that travel in general may aid students' global identity development. One study by Gretzel, Davis, Bowser, Jiang, and Brown (2014) suggests the possibility that topic-focused travel within the nation may be equally effective at encouraging prosocial values. Gretzel and colleagues surveyed U.S. college students attending a natural resources retreat in a national park. The students reported higher knowledge regarding environmental sustainability and felt efficacy to be a leader in solving global environmental problems. Thus, at least for this specific retreat, travel, while not international, may provide some benefits to students.

Taken together we feel confident in making the argument that study abroad is generally effective and beneficial for students. Students return reporting life changing experiences, greater psychological connection to the world, and better intercultural communication skills and confidence. Similar results were observed for teachers who have also traveled abroad as described earlier. However, the addition of classroom instruction combined with travel shows mixed results. More research is needed for both study abroad in general and the addition of class time to study abroad for contextualizing the trip for students. Additionally, more research is needed with respect to where traveled (e.g., Western vs. non-Western, English speaking or not), type and frequency of intergroup interactions, and the length of time abroad on global citizenship and related measures. In other words, much of the research paints a broad picture that study abroad is beneficial and omits what aspects of travel specifically influence students.

Service Learning

Beyond studying abroad, researchers have also explored whether service learning or participating in volunteer work abroad affects students' sense of self and attitudes. For example, Coryell, Wubbena, Stewart, Valverde-Poenie, and Spencer (2016) surveyed students, majority U.S. undergraduates, at the end of an international service learning experience helping rebuild after an earthquake in New Zealand. Student responses contained themes regarding a greater appreciation for different perspectives of the world, ability to problem solve and work cooperatively, greater empathy and felt connectedness with others, and a sense of global citizenship with respect to the need to act in a caring manner for global needs. Breitkreuz and Songer (2015) collected U.S. college students' perceptions of their improvement in different domains related to global citizenship following participation in a program that included an international service-learning component. The students reported self-improvement in areas such as cross-cultural sensitivity, respect for other cultures, understanding global issues, intercultural competency, and caring about people in other countries. However, because these reports were taken only after travel and not prior to it, the results may not reflect a growth in global citizenship identification or related values.

Le and Raven (2015) assessed attitudes of U.S. business students (undergraduate and graduate) who spent two weeks in either Vietnam or Cambodia conducting service learning (e.g., planting trees, aiding landmine victims) with a focus on the theme of global poverty. Students rated items related to felt efficacy to make a difference, awareness of needs in poorer countries, awareness of biases and prejudices, and students' understanding of their role as a global citizen above the midpoint of the measurement scale. A content analysis of students' reflection journals revealed a variety of themes such as having a responsible mindset, tolerance, cultural intelligence, cosmopolitan thinking, and interpersonal skills for intercultural communication. Foster, Cunningham, and Wrightsman (2015) also conducted pre and post surveys with U.S. high school students participating in a short-term service learning experience in Costa Rica. The results showed increases in understanding intercultural communication, understanding another's perspective, and empathy. However, the statistical analyses were not fully reported, hindering interpretation of the results.

Hartman (2014) provides evidence that global service learning can be enhanced with the addition of curriculum concerning global citizenship. Hartman conducted pre and post surveys on U.S. college students who engaged only in global service learning, or global service learning along with a global citizenship curriculum course. Students with the course scored higher on measures of globalism and civic engagement, while students in the service learning alone program did not show significantly higher scores. Sklad,

Friedman, Park, and Oomen (2016) assessed Dutch university students before and after participation in a service learning program that contained a heavy in-class learning emphasis on a slew of measures related to global competencies and attitudes. In general, the results showed that compared to a comparison sample, the students increased in global citizenship attitudes and beliefs. Together, the above findings suggest that service learning abroad combined with an in-class component may be more beneficial than service learning alone.

When examining the long-term impact of service learning for students, researchers find limited results suggesting potential benefits. Lough and McBride (2013) surveyed individuals just before, two weeks after returning, and two to three years after participating in service learning abroad. The researchers assessed global citizenship with a single item ("It would be better to be a citizen of the world than of any particular nation"), international engagement, and the belief that engagement at the national level can affect global change. The results showed that global citizenship did not change between pre and post service surveys. Lough, Sherraden, McBride, and Xiang (2014) conducted pre-, post-travel, and a third survey two to three years later for (1) individuals who participated in service learning abroad (anywhere from one month to one year of service) along with a (2) control sample of participants who traveled on their own (i.e., not part of program of service) and (3) individuals who did not travel. The majority of participants in these samples were U.S. citizens. While the service learning students did show increases over time with respect to intercultural relations (relationships with people from diverse backgrounds) the comparison group also showed a similar increase. Service learning students showed greater increase in concern for international issues than individuals who did not travel, but did not differ from individuals who traveled on their own (not in the volunteer program). The service-learning group also reported a greater increase in social capital (instrumental value of connections made with people of diverse backgrounds) compared to individuals who did not travel. The above studies highlight the need for caution in overstating the efficacy of service learning for long-term change in global citizenship. Furthermore, the findings from Lough et al. (2014) suggest that service learning may not benefit students above and beyond simply traveling abroad. Indeed, further research with respect to dissecting components of service learning, travel, and classroom components on global citizenship identification and related values is needed.

Researchers have also examined the benefits of service learning without traveling internationally. In a study with Chinese students who completed a service-learning project in Hong Kong, Ho (2016) found that students reported increased empathy and viewing the self as a responsible global citizen. Brunell (2013) asked U.S. college students to work on a project that was related to a global issue during a social justice–related course in political science. The students chose to work as a class on the topic of human trafficking and lead a campaign to raise money for an organization that aided women who had been trafficked. A survey conducted at the end of class suggested that students gained information about how to organize and work to mitigate a global issue through their experience. In effect, working locally to motivate action on a global issue provided an experience that could be applied to other issues and organizations when students exit college. Despite the lack of research in this area, the results suggest that service learning in one's local community may provide similar benefits for students without the need to travel abroad.

Together, the results provide initial evidence that service learning can promote global identification and prosocial values. However, service learning with an international travel component may not be any more beneficial than simply traveling in general. Service learning appears to be more beneficial when a classroom component is included. This may help frame the context in which the volunteer work will be conducted and reduce status/ethnocentrism which may hinder positive interactions with diverse others. Furthermore, there were mixed results with respect to long-term outcomes of participating in service learning. However, similar to study abroad, further research is needed about whether service learning within one's local community will have the same outcomes.

Global Activities

The academic literature in education is filled with classroom activities and suggested resources for engendering global citizenship in students. Some examples are activities such as role-playing (Banks, 2001), participatory action research (Kaukko & Fertig, 2016), school service clubs (Moffa, 2016), human rights learning communities (Kingston, MacCartney, & Miller, 2014), model United Nations (Gaudelli & Fernekes, 2004), and video conferencing with people in other cultures (Barnatt, Winter, Norman, Baker, & Wieczorek, 2014; Krutka & Carano, 2016). Furthermore, resources such as websites about global poverty and environmental issues (Cifuentes, Merchant, & Vural, 2011), films (Russell & Waters, 2013), and public datasets (Arabandi, Sweet, & Swords, 2014) have been proposed for teachers to use to engender global citizenship. Class activities are suggested to help students view a topic from different, non-mainstream, perspectives, reflect on experiences, induce greater interest and engagement, and make more connections with the curriculum in general (Banks, 2001; Barnatt et al., 2014; Kaukko & Fertig, 2016; Kingston et al., 2014). However, most of the suggestions in this area of education lack empirical support for their effectives in increasing global citizenship identification or prosocial values.

In one study, Blake, Pierce, Reysen, and Katzarska-Miller (2016) randomly assigned groups of students to participate in one of seven activities or listen to a short lecture (i.e., control condition). The activities included (1) students estimating percentages of things such as the number of people with access to clean drinking water for a village of 100 people, (2) estimating the number of countries that support different human rights, (3) role-playing talking to a person from another country, (4) a game in which students linked people, places, and things from the United States and related them to another country, (5) identifying where students' artifacts (e.g., backpack, phone, shoes) were made on a map of the world, (6) drawing a cartoon about how to resolve intercultural conflict, and (7) completing a writing task about stereotypes. After completing the assigned activity participants rated their degree of global citizenship identification. The degree of identification did not significantly differ between the activities and the control condition lecture.

The above study is a cautionary tale for teachers under the impression that short activities are somehow a magic bullet for promoting a global citizen identity. While short educational activities may appear to impact students, the activities should be tested with respect to whether they accomplish their intended goals. This is not to imply that some global citizen class activities do not increase identification, just that future researchers should test whether the activities work. Future researchers should strongly consider including a measure of global citizenship identification before (e.g., a week before) and after implementation of the activity. The activities used by Blake et al. (2016) were short (under 30 min) and the assessment of global citizenship was conducted immediately following the activity. Perhaps, more mentally intense, longer, and repeated variations of activities over time may show more fruitful results. Indeed, a better approach to encouraging global citizenship would be a whole school approach.

Whole School Approach

Bourn (2016) and Haigh (2008) note that, to date, the best outcomes for students has been observed when schools take a whole school approach—worked the themes related to global education into the vision and mission and included into as many aspects of school life as possible. Research shows that when students perceive the whole school as endorsing global citizenship they report greater global citizenship identification (Sherman, 2017). Unfortunately, perhaps the best method to kindle global citizen identity in schools is the one with the least amount of research to examine whether it is effective. Although there is not much research to promote the whole school approach, there are some criticisms. In interviews with teachers regarding a whole school approach to global education, Marshall (2007) reported that teachers were split and felt it was a contentious issue. While some teachers promoted this approach, others found it difficult to accommodate global issues in classes or across all topics within the class. The interviews highlighted the need for all teachers to buy in to the notion of a whole school approach. Without buy-in from the teachers, little progress will be made highlighting global citizenship in all classes. Haigh (2008) notes that many institutions are hypocritical in their promotion of global citizenship education. For example, on the one hand they promote environmental sustainability, but act in environmentally unfriendly ways. And mostly, they seek financial gains through promotion of the concept of global citizenship but do little to back up their claims in either support for students or faculty. This is a similar sentiment evidenced by faculty in Clifford and Montgomery's (2014) themes in faculty discussions. Research conducting cross-school examination of the degree of global education integration (with plenty of control variables included) is desperately needed.

CONCLUSION

In the present chapter we reviewed approaches, dimensions, goals, critiques, and evidence for strategies of inclusion of global citizen education. Global citizenship education while supposed to focus on interconnectedness, knowledge, skills, and attitudes/values is lacking in educational texts and lacking all dimensions when taught in the classroom. Teachers feel uneasy to include potentially controversial topics in classes and lack confidence regarding their knowledge and ability to include global citizenship in the classroom. Although there are some efforts to develop teacher-training programs, these are few and far between and lack consistent evidence of effectiveness. For educational institutions, teacher training is potentially the most important, and where they may find the best value for their money, with respect to infusing global education in their institutions. Researchers should also take note; there is a need to develop and assess programs for teachers. This will likely be a fruitful line of research inquiry in the coming years. We suggest focusing on aspects of teachers' normative environment and global awareness. These components predict global citizenship identification for everyone studied to date, teachers and students alike.

In the present chapter we also reviewed the evidence of effectiveness for the most popular strategies for inclusion of global citizenship education in schools. The data to date supports curriculum changes for inclusion of global citizen–related topics, travel (study abroad or on own), and service learning. However, the evidence remains mixed with respect to whether the addition of classes to travel enhances global citizenship identification. Both study abroad and service learning also shows some evidence of long-term benefits for students. While study abroad and international service learning can be expensive, we suggest greater research with respect to service learning in one's own community. Although knowing multiple languages is associated with identification with a global identity and related prosocial values, research is missing directly connecting this to language learning in school. Furthermore, research on short classroom activities is needed. Simply assessing students' ratings on a single item ("I strongly identify with global citizens") before and after an activity would greatly help in testing whether activities may be effective. As noted in the last chapter, identification is consistently linked to prosocial values. If change is observed on this single item we can infer that prosocial values will also be influenced. Together, the results reviewed support the various methods, with the exception of short activities, currently used to engender global citizenship identification. In the next chapter, we examine how global identity and related values are associated with another academic domain—business.

Chapter Seven

Global Citizenship in Business

Globalization has dramatically changed the face of business. Technology (e.g., geographically dispersed offices, international communication and collaboration), travel (e.g., international assignments), workplace culture (e.g., individuation, flexibility), and human resources (e.g., diversity) are just a few examples of areas in which businesses have observed drastic changes as globalization has intensified (Arabandi, 2011; Colbert, Yee, & George, 2016; Gonzalez-Loureiro, Kiessling, & Dabic, 2015; Stone & Deadrick, 2015). Factors related to globalization (e.g., foreign investment, international migration) also predict the odds of individuals viewing themselves as global citizens, especially for individuals in management (Kaya & Martin, 2016). Global citizenship in business research and theorizing has spanned decades under various labels such as corporate social responsibility. In the present chapter we review research from domains within the business literature highlighting global citizenship and related concepts. We begin this chapter focusing on skills and competencies that employers desire in students entering the workforce in relation to global citizenship. Next, we review the positive associations between global citizenship and the values and behaviors of employees. From a consumer perspective, we review research within business literature concerning consumers' preference for foreign products. In general, individuals with a global orientation prefer global brands and products. Next, we review research concerning corporate social responsibility and consumer activism. In this we highlight the notion that corporate social responsibility is global citizenship for companies and review the benefits of companies as global citizens, including favorable views from consumers as well as employees. In this section we also examine what aspects of the employees' work normative environment influences the model of antecedents and outcomes of global citizenship identification. Lastly, we review the association between global citizenship and reactions to companies that act irresponsibly.

GLOBAL COMPETENCIES

A common statement in the global citizenship education literature is the need to prepare students for the global workforce (Goren & Yemini, 2017a). Both U.S. non-students and high school students agree that knowledge of the world and international events will be important for their future careers (Hayward & Siaya, 2001). For example, when Bista and Saleh (2014) surveyed U.S. graduate students and alumni the majority agreed that a greater emphasis on global aspects in their education would have helped their chances for employment. However, what exactly employers would like to see from students entering the workforce remains a debatable topic. Researchers suggest that with globalization, both the contexts in which companies work and the diversity within companies requires new skills for successful intercultural communication (Andresen & Bergdolt, 2017; Tung, 2016). Coetzee (2014a) posits that one of the skills college graduates should have upon entering the workforce is global and moral citizenship, which includes communication skills, ability to apply and present information, and ethical and responsible behavior.

There is a longstanding tradition of asking employers what they want to see in college graduates. Over the years skills such as reading/writing, communication, creative thinking/problem solving, motivation, interpersonal communication, and leadership have consistently been identified as desired skills in employees (Carnevale, Gainer, & Meltzer, 1990; Stewart, Wall, & Marciniec, 2016). Dubey and Gunasekaran (2015) observed that companies broke down the skills of employees into hard (e.g., technical knowledge of environmentally friendly product components and technology) and soft skills (e.g., be a global citizen, leadership, teamwork, communication). These soft skills have changed slightly over time to reflect a more global orientation with the inclusion of global citizen as a desired attribute. For example, employers often list the importance of the hard skills, but also mention business ethics and social responsibility, as well as more generally being adaptive and flexible with changes in an interconnected and technologically advancing environment (Gerstein & Friedman, 2016; Ghannadian, 2013). In other words, the soft skills that employers are seeking appear to be shifting toward characteristics that are related to global citizenship. If global citizenship is a desired attribute in future employees, then we should see greater favorability toward individuals highlighting the identity during the hiring process.

Snider and Reysen (2014) provide some evidence of the positive label that global citizenship can have on individuals making employment decisions. In a series of studies the researchers examined individuals' willingness to hire an ex-offender. In the United States there is a consistent problem in the legal system of recidivism, and employment after release is one of the strongest predictors of desisting from reoffending (Tripodi, Kim, & Bender, 2010). However, the stigma associated with being an ex-offender hinders individuals from finding employment. Participants were presented with a description of an ex-offender who completed a global citizenship program while in prison or not. Across four studies, participants (U.S. undergraduate psychology and business students) indicated a greater wiliness to hire an ex-offender who had completed a global citizen program compared to one who had not. Furthermore, ex-offenders who had completed the global citizenship program were better liked and seen as more similar to the self than applicants who had not completed the program. A path model showed that manipulation of the program (global citizen vs. not) predicted liking and similarity to self, which in turn predicted less social distance from the applicant, and social distance predicted willingness to hire. Thus, the results suggest that global citizenship can mitigate the negative impact of past legal transgressions when applying for jobs. More importantly, the results show the added value for applicants of listing global citizenship and related values in applications and indicate that global citizenship is a desired attribute for potential employers. A note of caution that this study utilized undergraduate students and not actual employers, although one sample included business students as these individuals are likely to be in a hiring position in the future.

While global citizenship as a term is rarely used in the literature concerning employment, other terms such as "global competence", "intercultural competence", and "global mindset", are prevalent. Hunter, White, and Godbey (2006) interviewed business leaders regarding their perception of the components of global competence. The results revealed that businesses want employees to understand globalization and world history, and to be aware of global interconnectedness and world events. In another study, Deardorff (2004) interviewed 24 U.S. university administrators regarding their view of the components of intercultural competence for undergraduate students. Components such as cross-cultural awareness, respect for other cultures, global knowledge, cross-cultural communication skills, empathy, interpersonal skills, and communication were among the top rated components of intercultural competence. Thus, both employers and university administrators agree that students entering today's workplace will need intercultural competence. Additionally, many of the characteristics listed are related to global citizenship identification (e.g., awareness, interconnectedness, empathy). Below we briefly review the two commonly used terms in business literature regarding competence—cultural intelligence and global mindset (Andresen & Bergdolt, 2017).

Earley and Ang (2003) proposed cultural intelligence as an individual's ability to adapt to new and unfamiliar cultural settings. Cultural intelligence is measured with a scale, containing four dimensions: metacognitive (e.g., "I am conscious of the cultural knowledge I apply to cross-cultural interactions"), cognitive (e.g., "I know the cultural values and religious beliefs of other cultures"), motivational (e.g., "I enjoy interaction with people from different cultures"), and behavioral (e.g., "I use pause and silence differently to suit different cross-cultural situations") cultural intelligence (Ang et al., 2007). Antecedents include knowledge of other cultures and experience with culturally diverse people, and the construct is related to openness to experience, being a global leader, job adjustment, job performance, and effectiveness (Ott & Michailova, in press). The extent to which companies promote a global mindset is also suggested to increase employees' cultural intelligence (Ng et al., 2012), similar to our concept of normative environment as an antecedent to global citizenship identification. Some researchers (Bücker, Furrer, & Lin, 2015) questioned the factor structure of the measure and found two (rather than four) dimensions representing cultural knowledge and flexibility. However, number of factors notwithstanding, the results still show that endorsement of these items predicted effective intercultural communication. Thus, for jobs that require intercultural communication, higher cultural intelligence will provide better adaptation and global leadership (Kim & Van Dyne, 2012). A second attribute desired in potential future employees that is often referenced in the business literature is a global mindset.

The notion of a global mindset has been conceptualized and operationalized in a variety of ways; however, it is generally characterized by openness and cosmopolitanism, as well as effective functioning in complex business contexts (Andresen & Bergdolt, 2017; Levy, Beechler, Taylor, & Boyacigiller, 2007). In effect, a global mindset reflects awareness and openness to diversity and is an outcome of prior intercultural experiences (Lovvorn & Chen, 2011; Tung, 2014). Andresen and Bergdolt (2017) in comparing cultural intelligence and global mindset suggest that cultural intelligence is important for intercultural communication for individuals interacting with others, while global mindset is important for upper level management where individuals are making decisions about company standards, principles, and strategic development. Thus, constructs such as global mindset, cultural intelligence, along with intercultural sensitivity and cross-cultural competence share many similarities and facets and within business are important for successful management and global competency (Bücker & Poutsma, 2010). Just as with cultural intelligence, there are many similarities to concepts related to global citizenship identification (e.g., awareness, valuing diversity).

To summarize, students, non-students, and business leaders concur that the current business context requires students and educational institutions to focus more on global education. Given that businesses are more global and the workforce more diverse, beyond basic trade knowledge, intercultural communication along with characteristics similar to the outcomes of global citizenship identification are desired skills for employees. The majority of research within the business literature concerning intercultural competence advances the concepts of cultural intelligence and global mindset. Similar to the research presented in this book regarding one's normative environment and global awareness as predictors of global citizenship identification, knowledge of other cultures and experience with diverse others are posited as antecedents of cultural intelligence and a global mindset. We suspect that future research will find that global citizenship identification is closely related to both constructs. In other words, engendering global citizenship will likely lead to both cultural intelligence and the endorsement of global mindset variables. Furthermore, these variables are likely to be viewed as components of global citizens as employees.

GLOBAL CITIZENS AS EMPLOYEES

While a global orientation is desired by employers and promoted by universities, less research has examined the impact of employees with pro-global attitudes on the businesses. The little research that has been conducted suggests that the impact is positive. For example, Tran, Oh, and Choi (2016) examined the willingness of South Korean employees from five global companies to cooperate in a virtual team. Higher scores on a global mindset measure were positively related to wiliness to cooperate (e.g., share information). Furthermore, this association was mediated through employees' self-efficacy. Thus, global mindset is associated with both cooperativeness and self-efficacy within the workplace. Lisak and Erez (2015) examined leadership factors in business graduate students, from universities in eight countries, participating in multicultural team projects. Prior to assignment to teams of three or four, participants completed measures regarding global identity (e.g., "I relate to people from other parts of the world as if they were close acquaintances/associates"), cultural intelligence, and openness to cultural diversity (e.g., "I often spend time with people from cultural groups other than my own"). The project included stages such as getting to know one another, selection of team leader, and completion of project (guidelines for an expatriate who was assigned to overseas job). The students elected to be team leaders (vs. non-leaders) scored higher on global identity, cultural intelligence, and openness to diversity. In other words, individuals who scored higher on these constructs at the beginning of the study emerged as the leaders of their teams.

However, there is a lack of research examining employees' global citizenship and variables related to work. To address this gap, Reysen and Katzarska-Miller (2018a) asked 181 U.S. undergraduate college students to rate global citizenship identification along with various measures related to their job. All participants had indicated on a prescreen survey completed at the beginning of the semester that they are currently employed at a job where they have a boss. The results revealed that global citizenship identification (using a five-item measure "I would describe myself as a global citizen," "I strongly identify with global citizens," "I see myself as a global citizen," "I am glad to be a global citizen," "I feel strong ties with global citizens") was positively significantly related to various attitudes and perceptions related to work (see Table 7.1).

The results of the above study paint a beneficial picture of global citizens as employees. Global citizenship identification was positively associated with organizational identification. Organizational identification is a strong predictor of beneficial employee outcomes such as higher performance, reduced turnover, and organizational citizenship behaviors (Kreiner & Ashforth, 2004). Global citizenship identification was also strongly related to organizational citizenship behaviors (e.g., "I am always ready to lend a helping hand to others at work"; Ehrhart, 2004). Furthermore, it was related to job satisfaction (e.g., "All in all, I am satisfied with my job"; Bagger, Li, & Gutek, 2008) and two dimensions of work well-being: vigor (e.g., "At my work, I feel that I am bursting with energy") and absorption (e.g., "Time flies when I'm working"; Seppälä et al., 2008). Identifying with global citizens was positively related to viewing one's current employer as having procedural justice policies (e.g., "Thinking about the procedures used to arrive at decisions (e.g., rewards) in your job the procedures are free of bias"; Ehrhart, 2004) and endorsed business ethics in general (e.g., "Business has a social responsibility beyond making profits"; Giacalone, Jurkiewicz, & Deckop, 2008). Global citizenship identification was also related to three dimensions of job-crafting or proactively changing aspects of the job to fit with the individual: task (e.g., "So that the job I do suits me I undertake or seek for additional tasks"), relational (e.g., "So that the job I do suits me I invest in the relationships with people whom I get along with the best"), and cognitive job-crafting (e.g., "So that the job I do suits me I find personal meaning in my tasks and responsibilities at work"; Niessen, Weseler, & Kostova, 2016). Together, the results suggest that global citizens are likely to be identified with the organization, engaged, positive, energetic, helpful, ethical, and proactive in improving their fit in the job.

Beyond viewing their job favorably, well-being, and proactive helping at work, global citizenship identification was also related to employees' expectations of the organization they work for and personal values related to being a good employee. Global citizenship identification was positively associated with three dimensions of perceived obligations from their employer: relational (e.g., "The organization is obligated to provide job security,"), balanced

Table 7.1. Correlations between Employee Global Citizenship Identification and Work Related Measures

Variablo	Correlation
Organizational Identification	.30**
Work Well-Being	
Vigor	.20**
Dedication	.14
Absorption	.18*
Procedural Justice	.27**
Citizenship Behaviors	.39**
Job-Crafting	
Task	.23**
Relational	.17*
Cognitive	.19*
Organizational Obligations	
Relational	.15*
Balanced	.22**
Transactional	.25**
Job Satisfaction	.19*
Harmony/Disintegration	
Harmony	.25**
Disintegration	.10
Ethics	.16*
Materlialist-Postmaterialist	
Materialist	.01
Postmaterialist	.17*
Financial Locus of Control	
Internal	.25**
Chance	.09
External	-.05
Power	.05

Note. * $p < .05$, ** $p < .01$.

(e.g., "The organization is obligated to provide a wide scope of responsibility"), and transactional (e.g., "The organization is obligated to provide pay based on current level of performance"; Ho, Rousseau, & Leveque, 2006).

Thus, global citizens expect fair and appropriate behaviors and policies from the organizations in which they work. Global citizenship identification was positively related to harmony (e.g., "Maintaining interpersonal harmony is an important goal in life"), a variable that is associated with engendering a climate for positive and safe communication at work (Wang, Leung, & Zhou, 2014). It was also positively related to postmaterialist values (e.g., "Caring and compassion are essential to a business setting") while non-significantly related to materialist values (e.g., "The most important concern for a firm is making a profit, even if it means bending or breaking the rules;" Giacalone & Jurkiewicz, 2004). Lastly, global citizenship identification was positively correlated with an internal financial locus of control (e.g., "Whether or not I get to become wealthy depends mostly on my ability") and non-significantly related to other locus of control dimensions (Furnham, 1986). Together, the above values show global citizens as having high expectations of the organizations they work for, but also valuing maintaining harmony at work, caring about others more than rewards, and endorsing an internal locus of control regarding finances. In effect, the results suggest that businesses would benefit from hiring individuals who score high on global citizenship identification, and promoting the identity for employees of a company.

The research to date, although limited, paints a positive portrait of global citizens as employees. Global identity is related to both openness and cultural intelligence, and selection to serve in a leadership position in an intercultural work group. Employees' ratings of global citizenship identification are related to a wealth of positive beliefs, values, and behaviors that are desired in employees. Global citizens appear to be psychologically connected to the organization, satisfied with their work, proactively adapt their work to suit their needs, are energetic and absorbed in their work, believe that business should act ethically and expect that organizations to treat them fairly, endorse harmony and caring in the workplace, and view financial outcomes as intrinsically determined. Thus, global citizenship identification appears to be a good index to include in hiring decisions. However, given the limited work examining employee global citizenship, more research is needed to replicate and expand upon these findings.

CONSUMER PERSPECTIVE

Bennett (2004) describes global citizenship as the rise of consumers against corporations regarding issues of labor practices, environmental sustainability, human rights, and corporate responsibility. This argument coincides with the trend showing consumers displaying responsibility through their consumption choices (e.g., organic food, buying fair trade). However, responsibility is only part of the story as consumers also view multinational businesses as providing quality products and consumption of global brands as signifiers to others that one is a global citizen (Holt, Quelch, & Taylor, 2004). Given greater globalization, more companies have begun to focus their investment and marketing attention to global brands (brands that are marketed in multiple countries rather than in one country or limited area; Schuiling & Kapferer, 2004). This boom in business and marketing research has spawned various constructs and measures that attempt to measure segments of the market that are positively oriented toward purchasing foreign products (for a review see Bartsch, Riefler, & Diamantopoulos, 2016). Most research in this area has focused on whom and when people will buy products from foreign countries. Although not all the measures explicitly reference global citizenship, they all fall under the umbrella of global attitudes.

Consumer Cosmopolitanism

Cleveland et al. (2014) define cosmopolitanism as "a learned disposition: a general orientation reflecting a set of values, opinions, and competencies held by certain individuals; specifically a genuine, humanitarian appreciation for, desire to learn from and ability to engage with, peoples of different cultures" (p. 269). In their research they apply the concept of cosmopolitanism to consumer attributes and purchasing behaviors. Although various researchers have suggested consumer cosmopolitan scales (Altıntaş, Kurtulmuşoğlu, Kaufmann, Harcar, & Gundogan, 2013; Lawrence, 2012; Saran & Kalliny, 2012), few others have adopted them. One of the most widely used consumer cosmopolitan scales is part of a larger measure of acculturation to the global consumer culture from Cleveland and Laroche (2007). Cleveland and Laroche constructed the acculturation to global consumer culture scale to examine how people learn knowledge, skills, and behaviors that are appropriate in global consumer culture (i.e., culture that is not associated with any one nation, but is viewed as transnational and encompassing multiple countries). The notion of acculturation is based largely upon past research in psychology (e.g., Berry, 1997) regarding the cultural adaptation of individuals from one culture to another (e.g., marginalization, integration). The resulting measure contains seven subscales: (1) cosmopolitanism (e.g., "I am interested in learning more about people who live in other countries"), (2) exposure to marketing activities of multi-national corporations (e.g., "When I am watching TV, I often see advertising for products that are from outside my country"), (3) English language usage/exposure (e.g., "I feel very comfortable speaking in English"), (4) social interactions (e.g., "I prefer spending my vacations outside of the country that I live in"), (5) global mass media exposure (e.g., "I enjoy watching Hollywood films at the theatre"), (6) openness to and desire to emulate global consumer culture (e.g., "I think that my lifestyle is almost the same as that of people of my age-group in other countries"), and (7) self-identification with global consumer culture (e.g., "The way that I dress is influenced by the advertising activities of foreign or global companies"). Validity for the cosmopolitan dimension was demonstrated with positive relationships with societal interactions with others through travel and identification with global consumer culture (e.g., buying products from other countries). Of interest for the present discussion is only the cosmopolitanism dimension of this measure because of the its close association with global citizenship (see Chapters 1 and 2).

In subsequent research, Carpenter, Moore, Alexander, and Doherty (2013) examined demographic variables as predictors of acculturation and acculturation predicting food and fashion ethnocentrism (preference for domestic products). Younger age, greater education, and greater individualism predicted greater cosmopolitanism. Cosmopolitanism predicted lower product ethnocentrism. Cleveland, Laroche, and Papadopoulos (2015) surveyed individuals in eight (non-U.S.) countries to examine the association between learning English language and consumerism. Acquiring English was related to greater cosmopolitanism and consumption of global products. In a longitudinal examination of Dutch national identification and acculturation to global consumer culture, Sobol, Cleveland, and Laroche (2017) found that national identification tended to predict consumption of local products, while orientation toward global culture predicted greater consumption of global products. Other researchers have used short, five-item, measures of cosmopolitanism from the longer acculturation measure. In a sample of UK undergraduate students, Gonzalez-Jimenez (2016) found cosmopolitanism to be positively correlated with body appreciation, self-esteem, and purchasing clothes because they are fashionable and express individuality. And, consumer cosmopolitanism was positively related to foreign travel in a sample of Turkish citizens (Güngördü & Yumuşak, 2017). Thus, research, using this particular measure of consumer cosmopolitanism, shows relationships with desire to consume foreign products and knowing multiple languages.

After a review of prior measures (Riefler & Diamantopoulos, 2009), Riefler, Diamantopoulos, and Siguaw (2012) construed a consumer cosmopolitanism measure with three dimensions: open-mindedness (e.g., "I like having the opportunity to meet people from many different cultures"), diversity appreciation (e.g., "I enjoy being offered a wide range of products coming from various countries"), and consumption transcending borders (e.g., I like trying original dishes from other countries"). Consumer cosmopolitanism was negatively related to consumer ethnocentrism, risk aversion, consumers' need to enhance one's image, and positively related to consumer innovativeness, education, and international experience. Subsequent research with various samples has shown similar results. Al-Zayat and Bäcklund (2015) found a positive association between cosmopolitanism and loyalty to global brands. Zeugner-Roth, Žabkar, and Diamantopoulos (2015) found consumer cosmopolitanism to be positively related to foreign country attitudes, product judgments, and willingness to buy in samples of Austrians and Slovenians. In samples from Turkey and the United States cosmopolitanism was positively related to independent self-construal and willingness to buy foreign products, and negatively related to consumer ethnocentrism (Dogan & Yaprak, 2017). Cosmopolitanism was associated with concern for the environment and purchasing environmentally friendly products (Grinstein & Riefler, 2015). Similar to research with the other measure of consumer cosmopolitanism, higher scores on this scale are related to greater desire to consume global brands. Furthermore, the measure was associated with values similar to global citizenship (e.g., environmental sustainability).

Purchasing Global Brands

In a study examining predictors of global brand purchases, Holt and colleagues (2004) noted that a majority of participants viewed global brands as signifying membership in a global community. In effect, buying global brands was a way to be and show others that one is a global citizen. Building upon this finding, Strizhakova, Coulter, and Price (2008) developed a measure of the belief that purchasing global brands makes one a global citizen (e.g., "Buying global brands makes me feel like a citizen of the world"). The "belief in global citizenship" (their term) measure was also positively related to consumers' noted importance of branded products (purchasing a brand name product is important to the consumer). Research focusing on a belief in global products as signifiers of global citizenship shows that the association between the belief that global brands make consumers global citizens and purchase of global brands is mediated through perceived quality of global brands and use of brands to express identity (Strizhakova, Coulter, & Price, 2011). In other words, individuals who believe that global brands make them global citizens purchase them, in part, based on the beliefs that they are quality products, but also because they are identity expressions. Additionally, Gammoh, Koh, Okoroafo, and ELSamen (2015) found that cultural openness (e.g., enjoy learning about other countries), perceived quality (e.g., global brands are long-lasting) and social prestige (e.g., global brands are symbols of prestige) are positively associated with the belief that purchasing global brands makes consumers global citizens.

Global Identity

Westjohn (2009) surveyed U.S. participants and found that global identity, a measure adapted from Der-Karabetian and Ruiz (1997) (e.g., "I feel like I'm living in a global village"), is positively related to a global consumer orientation (enjoying products that are popular around the world), global brands, and globally oriented advertisements. Research utilizing this measure revealed that global identity was positively associated with favorable attitudes toward global consumer culture positioned–advertisements—ads that portray a brand as having a worldwide market (Westjohn, Singh, & Magnusson, 2012). Bartikowski and Walsh (2015), in a cross-national sample of postgraduate students from 21 countries, examined the relationship between national and global identity predicting reluctance to purchase foreign products through dimensions of universal-diverse orientation (Fuertes, Miville, Mohr, Sedlacek, & Gretchen, 2000). The universal-diverse orientation includes three dimensions—diversity of contact, relativistic appreciation, and discomfort with differences—that represent positive (diversity and appreciation) and negative (discomfort) attitudes toward cultural diversity. National identification predicted greater reluctance to purchase foreign products through lower universal-diverse orientation, and global identity predicted lower reluctance to purchase foreign products through greater universal-diverse orientation. In effect, global identity predicts greater universalism, which then predicts less reluctance to purchase foreign products.

Strizhakova and Coulter (2013) examined the relationship between global cultural identity and environmental consumer behaviors (e.g., willingness to pay extra for environmentally friendly products) in six countries. As part of the measures that were thought to tap global cultural identity was a scale of global connectedness (e.g., "I would describe myself as a global citizen"). Although the researchers use the term global connectedness, this scale is arguably a measure of global citizenship identification (see Chapter 4). Global connectedness was positively associated with concern and willingness to pay extra for environmentally friendly products, and likelihood to engage in environmentally friendly behaviors. Another line of research has also examined the associations between global identity and consumer attitudes toward global products, albeit with a different measure. As part of a series of studies showing the influence of global versus local identity priming on product evaluations, Zhang and Khare (2009) developed a 19-item measure of global and local identity with U.S. samples. Tu, Khare, and Zhang (2012) later shortened the measure such that four items assessed global identity (e.g., "I identify that I am a global citizen") and four items (with samples from UK, United States, and China) assessed local identity (e.g., "I identify that I am a local citizen"). The results across validity studies showed global identity as related to positive attitudes toward global products.

Subsequent research has shown that global identity is positively related to global brand attitudes (Guo, 2013). Bartsch, Diamantopoulos, Paparoidamis, and Chumpitaz (2016) tested a model with a sample of French participants that showed global identity predicting positive attitudes toward globalization, attitudes predicting identification with global brands, and identification predicting purchasing global brands. Lin and Wang (2016) examined monolingual Taiwanese individuals' perceptions of advertisements of products that contained either one or two languages (Chinese and English). Participants who indicated a higher global identity (with reference to global citizen) rated the advertisement and the product more favorably when the advertisement contained two rather than one language. In effect, highly identified global citizens gravitate toward globally marketed products and advertisements.

World-Mindedness

An early example of the relationship between world-mindedness and preference for global brands was provided by Rawwas, Rajendran, and Wuehrer (1996) who found that a measure of consumer world-mindedness (e.g., "I find imported goods more desirable than domestically produced products") was positively related to viewing foreign products as better quality than domestic products. Later research shows that world-mindedness is also positively related to purchasing foreign products (Parts & Vida, 2011; Topçu & Kaplan, 2015). Dutch participants' world-mindedness was positively associated with a favorable evaluation of ads with a global consumer culture positioning (Nijssen & Douglas, 2011). Beyond the research examining preference for global products, researchers have also examined consumers' attitudes toward fair trade products. In general, individuals are willing to pay more for fair trade products (De Pelsmacker, Driesden, & Rayp, 2005). Nijssen and Douglas (2008) found that Dutch participants' world-mindedness (e.g., "Even when consuming a particular foreign product does not fit the norms and values of my own culture, I still try it") was positively associated with favorable attitudes about fair-trade stores and grocery stores introducing an international food section. The above results supported the subsequent research by Reese and Kohlmann (2015) showing that participants' global identity predicted choice of a small fair-trade chocolate bar instead of a larger non-fair-trade chocolate.

Summary

In business and marketing, the main focus of research has been to identify measures to segment the market and examine who is, and when people are more likely, to buy global (vs. domestic) products. Although various measures have been proposed and used (e.g., consumer cosmopolitanism, global identity, world-mindedness), there is a consistent and clear trend showing higher scores on these measures are associated with a preference for global/ foreign products. Furthermore, there is also a preference for advertisements that are globally oriented. Another common trend in this research is the association between these measures and environmental sustainability, as shown in preference in purchasing environmentally friendly and fair trade products. In general, these measures show similarities with global citizenship identification, and indeed some measures contain items that could be said to be tapping global citizenship. Additionally, the measures are related to various constructs (e.g., valuing diversity, social justice, environmental sustainability) that are similar to the outcomes of global citizenship. However, the research is a far cry from the critical global citizenship espoused by theorists suggesting a dislike of large corporations. Perhaps global citizens, in general, are interested and desire consuming global products, just from ethical businesses. Support for corporations may only drop when the companies act in unethical ways.

CORPORATE SOCIAL RESPONSIBILITY

Corporate social responsibility (CSR) largely began to permeate business and academic domains in the 1950s in the United States with the idea that companies should, in addition to focusing on profit and business expansion, take actions that aided society (Taneja, Taneja, & Gupta, 2011). However, it was not until the 1970s in Western Europe, and its followed spread to the United States, that companies began releasing reports not only on company financials, but on social factors as well. Later, in the 2000s the reports on social factors included terms such as "sustainability", "corporate responsibility", and "corporate citizenship" (Fifka, 2013). Today, the majority of large companies report some sort of CSR-related activities (Bhattacharya, Korschun, & Sen, 2009). Dahlsrud (2008) coded the dimensions included in CSR definitions in the academic literature and examined the frequency of use of those dimensions. Five dimensions were identified, including (1) environmental (e.g., cleaner environment), (2) social (e.g., contribute to society), (3) economic (e.g., preserve profitability of business), (4) stakeholder (e.g., positive interaction with stakeholders), and (5) voluntariness (e.g., beyond legal obligations). The most cited definition of CSR was "a concept whereby companies integrate social and environmental concerns in their business operations and in their interaction with their stakeholders on a voluntary basis" (Commission of the European Communities, 2001, p. 6).

Carroll (1979) proposed the first model of corporate social performance including three responsibilities: economic (make profit), legal (obey the law), and ethical (obey society's ethical guidelines), with a later revision of adding a discretionary philanthropic category (be a good corporate citizen) (Carroll, 1991). Since this early model, subsequent researchers have, critiqued, revised, added concepts like moral responsibility, and introduced a process model of CSR (see Wood, 2010). From our perspective, CSR is the manifestation of companies acting like global citizens. In other words, companies, just like individuals, that exhibit social justice concerns, and other attitudes and behaviors that are prototypical of global citizens are global citizen companies. We are not alone in making this assertion. Logsdon and Wood (2002) distinguish corporate citizenship from global business citizenship with the latter adding the dimension of global human rights. The authors, in effect, suggest extending global citizenship at the individual level to that of the business organization. Logsdon and Wood (2005) note that global business citizenship is the subsequent evolution of CSR and suggest that companies follow universal ethical standards and local variations, reconcile conflicts between global and universal standards, and start a learning process beneficial to the organization but also the world. Thus, rather than taking advantage of lax rules or low standards in some parts of the world, companies should voluntarily hold high standards regardless of where the company is operating. In other words, engaging in practices that follow CSR makes companies global citizens.

CSR and Company Reputation

Over the years, researchers have used different measures of CSR. Wood (2010) reviewed the literature, with reference to her model of corporate social performance (principles, processes, and outcomes/impacts), to find researchers using indicators such as companies' CSR reports, percent given to charities, workplace safety records, pollution, percentage of women and minorities in upper management, community relations, number of lawsuits, customer ratings, company policies (e.g., affirmative action, environmental protection), political contributions, lobbying activities, product recalls, and employee perceptions. The long history of CSR has produced a wealth of research regarding the benefits of being corporate global citizens. For example, although some researchers note that the relationship between CSR and company financial performance is mixed (Fifka, 2013), in general, there is a small positive relationship between companies' CSR and financial performance (Allouche & Laroche, 2005; Orlitzky, Schmidt, & Rynes, 2003). Other research has focused on CSR and effects for stakeholders (e.g., consumers, employees).

Sen and Bhattacharya (2001) found that a company's CSR record is positively related to evaluation of the company. In general, CSR is associated with a company's reputation and consumers' loyalty. For example, Brammer and Pavelin (2006) found that CSR (broken down into social, community, environmental, and employee performance) was positively associated with the company's reputation (survey of chairmen and managing directors of large companies) for large UK businesses. Arora and Henderson (2007) manipulated advertisements to include a note about a donation to a charity included with a purchase of a product (vs. no mention of donation) to find that consumers were more willing to purchase the product with a prosocial benefit and reported a more favorable attitude of the company than products that did not have the CSR component. In other words, when the company was pairing a product with a CSR activity, customers responded with greater likelihood of purchase and higher perceived company reputation. Maignan, Ferrell, and Hult (1999) surveyed marketing executives as well as U.S. MBA students to find significant associations between perceived dimensions of CSR (economic, legal, ethical, discretionary) and perceived customer loyalty.

Beyond reputation and loyalty, CSR may also aid in protecting companies from bad press. Eisingerich, Rubera, Seifert, and Bhardwaj (2011) examined whether CSR acted as an insurance policy when consumers learned negative information about the company. The researchers first examined a model of CSR and the relationship with resistance to negative information and found an association. In a second study, the researchers first measured perceptions of CSR, customer orientation, service quality orientation, and customer expertise regarding their cell phone service provider. Five days later participants entered the laboratory and were randomly assigned to read a fictitious news article about the company having negative CSR, customer orientation, service quality orientation, or no negative information was provided. Participants who perceived the company's CSR positively at the first measurement time point showed greater resistance to the negative information about the company's CSR. However, this was domain specific. When negative information was reported about service or customer orientation, CSR did not protect the company. In other words, company CSR activities do provide some buffer against future mistakes, but mostly within that specific realm of CSR.

Employee Outcomes

Researchers have identified associations between CSR activities and positive outcomes for both potential and current employees. Turban and Greening (1997) found companies' CSR to be related to the perceived attractiveness as employers for U.S. business school seniors. Thus, the positive reputation afforded by CSR can attract employees. Once employed, employees show appreciation for CSR activities. Maignan et al. (1999) surveyed marketing executives as well as U.S. MBA students to find significant associations between perceived dimensions of CSR and perceived employee commitment to the company. Surveying employees in the media industry in Israel, Carmeli, Gilat, and Waldman (2007) found that employees' perception of the company as socially responsible to be positively related to their degree of organizational identification. Lin, Lyau, Tsai, Chen, and Chiu (2010) surveyed employees in Taiwan to find that perceptions of the company's CSR dimensions (e.g., legal, ethical) to be positively related to a variety of employee citizenship behaviors (e.g., altruism, conscientiousness, courtesy). Glavas and Piderit (2009) surveyed employees from seven U.S. companies to find that perceptions of the company's corporate citizenship to be positively related to employees' engagement, perception of high quality of relationships/ connections with others, and creative involvement at work.

Organizational Culture

CSR purportedly works best when it is integrated throughout the company. In other words, CSR is part of every aspect of the business creating an organizational culture that supports global citizenship. Galpin (2013) notes that global citizenship should be incorporated throughout the organization by including it in company mission, goals, values, and strategy. Some of the tactics for embedding global citizenship in the company that he suggests are including global citizenship concerns in selection of employees, training, rewards and incentives, rules and policies, and the physical environment. This approach is akin to the whole school strategy noted in the previous chapter. In essence, the company demonstrates to employees that management is concerned with global citizenship, while tying this concern to tangible and measurable outcomes for both the company and the employees. The extent to which supervisors and businesses encourage CSR can have an impact on employees (see Aguinis & Glavas, 2012).

As noted in Chapter 4, students' perception of their university as socially responsible influenced their own ratings of global citizenship identification. We expect similar impact of business CSR activities on employees (Aguinis & Glavas, 2012); the company, as part of employees' normative environment, should influence employees' global citizenship identification. To examine what aspects of the organization influence global citizenship, Katzarska-Miller and Reysen (2018b) surveyed students who were currently employed at a job where they had a boss. Participants completed measures regarding employees' perception of the organization (e.g., "My organization encourages me to be a global citizen"), upper management, immediate boss, and other employees as prescribing a global citizen identity along with measures of the model of antecedents and outcomes of global citizenship identification. All of the potential sources of normative influence (organization, management, boss, other employees) were correlated with the antecedents, global citizenship identification, and outcomes. Thus, there is a relationship between the organization and global citizenship identification. The four potential sources (i.e., organization, upper management, immediate boss, other employees) were then included as predictors of the model of antecedents and outcomes. Upper management and other employees, but not organization and boss, were significant predictors of employees' perception of their normative environment. The antecedents predicted identification, and global citizenship identification predicted the six prosocial outcomes. The perception of the upper management and other employees as prescribing a global citizen identity indirectly predicted global citizenship identification and prosocial outcomes. In effect, when controlling for one another, management and other employees were the most influential sources of the normative environment at work to influence individuals' global citizenship identification.

Summary

There is a long history of CSR research and theory in the business literature. The terminology has shifted over the years from "social performance" to the currently prevalent term "corporate social responsibility"; however, the basic core idea of doing good for stakeholders, and society in general, has stuck. Today's notion of CSR is the company being a good global citizen for all interested parties (e.g., employees, consumers, investors, society). CSR activities are related to positive outcomes such as financial performance, company reputation, product reputation, reduced risk, customer loyalty, employee commitment, organizational identification, employee citizenship behaviors, and employee engagement. Thus, there appear to be plenty of benefits for companies to integrate CSR values throughout the organization. Indeed, doing so can have an impact of employees' degree of global citizenship identification. However, not all companies act in socially responsible ways, which can lead to consumer protest.

CONSUMER ACTIVISM

As noted in Chapter 5, prior activist behaviors can predict individuals' degree of global citizenship identification. Individuals who are part of activist movements tend to describe themselves as global citizens (Schattle, 2005), are described by researchers as global citizens (Cable, Walsh, & Warland, 1998), or endorse the prosocial values and behaviors related to global citizenship. For example, Catalano (2013) interviewed U.S. participants of the Occupy Wall Street movement at four protest sites. When asked about the reasons they are participating in the movement, the responses reflected aspects of global citizenship such as demanding a fair society, inequality and economic disparity, human rights, environmental destruction by corporations, and general concern for social justice. Furthermore, the respondents noted that the issues regarding economic disparity were not limited to local or U.S. concerns, but are rather part of a larger global system of inequality. In effect, the respondents were noting a felt connection with others across the world.

While corporations report positive CSR activities, some companies may be actively harming employees and the environment (Raman, 2007). When corporations act in unethical or illegitimate ways, some consumers can become angry, leading to protest of the company (Cronin, Reysen, & Branscombe, 2012). Individuals' degree of global citizenship identification is strongly related to willingness to protest unethical companies (Snider et al., 2013). In two studies, Reysen, Katzarska-Miller, Gibson, Mohebpour, and Flanagan (2017) further examined the association between global citizenship identification and willingness to protest. In Study 1, participants, U.S. undergraduates, rated their degree of identification with global citizens, read about either an ethical or unethical company, and rated their willingness to protest the company. The results showed that global citizenship predicted a greater willingness to protest and individuals were more likely to protest an unethical company in general. However, these main effects were qualified by an interaction. When the company was engaging in ethical actions, global citizenship identification was unrelated to willingness to protest. However, when the company's actions were unethical, greater global citizenship identification predicted a greater willingness to protest. In other words, highly identified global citizens are not protesting corporations or large businesses in general, but rather willing to protest corporations that act unethically compared to low identified global citizens.

In Study 2, the researchers had participants read about an unethical company, but manipulated whether the company was domestic or foreign-based and whether the people harmed were part of one's or a foreign nation. Participants, U.S. undergraduates, rated their degree of global citizenship identification, read about an unethical company that was from the United States (vs. China) and harmed people in the United States (vs. China), and then rated their willingness to protest the company. The results showed a three-way interaction between global citizenship identification, company country of origin, and country of harmed consumers. Global citizenship identification was related to protest willingness when an ingroup company harmed the ingroup, but unrelated when an ingroup company harmed the outgroup. Global citizenship identification was also unrelated to protest when an outgroup company harmed the ingroup, but was marginally significantly related when an outgroup company harmed the outgroup. However, in general, the same trend emerged in that highly identified global citizens were willing to protest compared to low identified global citizens. Thus, the country of origin and who was harmed by the company's action were less important than the degree that individuals perceived themselves as global citizens under certain limiting conditions.

CONCLUSION

The present chapter reviewed the main areas of research concerning global citizenship in business. Starting with the oft-repeated notion that globalization necessitates global education for the current, and future, workplace, we reviewed the competencies sought by employers. Beyond the basic skills needed for a particular job, employers noted competencies and skills that are closely related to global citizenship (e.g., cultural intelligence, global mindset). Although more research is needed, there is also evidence that highlighting aspects of global citizenship in applications can aid in landing a job. Next, we reviewed the associations between global citizenship and positive characteristics of employees. Across a range of different variables, employee global citizenship identification was positively associated with beneficial employee values (e.g., postmaterialism, harmony), beliefs (e.g., ethics, job satisfaction), and behaviors (e.g., job-crafting, organizational citizenship behaviors). Thus, there is good reason for employers to value global citizenship from potential employees.

In the present chapter we also reviewed the vast array of measures (e.g., consumer cosmopolitanism, global identity) and their association with preference for global/foreign products. The results show a clear and consistent link regardless of type of measure. The various studies also highlighted many similarities between these diverse measures and global citizenship identification. However, future research is needed to disentangle the notion of the global citizen consumer and the global citizen activist. Perhaps, global citizens in general will show a preference for foreign products and only react with protest behaviors when a company is acting irresponsibly. To address this area, we selectively reviewed a portion of the vast literature concerning the business as a global citizen—corporate social responsibility. Both consumers and employees view businesses with strong CSR activities favorably. Lastly, we quickly reviewed the association between global citizenship and willingness to protest. In general, global citizens do support ethical companies, lending credence to the earlier notion that global citizens are consumers just with a preference for global products, but are likely to protest unethical companies (compared to non-global-citizens). The present chapter highlights links with related constructs in the business world, from hiring and employment to CSR and consumer responses when companies act unjustly. Overall, building upon CSR literature, global citizenship in business and marketing has a bright future for researchers.

Conclusion

Global Citizenship's Future

Across the chapters we have reviewed theory and research regarding global citizenship (and similar concepts) that make the compelling case that global citizenship is beneficial for society. Theorists and lay participants suggest that global citizenship is related to awareness of the world and interconnectedness with others, felt responsibility to act for the betterment of the world, valuing diversity, environmental sustainability, social justice concerns, empathy, and helping others. Empirical research confirms these assertions. Making a value judgment, we argue that these are positive values and behaviors. Furthermore, within specific domains (education and business) global citizen identity is related to positive variables such as academic motivation and grade point average for students, and support for ethics and job satisfaction for employees. Despite these positive associations, criticisms of the concept both in academia and public remain.

The main argument from academics (e.g., Bowden, 2003; Woolf, 2010) that decry the notion of a citizen of the world is because of the lack of a single world government. Although a valid point, the majority of the research indicates that global citizenship is best understood as a psychological orientation or identity. Standish (2012) argues that educating for global citizenship is a conscious attempt by advocates to stick social concerns and social change in education at the expense of factual knowledge. We contend that schools can teach values alongside factual knowledge, and global citizenship related values will aid students in functioning effectively in diverse societies and work environments (see Chapter 7).

In today's political climate, anti-globalism and greater nationalism are the prevailing sentiment. The president of the United States, Donald Trump, calls for "America first" while declining to enter into international partnerships regarding trade and climate change. Anti-globalist sentiment is also found in the UK with their recent "Brexit" vote (Cuervo-Cazurrra, Mudambi, & Pedersen, 2017). UK survey data shows that there exists a globalist versus nationalist policy divide that is partially explained by voters' age, class, education, and authoritarianism (Scotto, Sanders, & Reifler, 2018). Right-wing authoritarianism, along with social dominance orientation, is also related to support for Donald Trump (Choma & Hanoch, 2018), who as noted in the introduction holds an unfavorable view of the notion of global citizenship. Thus, at least in these two cultural spaces there appears to be a growing separation between those who wish greater cooperation and connection to other countries and those who do not. Needless to say, that while there are many benefits noted in the present work regarding outcomes of global citizenship, the concept remains controversial at least in the United States and UK.

SUMMARY OF AREAS IN NEED OF FURTHER RESEARCH

In this review we noted areas in need of greater research. Although there are cultural and contextual variations, we argue that there is greater similarity than differences in the components of global citizenship from academics and laypeople. We presented a model of global citizenship identification that includes the majority of these components, based upon theories from cultural and social psychology, and supported with a wealth of empirical research. Rather than viewing global citizenship as related to one particular value or behavior (e.g., global citizenship and environmentally sustainable behaviors), given the broad review of theory and research in this book, researchers may move closer toward a shared definition and understanding of global citizenship as related to a variety of prosocial outcomes. There exist many measures of related constructs (e.g., global identity, identification with the world) that show similarities with respect to correlations with similar variables. Examining similarities and differences in these associations, measures, and constructs is needed. Although we present a variety of factors that influence the model, there are variables still unexplored that may influence global citizenship identification and the model. Furthermore, we highlighted outcomes of global citizenship that are most frequently mentioned by lay participants, academics, and are consistently related in empirical research; however, there may be other outcomes yet to be identified, which may differ depending on context or time period. Within education, we highlighted the need for research regarding teacher training, and effectiveness of language instruction, classroom activities, and a whole school approach for engendering global citizenship. We presented initial evidence for examining global citizenship in business, employee factors and aspects of the organization that impact employees; however, more research can be conducted in this domain. For example, researchers may examine whether global citizenship identification is related to actual performance at work. Although we mentioned these holes in the literature throughout the book, there are many areas for researchers to explore in the future.

FUTURE DIRECTIONS

Despite criticisms and an unfavorable political climate in some countries, we contend that global citizenship has a bright future. While reviewing global citizenship programs at U.S. universities, Aktas and colleagues (2017) suggested that global citizenship may evolve into a dedicated discipline. As we have stated many times in this book, the majority of theory and research on global citizenship is within education. Although we focused on business in the previous chapter, global citizenship is spreading to other academic domains. For example, reference to global citizens is found in academic papers in disciplines such as agriculture (e.g., Zepeda & Reznickova, 2017), architecture (e.g., Hobbs, 2017), arts (e.g., Soongbeum, 2017), computer science (e.g., Aurigemma & Mattson, 2018), film (e.g., McLean, 2017), law (e.g., Walters & Zeller, 2017), medicine (e.g., Ilbawi et al., 2017), nursing (e.g., Kanbara, Yamamoto, Sugishita, Nakasa, & Moriguchi, 2017), social work (e.g., Briskman & Latham, 2017), and women's studies (e.g., Yu, 2018). In effect, the potential for usage of concepts related to global citizenship may move beyond education, business, and psychology. Below are a few broad questions in need of empirical investigation. These are a few of the questions that consistently resurfaced in our minds while working on this book that did not have clear answers and, thus, can direct future researchers.

What are the real life implications of global citizenship? Schattle (2008) presents an excellent overview of the pathways and practices of global citizenship distilled from interviews with self-identified global citizens. For his participants global citizenship was mainly related to actions such as working for advocacy groups, community associations, and activism more generally. However, overall, everyday individuals who were not part of an activist cause for the most part were not represented in this work. Thus, for individuals not working with an activist cause, how would global citizenship differ in daily life? While there is a wealth of research on individuals' perceptions of global citizenship (Chapter 3), further qualitative research from individuals outside of the public spotlight (e.g., activist organizations) can aid in understanding what are the everyday behaviors of global citizens. For example, a diary study with previously measured high and low identified global citizens may show dramatically different consumptive choices, relationship styles, and school/workplace behaviors. Furthermore, although there are many correlational studies examining values related to global citizenship, more research examining behavioral outcomes is needed. Just as Reese and Kohlmann (2015) showed that identification with the world community is related to choice of a fair trade chocolate bar over a larger mainstream chocolate, other behavioral measures may be used that reflect everyday choices. For example, highly identified global citizens may be more willing to write a letter to a member of Congress regarding a social justice issue, collect more names for a petition, interrupt a person making prejudicial statements, help a person in need, select global rather than national news to read, or choose artifacts for one's living space reflecting other cultures rather than domestic symbols (e.g., world flag alongside U.S. flag). Additionally, greater replication across cultural spaces would help to highlight the variation in behaviors associated with global citizenship. This is especially true for areas such as Africa and Middle Eastern regions where research is strongly lacking. As noted in Chapter 1, there are different types of global citizens, with people endorsing certain types (e.g., environmental) over others (e.g., spiritual) (Katzarska-Miller & Reysen, in press). We suspect that these types can vary in importance in different sociocultural settings and may be associated with conceptually relevant behaviors.

Is global citizenship exclusively a liberal political identity? As noted, global citizenship identification is positively correlated with a liberal political orientation (Katzarska-Miller et al., 2014). Furthermore, Reysen and Hackett (2017) find that global citizenship identification is related to activism for liberal causes. The values related to global citizenship appear to overlap with those prototypical of a liberal political orientation. Conservative political orientation is often related to concepts such as nationalism and ethnocentrism (Katzarska-Miller et al., 2014). Perhaps, as is a concern expressed by laypersons (e.g., Goren & Yemini, 2016), global citizenship is viewed as giving up or obviating one's national identity. Individuals with a conservative political orientation may view global citizenship as a threat to their national identity. Research with U.S. participants shows mixed results with some studies showing a positive correlation between national and global citizenship identification, while others show nonsignificant associations (Reysen & Katzarska-Miller, 2017a). However, using WVS data, Ariely (2018) finds that the correlation between national and world citizen identification differs depending on country, with a general trend of a negative correlation. Likely, the cultural context in which participants are sampled influences the degree that liberal or conservative individuals support global citizenship. In contexts in which global citizenship is not viewed as a threat toward one's nationalism, we would expect to see greater support. We suspect that political orientation may play a part in the mixed findings, however there may be other unaccounted for variables. Further research may also examine whether reducing the perceived threat to national identity increases support for global citizenship.

Is global citizenship a privileged identity? While conducting research on global citizenship, we have often wondered if it is a privileged identity, specific to WEIRD samples (Western, Educated, Industrialized, Rich, and Democratic: Henrich et al., 2010). While we can see wealthy individuals as philanthropists and activists for global causes (e.g., George Clooney, Bill Gates, Bono, Richard Branson), or those with Western education, or the money to travel around the world, we questioned if people living in challenging environments (e.g. poverty, oppression) would be less likely to view themselves as a global citizen. The present review resulted in inconsistent findings. On one hand, as discussed in Chapter 3, people who are under threat, in a highly nationalistic environment, or fighting for survival are not likely to view themselves as a global citizen. Similar to Malow's (1943) hierarchy of needs, lower needs (e.g., food, safety) must be met before higher needs can be sought or obtained. Related to this, Perdue (2014) reported that for African American students discrimination and oppression were more immediate concerns than thoughts of global citizenship. Pasha (2015) reported that the lack of travel hindered global citizenship for young students in Pakistan. On the other hand, other indicators in the research suggest the opposite. For example, Reysen, Katzarska-Miller, Gibson, et al. (2013) found that perceived knowledge predicted global citizenship better than factual knowledge. Thus, people may not need a prestigious degree to view themselves as global citizens. Additionally, researchers do not find income to be related to global citizenship. Indeed, Katzarska-Miller and colleagues (2012) found higher global citizenship identification for participants in Bulgaria and India (who had lower income) than those sampled in the United States. Similarly, utilizing public data from large surveys (e.g., WVS), Furia (2005) found small negative relationship between income and identification with the world as a whole.

Another aspect of privilege that is an implicit part of WEIRD samples is ethnicity. And although members of various ethnicities can reside in WEIRD spaces, whiteness is privileged within those spaces. Although we did not find other research, besides Perdue's (2014) study, we have wondered whether for multiethnic, multilingual, and/or immigrant people global citizen identity (even though not labeled as such) already is a part of how they see the self. Hence, all of the ways, particularly in education, to engender global citizenship, is based and marketed toward white students. Thus, future research should examine global citizenship from an intersectional perspective, and explore other variables that may provide evidence of global citizenship as a privileged identity.

Is there a negative side to global citizenship? Katzarska-Miller et al. (in press) found that a particular type—economic (e.g., "Free markets are good for everyone in the world," "Economic international development is good for everyone in the world")—of global citizen was positively correlated with ethnocentrism, right-wing authoritarianism, blind patriotism, military intervention, and traditional morality, while other types of global citizens showed low or nonsignificant associations with these variables. Beyond this particular type of global citizen, we did not find any necessarily negative outcomes of global citizenship in quantitative findings reviewed in this book. While this may be positive, we suspect there is dark side to global citizenship that just has not been explored yet. Research examining the common ingroup identity model suggests that focusing solely on one superordinate group may threaten subgroup distinctiveness and avoid discussion of inequality while maintaining a status quo (Dovidio et al., 2012; Hornsey & Hogg, 2002). Use of global citizenship may be used by advantaged groups, similar to a color-blind perspective, to silence discussions of inequality by disadvantaged groups. Furthermore, advantaged groups may change the meaning or prototypical content of global citizenship. At present, lay perceptions of global citizenship tend to view the construct as social justice activism and individuals acting for the benefit of the world; however, this bottom-up perspective may change in the future. Corporations or governments may coopt the term "global citizen" and subsequently change the meaning to fit their agendas. In effect, change the normative content of the identity to fit the desires of those in power. For example, UK's International Citizen Service sends volunteers to other countries to fight global poverty, but omits political and historical causes of that poverty from a critical perspective in promotional and pedagogical materials (Griffiths, 2017). Another potential negative outcome may be extreme global citizenship. Activism can vary in the degree of risk to the activists and others. For example, writing a letter to a politician holds lower risk than sabotaging logging equipment. Individuals who are highly identified global citizens may endorse more extreme versions of activism (e.g., causing bodily harm to another person who is perceived as acting in unjust manner). The above are just a few possible downsides to global citizenship that may be explored in the future.

What are the possible future directions researchers may take? In Chapter 4 we presented a long list of variables that showed positive, negative, and non-significant associations with global citizenship identification. For example, global citizenship identification was positively related to big five personality variables of agreeableness, conscientiousness, emotional stability, and intellectualism/openness, as well as correlations with religious motivations. However, the variables presented are just a few of the variety of constructs that have been shown by social psychologists to be important attitudes and beliefs for individuals' behavior and lives. Future researchers may examine the associations between global citizenship identification and other constructs. For example, given the strong association between global citizenship and environmental concern, identification with global citizens may be strongly associated with individuals' connection to animals or their tendency to anthropomorphize. Global citizenship may also be related to variables such as locus of control and perceived attribution of behaviors. In Chapter 7 we showed that identification was related to an internal financial locus of control, but no research has explored whether identification is related to the tendency to make a fundamental attribution error or ultimate attribution error. Furthermore, thinking styles (e.g., analytical thinking) and moral decision-making may be associated with identification. Although research shows that identification is related to intergroup helping, it may be related to other aspects of intergroup relations (e.g., negotiation style). In general, there are a variety of areas within psychology that can be examined in relation to global citizenship identification.

CONCLUSION

Global citizenship is associated with a variety of prosocial values and behaviors. Despite criticisms, the concept has endured, and is beginning to spread to other academic domains and gaining greater coverage in the popular media. In the present work we reviewed what research has been done on global citizenship and related concepts, identified areas where more work is needed, presented a model that includes the most frequently mentioned components, and speculated on where global citizenship may go next. There tends to be a disciplinary split between theorists and empirical researchers with little cross-disciplinary discussion. A review of the literature suggests there is a common ground. In effect, the present work reviews what has been done to aid researchers moving forward.

References

Adler, A. (1954). *Understanding human nature,* ed. and trans. W. B. Wolfe. Greenwich, CT: Fawcett. (Original work published 1927).

Aguinis, H., & Glavas, A. (2012). What we know and don't know about corporate social responsibility: A review and research agenda. *Journal of Management, 38,* 932–968. doi:10.1177/0149206311436079

Ahmad, R. E. (2013). Global citizen in the twenty first century: Challenges and opportunities in the post 9/11 era. *International Affairs and Global Strategy, 16,* 42–45.

Ahn, S.-Y. (2015). Criticality for global citizenship in Korean English immersion camps. *Language and Intercultural Communication, 15,* 533–549. doi:10.1080/ 14708477.2015.1049612

Aktas, F., Pitts, K., Richards, J. C., & Silova, I. (2017). Institutionalizing global citizenship: A critical analysis of higher education programs and curricula. *Journal of Studies in International Education, 21,* 65–80. doi:10.1177/1028315316669815

Allan, A., & Charles, C. (2015). Preparing for life in the global village: Producing global citizen subjects in UK schools. *Research Papers in Education, 30,* 25–43. doi:10.1080/ 02671522.2013.851730

Allouche, J., & Laroche, P. (2005). A meta-analytical investigation of the relationship between corporate social and financial performance. *Revue de Gestion des Ressources Humaines, 57,* 8–41.

Al Sarhan, K. A., Abbadneh, S. A., & Abu-Nair, N. S. (2015). A suggested model for the global citizen from the viewpoint of educational leaders in Jordan. *European Journal of Social Sciences, 47,* 247–261.

Altheide, D. L. (1997). The news media, the problem frame, and the production of fear. *The Sociological Quarterly, 38,* 647–668. doi:10.1111/j.1533–8525.1997.tb00758.x

Altheide, D. L., & Michalowski, R. S. (1999). Fear in the news: A discourse of control. The Sociological Quarterly, 40, 475–503. doi:10.1111/j.1533–8525.1999.tb01730.x

Altıntaş, M. H., Kurtulmuşoğlu, F. B., Kaufmann, H. R., Harcar, T., & Gundogan, N. (2013). The development and validation of a consumer cosmopolitanism scale: The polar opposite of xenophobic attitudes. *Economic Research, 26,* 137–154.

Alvarez, L., Boussalis, C., Merolla, J. L., & Peiffer, C. A. (in press). Love thy neighbor: Social identity and public support for humanitarian aid. *Development Policy Review.* doi:10.1111/ dpr.12329

Alviar-Martin, T., & Baildon, M. C. (2016). Context and curriculum in two global cities: A study of discourses of citizenship in Hong Kong and Singapore. *Education Policy Analysis Archives, 24,* 1–27. doi:10.14507/epaa.24.2140

Al-Zayat, Z., & Bäcklund, J. (2015). *The association between cosmopolitanism and global brand loyalty: A quantitative study in developing and developed countries* (Unpublished master's thesis). Linnaeus University, Växjö, Sweden.

Andreotti, V. (2006). Soft versus critical global citizenship education. *Policy & Practice: A Development Education Review, 3,* 40–51. doi:10.1057/9781137324665_2

Andreotti, V. D. O., Pashby, K. (2013). Digital democracy and global citizenship education: Mutually compatible or mutually complicit? *The Educational Forum, 77,* 422–437. doi:10.1080/00131725.2013.822043

Andresen, M., & Bergdolt, F. (2017). A systematic literature review on the definitions of global mindset and cultural intelligence—merging two different research streams. *The International al Journal of Human Resource Management, 28,* 170–195. doi:10.1080/09585192.2016.1243568

Andrighetto, L., Mari, S., Volpato, C., & Behluli, B. (2012). Reducing competitive victimhood in Kosovo: The role of extended contact and common ingroup identity. *Political Psychology, 33,* 513–529. doi:10.1111/j.1467–9221.2012.00887.x

Andrzejewski, J., & Alessio, J. (1999). *Education for global citizenship and social responsibility.* (Monograph). Burlington, VT: John Dewey Project on Progressive Education.

Ang, S., Van Dyne, L., Koh, C., Ng, K. Y., Templer, K. J., Tay, C., & Chandrasekar, N. A. (2007). Cultural intelligence: Its measurement and effects on cultural judgment and decision making, cultural adaptation and task performance. *Management and Organizational Review, 3,* 335–371. doi:10.1111/j.1740 8784.2007.00082.x

Angwenyi, D. M. (2014). *Travel abroad: A study of the perceived influence of high school students' experiences of short-term travel or study abroad prior to college* (Doctoral dissertation). Retrieved from ProQuest Dissertations and Theses. (UMI No. 3617506)

Antonis, S., Lia, F., Nikos, B., Antonis, G., & Pavlos, P. (2012). 'Categories we share': Mobilising common in-groups in discourse on contemporary immigration in Greece. *Journal of Community Applied & Social Psychology, 43,* 347–361. doi:10.1002/casp.2128

Arabandi, B. (2011). Globalization, flexibility and new workplace culture in the United States and India. *Sociology Compass, 5,* 525–539. doi:10.1111/j.1751–9020.2011.00389.x

Arabandi, B., Sweet, S., & Swords, A. (2014). Testing the flat world thesis: Using a public dataset to engage students in the global inequality debate. *Teaching Sociology, 42,* 267–276. doi:10.1177/0092055X14542352

Arcaro, T. (2009). Beyond the pledge of allegiance: Becoming a responsible world citizen. In T. Arcaro & R. Haskell (Eds.), *Understanding the global experience: Becoming a responsible world citizen* (pp. 3–25). New York: Allyn & Bacon.

Ariely, G. (2018). Globalization and global identification: A comparative multilevel analysis. *National Identities, 20,* 125–141. doi:10.1080/14608944.2015.1136610

Arnett, J. J. (2002). The psychology of globalization. *American Psychologist, 57,* 774–783. doi:10.1037/0003–066X.57.10.774

Arnett, J. J. (2008). The neglected 95%: Why American psychology needs to become less American. *American Psychologist, 63,* 602–614. doi:10.1037/0003–066X.63.7.602

Arnocky, S., Stroink, M., & Decicco, T. (2007). Self-construal predicts environmental concern, cooperation, and conservation. *Journal of Environmental Psychology, 27,* 255–264. doi:10.1016/j.jenvp.2007.06.005

Arnold, E. V. (1971). *Roman Stoicism: Being lectures on the history of the Stoic philosophy with special reference to its development within the Roman empire.* Freeport, NY: Books for Libraries Press.

Arora, N., & Henderson, T. (2007). Embedded premium promotion: Why it works and how to make it more effective. *Marketing Science, 26,* 514–531. doi:10.1287/mksc.1060.0247

Ashforth, B. E., Harrison, S. H., Corley, K. G. (2008). Identification in organizations: An examination of four fundamental questions. *Journal of Management, 34,* 325–374. doi:10.1177/0149206308316059

Ashmore, R. D., Deaux, K., & McLaughlin-Volpe, T. (2004). An organizing framework for collective identity: Articulation and significance of multidimensionality. *Psychological Bulletin, 130,* 80–114. doi:10.1037/0033–2909.130.1.80

Associated Press. (2008, July 24). Obama delivers Berlin address: "A world that stands as one." Retrieved from http://www.washingtonpost.com/wp-dyn/content/article/2008/07/24/AR2008072402293_pf.html

Assis, N., Reysen, S., Gibson, S., & Hendricks, L. (2018). *Perception of university responsibility and global citizenship identification.* Manuscript submitted for publication.

Aurigemma, S., & Mattson, T. (2018). Exploring the effect of uncertainty avoidance on taking voluntary protective security actions. *Computers & Security, 73,* 219–234. doi:10.1016/j.cose.2017.11.001

Bagger, J., Li, A., & Gutek, B. A. (2008). How much do you value your family and does it matter? The joint effects of family identity salience, family-interference-with-work, and gender. *Human Relations, 61,* 187–211. doi:10.1177/0018726707087784

Bahçekapili, H. G., & Yilmaz, O. (2017). The relation between different types of religiosity and analytic cognitive style. *Personality and Individual Differences, 117,* 267–272. doi:10.1016/j.paid.2017.06.013

Balbağ, N. L., & Türkcan, B. (2017). Elementary school 4th grade students and teachers' perceptions of global citizenship. *Turkish Online Journal of Qualitative Inquiry, 8,* 216–249. doi:10.17569/tojqi.270274

Banks, J. A. (2001). Citizenship education and diversity: Implications for teacher education. *Journal of Teacher Education, 52,* 5–16. doi:10.1177/0022487101052001002

Banks, J. A. (2008). Diversity, group identity, and citizenship education in a global age. *Educational Researcher, 37,* 129–139. doi:10.3102/0013189X08317501

Barnatt, J., Winter, M., Norman, V., Baker, D., & Wieczorek, S. (2014). Using cultural artifacts to understand self and other: A global exchange in elementary classrooms. *The Ohio Social Studies Review, 51,* 7–17.

Barth, M., Jugert, P., Wutzler, M., & Fritsche, I. (2015). Absolute moral standards and global identity as independent predictors of collective action against global injustice. *European Journal of Social Psychology, 45,* 918–930. doi:10.1002/ejsp.2160

Bartikowski, B., & Walsh, G. (2015). Attitude toward cultural diversity: A test of identity-related antecedents and purchasing consequences. *Journal of Business Research, 68,* 526–533. doi:10.1016/j.jbusres.2014.09.010

Bartsch, F., Diamantopoulos, A., Paparoidamis, N. G., & Chumpitaz, R. (2016). Global brand ownership: The mediating roles of consumer attitudes and brand identification. *Journal of Business Research, 69,* 3629–3635. doi:10.1016/j.jbusres.2016.03.023

Bartsch, F., Riefler, P., & Diamantopoulos, A. (2016). A taxonomy and review of positive consumer dispositions toward foreign countries and globalization. *Journal of International Marketing, 24,* 82–110. doi:10.1509/jim.15.0021

Batson, C. D., Schoenrade, P. A., & Ventis, W. L. (1993). *Religion and the individual: A social-psychological perspective.* New York: Oxford University Press.

Bayram, A. B. (2015). What drives modern Diogenes? Individual values and cosmopolitan allegiance. *European Journal of International Relations, 21,* 451–479. doi:10.1177/1354066114541879

Beja, E. L., Jr. (2013). Subjective well-being approach to the valuation of international development: Evidence for the millennium development goals. *Social Indicators Research, 111,* 141–159. doi:10.1007/s11205-011-9987-2

Belt, A. A. S. (2016). *Does global citizenship education predict identification with all humanity?* (Doctoral dissertation). Retrieved from ProQuest Dissertations and Theses. (No. 1829630217)

Beltramo, J. L., & Duncheon, J. C. (2013). Globalization standards: A comparison of U.S. and non-U.S. social studies curricula. *The Journal of Social Studies Research, 37,* 97–109. doi:10.1016/j.jssr.2013.03.003

Bennett, W. L. (2004). Branded political communication: Lifestyle politics, logo campaigns, and the rise of global citizenship. In M. Micheletti, A. Follesdal, & D. Stolle (Eds.), *Politics, products and markets: Exploring political consumerism, past and present* (pp. 101–126). New Brunswick, NJ: Transaction Publishers.

Bergen, J. K., & McLean, L. R. (2014). Students as citizens: Conceptions of citizenship in a social studies curriculum. *Transnational Curriculum Inquiry, 2,* 1–24.

Bernstein, M. (2005). Identity politics. *Annual Review of Sociology, 31,* 47–74. doi:10.1146/annurev.soc.29.010202.100054

Berry, J. W. (1997). Immigration, acculturation, and adaptation. *Applied Psychology, 46,* 5–34. doi:10.1111/j.1464–0597.1997.tb01087.x

Beugelsdijk, S., Maseland, R., & van Hoorn, A. (2015). Are scores on Hofstede's dimensions of national culture stable over time? A cohort analysis. *Global Strategy Journal, 5,* 223–240. doi:10.1002/gsj.1098

Bhattacharya, C. B., Korschun, D., & Sen, S. (2009). Strengthening stakeholder-company relationships through mutually beneficial corporate social responsibility initiatives. *Journal of Business Ethics, 85,* 257–272. doi:10.1007/s10551–008–9730–3

Bird, J., & Maher, T. V. (2017). Turning fans into heroes: How the Harry Potter alliance uses the power of story to facilitate fan activism and bloc recruitment. In J. Earl & D. A. Rohlinger (Eds.), *Social movements and media: Studies in media and communications* (Vol. 14, pp. 23–54). Bingley, UK: Emerald Publishing Limited. doi:10.1108/S2050–206020170000014002

Birdsall, N., Meyer, C., & Sowa, A. (2013). *Global markets, global citizens, and global governance in the 21st century. CGD Working Paper 329.* Washington, DC: Center for Global Development.

Bista, K., & Saleh, A. (2014). Assessing the need for graduate global education programs in the United States. *Journal of International and Global Studies, 5,* 19–39.

Blake, M. E., Pierce, L., Gibson, S., Reysen, S., & Katzarska-Miller, I. (2015). University environment and global citizenship identification. *Journal of Educational and Developmental Psychology, 5,* 97–107. doi:10.5539/jedp.v5n1p97

Blake, M. E., Pierce, L., Reysen, S., & Katzarska-Miller (2016). [Educational activities and global citizenship identification]. Unpublished raw data.

Blake, M. E., & Reysen, S. (2014). The influence of possible selves on global citizenship identification. *International Journal of Development Education and Global Learning, 6,* 63–78. doi:10.18546/IJDEGL.06.3.05

Blondin, J. E. (2015). Strategies for the development of an intercultural environment. In R. D. Williams & A. Lee (Eds.), *Internationalizing higher education: Critical collaborations across the curriculum* (pp. 87–100). Rotterdam, The Netherlands: Sense Publishers. doi:10.1007/978–94–6209–980–7_6

Bonds-Raacke, J., & Raacke, J. (2010). Myspace and Facebook: Identifying dimensions of uses and gratifications for friend networking sites. *Individual Differences Research, 8,* 27–33.

Bourn, D. (2016). Global learning and the school curriculum. *Management in Education, 30,* 121–125. doi:10.1177/0892020616653178

Bourn, D., & Shiel, C. (2009). Global perspectives: Aligning agendas? *Environmental Education Research, 15,* 661–677. doi:10.1080/13504620903244167

Bowden, B. (2003). The perils of global citizenship. *Citizenship Studies, 7,* 349–362. doi:10.1080/1362102032000098913

Brammer, S. J., & Pavelin, S. (2006). Corporate reputation and social performance: The importance of fit. *Journal of Management, 43,* 435–455. doi:10.1111/j.1467–6486.2006.00597.x

Braskamp, L. A. (2008). Developing global citizens. *Journal of College and Character, 10,* 1–5. doi:10.2202/1940–1639.1058

Braskamp, L. A., Braskamp, D. C., & Engberg, M. E. (2014). *Global Perspective Inventory (GPI): Its purpose construction, potential uses, and psychometric characteristics.* Global Perspective Institute, Inc.: Chicago, IL.

Braun, M., Behr, D., & Medrano, J. D. (in press). What do respondents mean when they report to be "citizens of the world"? Using probing questions to elucidate international differences in cosmopolitanism. *Quality & Quantity.* doi:10.1007/s11135–017–0507–6

Breitkreuz, K. R., & Songer, T. D. (2015). The emerging 360 degree model for global citizenship education. *International Journal of Research on Service-Learning and Community Engagement, 3,* 1–13.

Brewer, M. B. (1991). The social self: On being the same and different at the same time. *Personality and Social Psychology Bulletin, 17,* 475–482. doi:10.1177/0146167291175001

Brincat, S. (2009). Hegel's gesture towards radical cosmopolitanism. *Journal of Critical Globalisation Studies, 1,* 47–65.

Briskman, L., & Latham, S. (2017). Refugees, Islamophobia, and Ayaan Hirsi Ali: Challenging social work co-option. *Affilia: Journal of Women and Social Work, 32,* 108–111. doi:10.1177/0886109916685801

Brunell, L. A. (2013). Building global citizenship: Engaging global issue, practicing civic skills. *Journal of Political Science Education, 9,* 16–33. doi:10.1080/15512169.2013.747833

Buchan, N. R., Brewer, M. B., Grimalda, G., Wilson, R. K., Fatas, E., & Foddy, M. (2011). Global social identity and global cooperation. *Psychological Science, 22,* 821–828. doi:10.1177/0956797611409590

Bücker, J., Furrer, O., & Lin, Y. (2015). Measuring cultural intelligence (CQ): A new test of the CQ scale. *International Journal of Cross Cultural Management, 15,* 259–284. doi:10.1177/1470595815606741

Bücker, J., & Poutsma, E. (2010). Global management competencies: A theoretical foundation. *Journal of Managerial Psychology, 25,* 829–844. doi:10.1108/02683941011089116

Buckner, E., & Russell, S. G. (2013). Portraying the global: Cross-national trends in textbooks' portrayal of globalization and global citizenship. *International Studies Quarterly, 57,* 738–750. doi:10.1111/isqu.12078

Byker, E. J. (2016). Developing global citizenship consciousness: Case studies of critical cosmopolitan theory. *Journal of Research in Curriculum and Instruction, 20,* 264–275.

Cable, S., Walsh, E. J., & Warland, R. H. (1998). Differential paths to politicalactivism: Comparisons of four mobilization processes after the Three Mile Island accident. *Social Forces, 66,* 951–969. doi:10.2307/2579430

Camilleri, R.-A. (2016). Global education and intercultural awareness in eTwinning. *Cogent Education, 3,* 1–13. doi:10.1080/2331186X.2016.1210489

Canton, K., Schott, C., & Daniele, R. (2014). Tourism's imperative for global citizenship. *Journal of Teaching in Travel and Tourism, 14,* 123–128. doi:10.1080/15313220.2014.907955

Capozza, D., Vezzali, L., Trifiletti, E., Falvo, R., & Favara, I. (2010). Improving intergroup relationships within and outside the contact situation: The role of common ingroup identity and emotions of empathy and anxiety. *Testing, Psychometrics, Methodology in Applied Psychology, 17,* 17–36.

Carano, K. T (2013). Global educators' personal attribution of a global perspective. *Journal of International Social Studies, 3,* 4–18.

Cargile, A. C., Bradac, J. J., & Cole, T. (2006). Theories of intergroup conflict: A report of lay attributions. *Journal of Language and Social Psychology, 25,* 47–63. doi:10.1177/0261927X05284479

Carmeli, A., Gilat, G., & Waldman, D. A. (2007). The role of perceived organizational performance in organizational identification, adjustment and job performance. *Journal of Management Studies, 44,* 972–992. doi:10.1111/j.1467–6486.2007.00691.x

Carmichael, J. T., & Brulle, R. J. (2017). Elite cues, media coverage, and public concern: An integrate path analysis of public concern opinion on climate change, 2001–2013. *Environmental Politics, 26,* 232–252. doi:10.1080/09644016.2016.1263433

Carnevale, A. P., Gainer, L. J., & Meltzer, A. S. (1990). *Workplace basics: The essential skills employers want.* San Francisco, CA: Jossey-Bass Publishers.

Carpenter, J. M., Moore, M., Alexander, N., & Doherty, A. M. (2013). Consumer demographics, ethnocentrism, cultural values, and acculturation to the global consumer culture: A retail perspective. *Journal of Marketing Management, 29,* 271–291. doi:10.1080/0267257X.2013.766629

Carr, P. R., Pluim, G., & Howard, L. (2014). Linking global citizenship education and education for democracy through social justice: What can we learn from the perspectives of teacher-education candidates? *Journal of Global Citizenship and Equity Education, 4,* 1–21.

Carroll, A. B. (1979). A three-dimensional conceptual model of corporate performance. *Academy of Management Review, 4,* 497–505. doi:10.5465/AMR.1979.4498296

Carroll, A. B. (1991). The pyramid of corporate social responsibility: toward the moral management of organizational stakeholders. *Business Horizons, 34,* 39–48. doi:10.1016/0007–6813(91)90005–G

Castro, P., Lundgren, U., & Woodin, J. (2015). International mindedness through the looking glass: Reflections on a concept. *Journal of Research in International Education, 14,* 187–197. doi:10.1177/1475240915614202

Catalano, T. A. (2013). Occupy: A case illustration of social movements in global citizenship education. *Education, Citizenship and Social Justice, 8,* 276–288. doi:10.1177/1746197913497661

Chadborn, D., Edwards, P., & Reysen, S. (in press). Reexamining differences between fandom and local sense of community. *Psychology of Popular Media Culture.* doi:10.1037/ppm0000125

Chadborn, D., & Reysen, S. (in press). Moved by the masses: A social identity perspective on inspiration. *Current Psychology.* doi:10.1007/s12144–016–9545–9

Chang, C.-W. (2016). I studied abroad, therefore I am a global citizen? An initial study on relationship between global citizenship and international mobility experiences. *Asian Journal of Education, 17,* 131–147.

Chang, Y.-J. (2015). Being a part of the globalized world? Globalization, English, and world membership from students' perspectives. *English Teaching and Learning, 39,* 69–97. doi:10.6330/ETL.2015.39.1.03

Chavis, D. M., Hogge, J. H., McMillan, D. W., & Wandersman, A. (1986). Sense of community through Brunswik's lens: A first look. *Journal of Community Psychology, 14,* 24–40. doi:10.1002/1520–6629(198601)14:124::AID-JCOP2290140104>3.0.CO;2–P

Che, S. M., Spearman, M., & Manizade, A. (2009). Constructive disequilibrium: Cognitive and emotional development through dissonant experiences in less familiar destinations. In R. Lewin (Ed.), *The handbook of practice and research in study abroad: Higher education and the quest for global citizenship* (pp. 99–116). New York: Routledge.

Chen, S. X., Lam, B. C. P., Hui, B. P. H., Ng, J. C. K., Mak, W. W. S., Guan, Y., Buchtel, E. E., Tang, W. C. S., & Lau, V. C. Y. (2016). Conceptualizing psychological processes in response to globalization: Components, antecedents, and consequences of global orientations. *Journal of Personality and Social Psychology, 110,* 302–331. doi:10.1037/a0039647

Cheon, S.-H. (2017). *Primary school teachers' global citizenship types and perceptions of global citizenship education: Focusing on Seoul, South Korea* (Unpublished master's thesis). Seoul National University, Seoul, South Korea.

Chickering, A., & Braskamp, L. A. (2009). Developing a global perspective for personal and social responsibility. *Peer Review, 11,* 27–30.

Chiu, C., Gries, P., Torelli, C. J., & Cheng, S. Y. Y. (2011). Toward a social psychology of globalization. *Journal of Social Issues, 67,* 663–676. doi:10.1111/j.1540–4560.2011.01721.x

Cho, Y. H., & Chi, E. (2015). A comparison of attitudes related to global citizenship between Korean- and US-educated Korean university students. *Asia Pacific Journal of Education, 35,* 213–225. doi:10.1080/02188791.2014.924393

Choma, B. L, & Hanoch, Y. (2017). Cognitive ability and authoritarianism: Understanding support for Trump and Clinton. *Personality and Individual Differences, 106,* 287–291. doi:10.1016/j.paid.2016.10.054

Chui, W. H., & Leung, E. W. Y. (2014). Youth in a global world: Attitudes toward globalization and global citizenship among university students in Hong Kong. *Asia Pacific Journal of Education, 34,* 107–124. doi:10.1080/02188791.2013.810143

Cialdini, R. B., & Goldstein, N. J. (2004). Social influence: Compliance and conformity. *Annual Review of Psychology, 55,* 591–621. doi:10.1146/annurev.psych.55.090902.142015

Cifuentes, L., Merchant, Z., & Vural, Ö. F. (2011). Web 2.0 technologies forge the way for global citizenship. *Mustafa Kemal University Journal of Social Sciences Institute, 8,* 295–312.

Clark, E. B., & Savage, G. C. (2017). Problematizing 'global citizenship' in an international school. In S. Choo, D. Sawch, A. Villanueva, & R. Vinz (Eds.), *Educating for the 21st century: Perspectives, policies and practices from around the world* (pp. 405–424). Singapore: Springer. doi:10.1007/978–981–10–1673–8_22

Clark, I., III, Flaherty, T. B., Wright, N. D., & McMillen, R. M. (2009). Student intercultural proficiency from study abroad programs. *Journal of Marketing Education, 31,* 173–181. doi:10.1177/0273475309335583

Clayton, M. J., Cavanagh, K. V., & Hettche, M. (2013). The communication of global citizenship through public service announcements: A US study. *Journal of Marketing for Higher Education, 23,* 1–14. doi:10.1080/08841241.2013.802756

Cleveland, M., Erdoğan, S., Arikan, G., & Poyraz, T. (2012). Cosmopolitanism, individual-level values and cultural-level values: A cross-cultural study. *Journal of Business Research, 64,* 934–943. doi:10.1016/j.jbusres.2010.11.015

Cleveland, M., & Laroche, M. (2007). Acculturation to the global consumer culture: Scale development and research paradigm. *Journal of Business Research, 60,* 249–259. doi:10.1016/j.jbusres.2006.11.006

Cleveland, M., Laroche, M., & Papadopoulos, N. (2015). You are what you speak? Globalization, multilingualism, consumer dispositions and consumption. *Journal of Business Research, 68,* 542–552. doi:10.1016/j.jbusres.2014.09.008

Cleveland, M., Laroche, M., Takahashi, I., & Erdoğan, S. (2014). Cross-linguistic validation of a unidimensional scale for cosmopolitanism. *Journal of Business Research, 67,* 268–277. doi:10.1016/j.jbusres.2013.05.013

Clifford, V., & Montgomery, C. (2014). Challenging conceptions of Western higher education and promoting graduates as global citizens. *Higher Education Quarterly, 68,* 28–45. doi:10.1111/hequ.12029

Coats, S., Smith, E. R., Claypool, H. M., & Banner, M. J. (2000). Overlapping mental representations of self and in-group: Reaction time evidence and its relationship with explicit measures of group identification. *Journal of Experimental Social Psychology, 36,* 304–315. doi:10.1006/jesp.1999.1416

Coetzee, M. (2014a). Exploring the mediating role of graduate attributes in relation to academic self-directedness in open distance learning. *Higher Education Research and Development, 33,* 1085–1098. doi:10.1080/07294360.2014.911260

Coetzee, M. (2014b). Measuring student graduateness: Reliability and construct validity of the graduate skills and attributes scale. *Higher Education Research and Development, 33,* 887–902. doi:10.1080/07294360.2014.890572

Colbert, A., Yee, N., & George, G. (2016). The digital workforce and the workplace of the future. *Academy of Management Journal, 59,* 731–739. doi:10.5465/amj.2016.4003

Commission of the European Communities. (2001). *Promoting a European framework for corporate social responsibility.* Brussels, Belgium: Commission of the European Communities.

Connell, C. (2016). The ascent of global learning: Colleges and universities are revamping curricula and engaging faculty to achieve global learning outcomes. *International Educator, 25,* 16–23.

Contorno, L. (2012). The influence of cosmopolitan values on environmental attitudes: An international comparison. *Res Publica—Journal of Undergraduate Research, 17,* 14–39.

Coryell, J. E., Wubbena, Z. C., Stewart, T., Valverde-Poenie, T. C., & Spencer, B. J. (2016). International service-learning: Study abroad and global citizenship development in a post-disaster locale. In D. Velliaris (Ed.), *Handbook of research on study abroad programs and outbound mobility* (pp. 420–445). Hershey, PA: IGI Global. doi:10.4018/978–1–5225–0169–5.ch017

Crimston, D., Bain, P. G., Hornsey, M. J., Bastian, B. (2016). Moral expansiveness: Examining variability in the extension of the moral world. *Journal of Personality and Social Psychology, 111,* 636–653. doi:10.1037/pspp0000086

Crisp, R. J., & Hewstone, M. (1999). Differential evaluation of crossed category groups: Patterns, processes, and reducing intergroup bias. *Group Processes and Intergroup Relations, 2,* 307–333. doi:10.1177/1368430299024001

Crisp, R. J., & Hewstone, M. (2007). Multiple social categorization. *Advances in Experimental Social Psychology, 39,* 163–254. doi:10.1016/S0065-2601(06)39004-1

Crisp, R. J., Turner, R. N., Hewstone, M. (2010). Common ingroups and complex identities: Routes to reducing bias in multiple category contexts. *Group Dynamics: Theory, Research, and Practice, 14*, 32–46. doi:10.1037/a0017303

Cronin, T., Reysen, S., & Branscombe, N. R. (2012). Wal-Mart's conscientious objectors: Perceived illegitimacy, moral anger, and retaliatory consumer behavior. *Basic and Applied Social Psychology, 34*, 322–335. doi:10.1080/01973533.2012.693347

Croucher, S. (2015). From world citizenship to purified patriotism: Obama's nation-shaping in a global era. *Identities: Global Studies in Culture and Power, 22*, 1–18. doi:10.1080/1070289X.2014.969270

Cuervo-Cazurrra, A., Mudambi, R., & Pedersen, T. (2017). Globalization: Rising skepticism. *Global Strategy Journal, 7*, 155–158. doi:10.1002/gsj.1156

Cui, Q. (2016). Assessment of pre-service teachers' global-mindedness. *SAGE Open, 6*, 1–9. doi:10.1177/2158244016663284

Curtin, N., Stewart, A. J., & Duncan, L. E. (2010). What makes the political personal? Openness, personal political salience, and activism. *Journal of Personality, 78*, 943–968. doi:10.1111/j.1467–6494.2010.00638.x

Dahlsrud, A. (2008). How corporate social responsibility is defined: An analysis of 37 definitions. *Corporate Social Responsibility and Environmental Management, 15*, 1–13. doi:10.1002/csr.132

Davies, L. (2006). Global citizenship: Abstraction or framework for action? *Educational Review, 58*, 5–25. doi:10.1080/00131910500352523

Deardorff, D. K. B. (2004). *The identification and assessment of intercultural competence as a student outcome of internationalization at institutions of higher education in the United States* (Doctoral dissertation). Retrieved from ProQuest Dissertations and Theses. (No. 3128751)

de Jong, S. (2013). Intersectional global citizenship: Gendered and racialized renderings. *Politics, Groups, and Identities, 1*, 402–416. doi:10.1080/21565503.2013.816245

De Pelsmacker, P., Driesen, L., & Rayp, G. (2005). Do consumers care about ethics? Willingness to pay for fair-trade coffee. *The Journal of Consumer Affairs, 39*, 363–385. doi:10.1111/j.1745–6606.2005.00019.x

Der-Karabetian, A. (1992). World-mindedness and the nuclear threat: A multinational study. *Journal of Social Behavior and Personality, 7*, 293–308.

Der-Karabetian, A., & Alfaro, M. (2015). Psychological predictors of sustainable behavior in college samples from the United States, Brazil and the Netherlands. *American International Journal of Social Science, 4*, 29–39.

Der-Karabetian, A., Cao, Y., & Alfaro, M. (2014). Sustainable behavior, perceived globalization impact, world-mindedness, identity, and perceived risk in college samples from the United States, China, and Taiwan. *Ecopsychology, 6*, 218–233. doi:10.1089/eco.2014.0035

Der-Karabetian, A., & Ruiz, Y. (1997). Affective bicultural and global-human identity scales for Mexican-American adolescents. *Psychological Reports, 80*, 1027–1039. doi:10.2466/pr0.1997.80.3.1027

Der-Karabetian, A., Stephenson, K., & Poggi, T. (1996). Environmental risk perception, activism and world-mindedness among samples of British and U.S. college students. *Perceptual and Motor Skills, 83*, 451–462. doi:10.2466/pms.1996.83.2.451

Diessner, R., Iyer, R., Smith, M. M., & Haidt, J. (2013). Who engages with moral beauty? *Journal of Moral Education, 42*, 139–163. doi:10.1080/03057240.2013.785941

Diogenes. (1965). *Lives of eminent philosophers*, ed. and trans. R. D. Hicks. Cambridge, MA: Harvard University Press.

Diven, P. J., & Constantelos, J. (2011). The domestic foundations of confidence in the United Nations. *Peace Studies Journal, 4*, 1–23.

Dobson, A. (2006). Thick cosmopolitanism. *Political Studies, 54*, 165–184. doi:10.1111/j.1467–9248.2006.00571.x

Dogan, M., & Yaprak, A. (2017). Self-construal and willingness to purchase foreign products: The mediating roles of consumer cosmopolitanism and ethnocentrism. In M. Stieler (Eds.), *Creating marketing magic and innovative future marketing trends: Developments in market-*

ing science: Proceedings of the academy of marketing science (pp. 1499–1511). New York: Springer. doi:10.1007/978–3–319–45596–9_277

Dovidio, J. F., Saguy, T., Gaertner, S. L., & Thomas, E. L. (2012). From attitudes to (in)action: The darker side of "we". In J. Dixon & M. Levine (Eds.), *Beyond prejudice: Extending the social psychology of conflict, inequality and social change* (pp. 248–269). Cambridge, UK: Cambridge University Press.

Dower, N. (2002a). Global citizenship: Yes or no?. In N. Dower & J. Williams (Eds.), *Global citizenship: A critical introduction* (pp. 30–40). New York: Routledge.

Dower, N. (2002b). Global ethics and global citizenship. In N. Dower & J. Williams (Eds.), *Global citizenship: A critical introduction* (pp. 146–157). New York: Routledge.

Dower, N. (2008). Are we all global citizens or are only some of us global citizens? The relevance of this question to education. In A. A. Abdi & L. Shultz (Eds.), *Educating for human rights and global citizenship* (pp. 39–53). Albany, NY: State University of New York Press.

Dower, N. (2014). Global ethics: Dimensions and prospects. *Journal of Global Ethics, 10,* 8–15. doi:10.1080/17449626.2014.896575

Dubey, R., & Gunasekaran, A. (2015). Shortage of sustainable supply chain talent: An industrial training framework. *Industrial and Commercial Training, 47,* 86–94. doi:10.1108/ICT-08–2014–0052

Dudley, D. R. (1937). *A history of cynicism: From Diogenes to the 6th century A.D.* London: Methuen & Co.

Dzhuryak, I. (2013, June). *Content analysis of outcome assessment of global learning foundations courses: A case study.* Paper presented at the 12th annual South Florida Education Research Conference, Miami, FL.

Earley, P. C., & Ang, S. (2003). *Cultural intelligence: Individual interactions across cultures.* Stanford, CA: Stanford University Press.

Edwin, C. N., Obi-Nwosu, H., Atalor, A., & Okoye, C. A. F. (2016). Toward globalization: Construct validation of global identity scale in a Nigerian sample. *Psychology & Society, 8,* 85–99.

Ehrhart, M. G. (2004). Leadership and procedural justice climate as antecedents of unit-level organizational citizenship behavior. *Personnel Psychology, 57,* 61–94. doi:10.1111/j.1744–6570.2004.tb02484.x

Eisingerich, A. B., Rubera, G., Seifert, M., & Bhardwaj, G. (2011). Doing good and doing better despite negative information?: The role of corporate social responsibility in consumer resistance to negative information. *Journal of Service Research, 14,* 60–75. doi:10.1177/1094670510389164

Embrick, D. G. (2011). The diversity ideology in the business world: A new oppression for a new age. *Critical Sociology, 37,* 541–556. doi:10.1177/0896920510380076

Engberg, M. E. (2013). The influence of study away experiences on global perspective-taking. *Journal of College Student Development, 54,* 466–480. doi:10.1353/csd.2013.0073

Engberg, M. E., Davidson, L. M., Manderino, M., & Jourian, T. J. (2016). Examining the relationship between intercultural engagement and undergraduate students' global perspective. *Multicultural Education Review, 8,* 253–274. doi:10.1080/2005615X.2016.1237417

Erskine, T. (2002). 'Citizen of nowhere' or 'the point where circles intersect'? Impartialist and embedded cosmopolitanisms. *Review of International Studies, 28,* 457–478. doi:10.1017/S0260210502004576

Falk, R. (1993). The making of global citizenship. In J. Brecher, J. B. Childs, & J. Cutler (Eds.), *Global visions: Beyond the new world order* (pp. 39–52). Boston, MA: South End Press.

Farrell, J. E., Hook, J. N., Zhang, H., Mosher, D., Aten, J. D., Van Tongeren, D. R., & Davis, D. E. (2018). Religious attitudes and behaviors toward individuals who hold different religious beliefs and perspectives: An exploratory qualitative study. *Psychology of Religion and Spirituality, 10,* 63–71. doi:10.1037/rel0000143

Fattori, F., Pozzi, M., Marzana, D., & Mannarini, T. (2015). A proposal for an integrated model of prosocial behavior and collective action as the expression of global citizenship. *European Journal of Social Psychology, 45,* 907–917. doi:10.1002/ejsp.2154

Faulkner, N. (2017). Motivating cosmopolitan helping: Thick cosmopolitanism, responsibility for harm, and collective guilt. *International Political Science Review, 38,* 316–331. doi:10.1177/0192512116630750

Faulkner, N. (2018). "Put yourself in their shoes": Testing empathy's ability to motivate cosmopolitan behavior. *Political Psychology, 39,* 217–228. doi:10.1111/pops.12411

Ferrari, C. M., & Fine, J. B. (2016). Developing global perspectives in short-term study abroad: High-impact learning through curriculum, co-curriculum and community. *Journal of Global Initiatives, 10,* 109–122.

Fielding, K. S., McDonald, R., & Louis, W. R. (2008). Theory of planned behaviour, identity and intentions to engage in environmental activism. *Journal of Environmental Psychology, 28,* 318–326. doi:10.1016/j.jenvp.2008.03.003

Fifka, M. S. (2013). Corporate responsibility reporting and its determinants in comparative perspective—a review of the empirical literature and a meta-analysis. *Business Strategy and the Environment, 22,* 1–35. doi:10.1002/bse.729

Foster, A. M. M., Cunningham, H. B., Wrightsman, K. R. (2015). Using service-learning as a tool to develop intercultural understanding. *Journal of International Social Studies, 5,* 54–68.

Friedman, J. Z. (in press). The global citizenship agenda and the generation of cosmopolitan capital in British higher education. *British Journal of Sociology of Education.* doi:10.1080/01425692.2017.1366296

Friedman, T. L. (2005). *The world is flat: A brief history of the twenty-first century.* New York: Farrar, Straus and Giroux.

Fuertes, J. N., Miville, M. L., Mohr, J. J., Sedlacek, W. E., & Gretchen, D. (2000). Factor structure and short form of the Miville-Guzman Universality-Diversity scale. *Measurement and Evaluation in Counseling and Development, 33,* 157–169.

Furia, P. A. (2005). Global citizenship, anyone? Cosmopolitanism, privilege and public opinion. *Global Society, 19,* 331–359. doi:10.1080/13600820500242415

Furnham, A. (1986). Economic locus of control. *Human Relations, 39,* 29–43. doi:10.1177/001872678603900102

Gaertner, S. L., & Dovidio, J. F. (2008). Addressing contemporary racism: The common ingroup identity model. In C. Willis-Esqueda (Ed.), *Motivational aspects of prejudice and racism* (pp. 111–133). New York: Springer. doi:10.1007/978-0-387-73233-6_5

Gaertner, S. L., Dovidio, J. F., Anastasio, P. A., Bachman, B. A., & Rust, M. C. (1993). The common ingroup identity model: Recategorization and the reduction of intergroup bias. *European Review of Social Psychology, 4,* 1–26. doi:10.1080/14792779343000004

Galinova, E. (2015). Promoting holistic global citizenship in college. In R. D. Williams & A. Lee (Eds.), *Internationalizing higher education: Critical collaborations across the curriculum* (pp. 17–34). Rotterdam, The Netherlands: Sense Publishers.

Galpin, T. (2013). Creating a culture of global citizenship. *Journal of Corporate Citizenship, 49,* 34–47.

Gammoh, B. S., Koh, A. C., Okoroafo, S. C., & ELSamen, A. A. (2015). Antecedents of belief in global citizenship: A two-country empirical investigation. *Journal of Global Marketing, 28,* 52–66. doi:10.1080/08911762.2014.959630

Gaudelli, W., & Fernekes, W. R. (2004). Teaching about global human rights for global citizenship. *The Social Studies, 95,* 16–26. doi:10.3200/TSSS.95.1.16–26

Gaudelli, W., & Heilman, E. (2009). Reconceptualizing geography as democratic global citizenship education. *Teachers College Record, 111,* 2647–2677.

Gerstein, M., & Friedman, H. H. (2016). Rethinking higher education: focusing on skills and competencies. *Psychosociological Issues in Human Resource Management, 4,* 104–121.

Gerzon, M. (2010). *American citizen, global citizen: How expanding our identities makes us safer, stronger, wiser—and builds a better world.* Boulder, CO: Spirit Scope Publishing.

Ghannadian, F. F. (2013). What employers want, what we teach. *BizEd, 12,* 40–44.

Giacalone, R. A., & Jurkiewicz, C. L. (2004). The interaction of materialist and postmaterialist values in predicting dimensions of personal and social identity. *Human Relations, 57,* 1379–1405. doi:10.1177/0018726704049414

Giacalone, R. A., Jurkiewicz, C. L., & Deckop, J. R. (2008). On ethics and social responsibility: The impact of materialism, postmaterialism, and hope. *Human Relations, 61,* 483–514. doi:10.1177/0018726708091019

Gibson, K. L., Rimmington, G. M., & Landwehr-Brown, M. (2008). Developing global awareness and responsible world citizenship with global learning. *Roeper Review, 30,* 11–23. doi:10.1080/02783190701836270

Gibson, S. A., & Reysen, S. (2013). Representations of global citizenship in a school environment. *International Journal of Education Research, 8,* 116–128.

Gibson, S. A., Reysen, S., & Katzarska-Miller, I. (2014). Independent and interdependent self-construal and global citizenship. *International Journal of Business and Public Administration, 11,* 62–72.

Giugni, M. (2008). Political, biographical, and cultural consequences of social movements. *Sociology Compass, 2,* 1582–1600. doi:10.1111/j.1751–9020.2008.00152.x

Glavas, A., & Piderit, S. K. (2009). How does doing good matter? Effects of corporate citizenship on employees. *Journal of Corporate Citizenship, 36,* 51–70.

GlobeScan. (2016, April 27). Global citizenship a growing sentiment among citizens in emerging economies: Global poll. Retrieved from https://globescan.com/wp-content/uploads/2016/04/BBC_GlobeScan_Identity_Season_Press_Release_April%2026.pdf

Golay, P. A. (2006). *The effects of study abroad on the development of global-mindedness among students enrolled in international programs at Florida State University* (Doctoral dissertation). Retrieved from ProQuest Dissertations and Theses. (No. 3232382)

Golmohamad, M. (2008). Global citizenship: From theory to practice, unlocking hearts and minds. In M. A. Peters, H. Blee, & A. Britton (Eds.), *Global citizenship education: Philosophy, theory and pedagogy* (pp. 521–533). Rotterdam, The Netherlands: Sense Publishers.

Gonzales, R. D. L. C., & Lopez, M. Y. (2016). *Foreign language learning motivation questionnaire: Further examination of a six-factor model.* Unpublished manuscript, Graduate School, University of Santo Tomas, Manila, Philippines.

Gonzalez-Jimenez, H. (2016). Associations between cosmopolitanism, body appreciation, self-esteem and sought functions of clothing. *Personality and Individual Differences, 101,* 110–113. doi:10.1016/j.paid.2016.05.056

Gonzalez-Loureiro, M., Kiessling, T., & Dabic, M. (2015). Acculturation and overseas assignments: A review and research agenda. *International Journal of Intercultural Relations, 49,* 239–250. doi:10.1016/j.ijintrel.2015.05.003

Goodale, M. (2006). Reclaiming modernity: Indigenous cosmopolitanism and the coming of the second revolution in Bolivia. *American Ethnologist, 33,* 634–649. doi:10.1525/ae.2006.33.4.634

Goplen, J., & Plant, E. A. (2015). A religious worldview: Protecting one's meaning system through religious prejudice. *Personality and Social Psychology Bulletin, 41,* 1474–1487. doi:10.1177/0146167215599761

Goren, H., & Yemini, M. (2016). Global citizenship education in context: Teacher perceptions at an international school and a local Israeli school. *Compare: A Journal of Comparative and International Education, 46,* 832–853. doi:10.1080/03057925.2015.1111752

Goren, H., & Yemini, M. (2017a). Global citizenship education redefined—A systematic review of empirical studies on global citizenship education. *International Journal of Educational Research, 82,* 170–183. doi:10.1016/j.ijer.2017.02.004

Goren, H., & Yemini, M. (2017b). The global citizenship education gap: Teacher perceptions of the relationship between global citizenship education and students' socio-economic status. *Teaching and Teacher Education, 67,* 9–22. doi:10.1016/j.tate.2017.05.009

Greenaway, K. H., & Louis, W. R. (2010). Only human: Hostile human norms can reduce legitimization of intergroup discrimination by perpetrators of historical atrocities. *British Journal of Social Psychology, 49,* 765–783. doi:10.1348/014466609X479202

Greenaway, K. H., Loius, W. R., & Wohl, M. J. A. (2012). Awareness of common humanity reduced empathy and heightens expectations of forgiveness for temporally distant wrongdoing. *Social Psychological and Personality Science, 3,* 446–454. doi:10.1177/1948550611425861

Greenaway, K. H., Quinn, E. A., & Louis, W. R. (2011). Appealing to common humanity increases forgiveness but reduces collective action among victims of historical atrocities. *European Journal of Social Psychology, 41,* 569–573. doi:10.1002/ejsp.802

Gretzel, U., Davis, E. B., Bowser, G., Jiang, J., & Brown, M. (2014). Creating global leaders with sustainability mindsets—insights from the RMSSN summer academy. *Journal of Teaching in Travel & Tourism, 14,* 164–183. doi:10.1080/15313220.2014.907958

Griffiths, M. (2017). 'It's all bollocks!' and other critical standpoints on the UK Government's vision of global citizenship. *Identities: Global Studies in Culture and Power, 24,* 398–416. doi:10.1080/1070289X.2016.1161515

Grinstein, A., & Riefler, P. (2015). Citizens of the (green) world? Cosmopolitan orientation and sustainability. *Journal of International Business Studies, 46,* 694–714. doi:10.1057/jibs.2015.1

Grudzinski-Hall, M. N. (2007). *How do college and university undergraduate level global citizenship programs advance the development and experiences of global competencies?* (Doctoral dissertation). Retrieved from ProQuest Dissertations and Theses. (No. 3261868)

Günel, E., & Pehlivan, A. (2016). Pre-service social studies teachers' perception of global citizenship. *Journal of Education and Future, 10,* 51–69.

Güngördü, A., & Yumuşak, T. (2017). Examining consumer cosmopolitanism and foreign travelling in the context of consumer behavior. *Journal of Business Research Turk, 9,* 271–280.

Guo, X. (2013). Living in a global world: Influence of consumer global orientation on attitudes toward global brands from developed versus emerging countries. *Journal of International Marketing, 21,* 1–22. doi:10.1509/jim.12.0065

Hackett, J. D. (2014). "The response": A day of prayer and protest. *Politics, Bureaucracy, and Justice, 4,* 45–53.

Hackett, J. D., Omoto, A. M., & Matthews, M. (2015). Human rights: the role of psychological sense of global community. *Peace and Conflict: Journal of Peace Psychology, 21,* 47–67. doi:10.1037/pac0000086

Haigh, M. (2008). Internationalisation, planetary citizenship and higher education inc. *Compare, 38,* 427–440. doi:10.1080/03057920701582731

Hall, D. L., Matz, C. M., & Wood, W. (2010). Why don't we practice what we preach? A meta-analytic review of religious racism. *Personality and Social Psychology Review, 14,* 126–139. doi:10.1177/1088868309352179

Hamer, K., Penczek, M., & Bilewicz, M. (2017). "Humanum ignoscere est". The relationship of national and supranational identifications with intergroup forgiveness. *Personality and Individual Differences, 105,* 257–263. doi:10.1016/j.paid.2016.09.058

Hanson, R. A. (2017). *Intergroup contact through study abroad: An investigation of effects of study abroad on student engagement with racial and religious diversity* (Master's thesis). Retrieved from ProQuest Dissertations and Theses. (No. 10275038)

Hanvey, R. G. (1976). *An attainable global perspective.* New York: Global Perspectives in Education.

Harshman, J. R., & Augustine, T. A. (2013). Fostering global citizenship education for teachers through online research. *The Educational Forum, 77,* 450–463. doi:10.1080/00131725.2013.822040

Hartman, E. (2014). Educating for global citizenship: A theoretical account and quantitative analysis. *eJournal of Public Affairs, 3,* 1–42.

Haslam, N., & Loughnan, S. (2014). Dehumanization and infrahumanization. *Annual Review of Psychology, 65,* 399–423. doi:10.1146/annurev-psych-010213-115045

Haugestad, A. K. (2004). Norwegians as global neighbors and global citizens. In A. K. Haugestad, & J. D. Wolfhorst (Eds.), Future as fairness: Ecological justice and global citizenship (pp. 218–240). New York: Rodopi.

Hayward, F. M., & Siaya, L. M. (2001). *Public experience, attitudes, and knowledge: A report on two national surveys about international education.* Washington, DC: American Council on Education.

He, B. (2005). Citizenship and cultural equality. In S. Tan (Ed.), *Challenging citizenship: Group membership and cultural identity in a global age* (pp. 151–168). Aldershot, UK: Ashgate.

Heater, D. (1997). The reality of multiple citizenship. In I. Davies & A. Sobisch (Eds.), *Developing European citizens* (pp. 21–48). Sheffield, UK: Hallam University Press.

Heater, D. (2000). Does cosmopolitan thinking have a future? *Review of International Studies, 26,* 179–197. doi:10.1017/S0260210500001790

Heater, D. (2002). *World citizenship: Cosmopolitan thinking and its opponents.* London: Continuum.

Hendershot, K. (2010). *Transformative learning and global citizenship identity development in undergraduates: A case study* (Doctoral dissertation). Retrieved from ProQuest Dissertations and Theses. (UMI No. 3389956)

Henrich, J., Heine, S. J., & Norenzayan, A. (2010). The weirdest people in the world? *Behavioral and Brain Sciences, 33,* 61–135. doi:10.1017/S0140525X0999152X

Hett, E. J. (1993). *The development of an instrument to measure global-mindedness* (Unpublished doctoral dissertation). University of San Diego, San Diego, CA.

Hicks, D. (2003). Thirty years of global education: A reminder of key principles and precedents. *Educational Review, 55,* 265–275. doi:10.1080/0013191032000118929

Ho, A. P. Y. (2016). Can service learning cultivate empowering experiences for students? Insight from empowerment pedagogy. *Proceedings of the 2nd International Conference on Service-Learning, 1–2,* 119–123.

Ho, V. T., Rousseau, D. M., & Levesque, L. L. (2006). Social networks and the psychological contract: Structural holes, cohesive ties, and beliefs regarding employer obligations. *Human Relations, 59,* 459–481. doi:10.1177/0018726706065370

Hobbs, J. J. (2017). Heritage in the lived environment of the United Arab Emirates and the Gulf region. *Archnet-IJAR: International Journal of Architectural Research, 11,* 55–82. doi:10.26687/archnet-ijar.v11i2.1240

Hogg, M. A., & Abrams, D. (1988). *Social identifications: A social psychology of intergroup relations and group processes.* London: Routledge.

Hogg, M. A., & McGarty, C. (1990). Self-categorization and social identity. In D. Abrams & M. A. Hogg (Eds.), *Social identity theory: Constructive and critical advances* (pp. 10–27). New York: Springer-Verlag.

Hogg, M. A., & Smith, J. R. (2007). Attitudes in social context: A social identity perspective. *European Review of Social Psychology, 18,* 89–131. doi:10.1080/10463280701592070

Holt, D. B., Quelch, J. A., & Taylor, E. L. (2004). How global brands compete. *Harvard Business Review, 82,* 68–75.

Hong, Y.-Y., Levy, S. R., & Chiu, C.-Y. (2001). The contribution of the lay theories approach to the study of groups. *Personality and Social Psychology Review, 5,* 98–106. doi:10.1207/S15327957PSPR0502_1

Hornsey, M. J., & Hogg, M. A. (2002). The effects of status on subgroup relations. *British Journal of Social Psychology, 41,* 203–218. doi:10.1348/014466602760060200

Horsley, M., Newell, S., & Stubbs, B. (2005). The prior knowledge of global education of pre-service teacher education students. *Citizenship, Social and Economics Education, 6,* 137–155. doi:10.2304/csee.2004.6.3.137

Hunter, B., White, G. P., & Godbey, G. C. (2006). What does it mean to be globally competent? *Journal of Studies in International Education, 10,* 267–285. doi:10.1177/1028315306286930

Ibrahim, T. (2005). Global citizenship education: Mainstreaming the curriculum? *Cambridge Journal of Education, 35,* 177–194. doi:10.2304/csee.2004.6.3.137

Ilbawi, A. M., Ayoo, E., Bhadelia, A., Chidebe, R. C. W., Fadelu, T., Herrera, C. A., . . . Yap, M. L. (2017). Advancing access and equity: The vision of a new generation in cancer control. *The Lancet Oncology, 18,* 172–175. doi:10.1016/S1470-2045(17)30041-4

Inglis, D. (2014). Cosmopolitanism's sociology and sociology's cosmopolitanism: Retelling the history of cosmopolitan theory from Stoicism and Durkheim and beyond. *Distinktion: Scandinavian Journal of Social Theory, 15,* 69–87. doi:10.1080/1600910X.2013.809662

Ip, G. (2017, January 6). We are not the world. *Wall Street Journal*. Retrieved from http://www.wsj.com/articles/we-arent-the-world-1483728161

Iyer, R., Koleva, S., Graham, J., Ditto, P., & Haidt, J. (2012). Understanding libertarian morality: The psychological dispositions of self-identified libertarians. *PLoS ONE, 7*, e42366. doi:10.1371/journal.pone.0042366

Jaberi, E. (2014). *Global citizenship through the eyes of the grade seven elementary students: A case study* (Unpublished master's thesis). University of Western Ontario, London, Ontario, Canada.

Jack, A. I., Friedman, J. P., Boyatzis, R. E., & Taylor, S. N. (2016). Why do you believe in God? Relationships between religious belief, analytic thinking, mentalizing and moral concern. *PLoS ONE, 11*, e0149989. doi:10.1371/journal.pone.0149989

Jaffee, A. T., Watson, V. W. M., & Knight, M. G. (2014). Toward enacted cosmopolitan citizenship: New conceptualizations of African immigrants' civic learning and action in the United States. *Journal of Global Citizenship and Equity Education, 4*, 1–18.

James, A., Fine, M., & Lester, A. (2015). A re-investigating of the religious orientation-moral reasoning relationship: A relational developmental systems perspective. *Journal of Beliefs & Values, 36*, 244–251. doi:10.1080/13617672.2015.1051362

Jenkins, H. (1992). *Textual poachers: Television fans and participatory culture*. New York: Routledge.

Jenkins, S. T., Reysen, S., & Katzarska-Miller, I. (2012). Ingroup identification and personality. *Journal of Interpersonal Relations, Intergroup Relations and Identity, 5*, 9–16.

Jing, H. (2013). Global awareness: Foreign language teachers' beliefs and practices. *Intercultural Communication Studies, 22*, 95–116.

Johnson, M. K., Rowatt, W. C., & LaBouff, J. P. (2012). Religiosity and prejudice revisited: Ingroup favoritism, out-group derogation, or both? *Psychology of Religion and Spirituality, 4*, 154–168. doi:10.1037/a0025107

Jung, S. (2012). Fan activism, cybervigilantism, and othering mechanisms in K-pop fandom. *Transformative Works and Fan Activism, 10*. doi:10.3983/twc.2012.0300

Kanbara, S., Yamamoto, Y., Sugishita, T., Nakasa, T., & Moriguchi, I. (2017). Japanese experience of evolving nurses' roles in changing social contexts. *International Nursing Review, 64*, 181–186. doi:10.1111/inr.12365

Kant, I. (1963). *On history*, ed. and trans. L. W. Beck, R. E. Anchor, & E. L. Fackenheim. Indianapolis, IN: Bobbs-Merrill.

Kaowiwattanakul, S. (2016). Role of international study experiences in the personal and professional development of university lecturers in the humanities and social sciences fields in Thailand. *The International Education Journal: Comparative Perspectives, 15*, 58–71.

Katzarska-Miller, I., Barnsley, C. A., & Reysen, S. (2014). Global citizenship identification and religiosity. *Archive for the Psychology of Religion, 36*, 344–367. doi:10.1163/15736121–12341291

Katzarska-Miller, I., & Reysen, S. (in press). Measuring types of global citizens. *Journal of Global Citizenship and Equity Education*.

Katzarska-Miller, I., & Reysen, S. (2018a). [Lay definitions of humans]. Unpublished raw data.

Katzarska-Miller, I., & Reysen, S. (2018b). [Workplace predictors of antecedents and outcomes of global citizenship identification]. Unpublished raw data.

Katzarska-Miller, I., Reysen, S., Kamble, S. V., & Vithoji, N. (2012). Cross-national differences in global citizenship: Comparison of Bulgaria, India, and the United States. *Journal of Globalization Studies, 3*, 166–183.

Kaukko, M., & Fertig, M. (2016). Linking participatory action research, global education, and social justice: Emerging issues from practice. *International Journal of Development Education and Global Learning, 7*, 24–46. doi:10.18546/IJDEGL.07.3.03

Kaya, Y., & Martin, N. D. (2016). Managers in the global economy: A multilevel analysis. *The Sociological Quarterly, 57*, 232–255. doi:10.1111/tsq.12111

Kennedy, R. (2013). The role of supranational identity in promoting democratic values. *European Union Politics, 14*, 228–249. doi:10.1177/1465116512466604

Kerkhoff, S. N. (2017). Designing global futures: A mixed methods study to develop and validate the teaching for global readiness scale. *Teaching and Teacher Education, 65,* 91–106. doi:10.1016/j.tate.2017.03.011

Killick, D. (2012). Seeing-ourselves-in-the-world: Developing global citizenship through international mobility and campus community. *Journal of Studies in International Education, 16,* 372–389. doi:10.1177/1028315311431893

Killick, D. (2013). Global citizenship, sojourning students and campus communities. *Teaching in Higher Education, 18,* 721–735. doi:10.1080/13562517.2013.836087

Kim, Y. J., & Van Dyne, L. (2012). Cultural intelligence and international leadership potential: The importance of contact for members of the majority. *Applied Psychology: An International Review, 61,* 272–294. doi:10.1111/j.1464–0597.2011.00468.x

Kingston, L. N., MacCartney, D., & Miller, A. (2014). Facilitating student engagement: Social responsibility and freshmen learning communities. *Teaching and Learning Inquiry: The ISSOTL Journal, 2,* 63–80.

Kirkwood-Tuker, T. F., Morris, J. D., & Lieberman, M. G. (2010). What kind of teachers will teach our children? The worldmindedness of undergraduate elementary and secondary social studies teacher candidates at five Florida public universities. *International Journal of Development Education and Global Learning, 3,* 5–28. doi:10.18546/IJDEGL.03.3.02

Kreiner, G. E., & Ashforth, B. E. (2004). Evidence toward an expanded model of organizational identification. *Journal of Organizational Behavior, 25,* 1–27. doi:10.1002/job.234

Krutka, D. G., & Carano, K. T. (2016). Videoconferencing for global citizenship education: Wise practices for social studies educators. *Journal of Social Studies Education Research, 7,* 109–136.

Kuehl, R. A. (2011). *Toward a feminist rhetorical theory of global citizenship* (Doctoral dissertation). Retrieved from ProQuest Dissertations and Theses. (UMI No. 3457096)

Kuleta-Hulboj, M. (2016). The global citizen as an agent of change: Ideals of the global citizen in the narratives of Polish NGO employees. *Journal for Critical Education Policy Studies, 14,* 220–250.

Kunst, J. R., & Sam, D. L. (2013). Expanding the margins of identity: A critique of marginalization in a globalized world. *International Perspectives in Psychology: Research, Practice, Consultation, 2,* 225–241. doi:10.1037/ipp0000008

Langran, I. V., Langran, E., & Ozment, K. (2009). Transforming today's students into tomorrow's global citizens: Challenges for U.S. educators. *New Global Studies, 3,* 1–21. doi:10.2202/1940–0004.1056

Larsen, M. A. (2014). Critical global citizenship and international service learning: A case study of the intensification effect. *Journal of Global Citizenship and Equity Education, 4,* 1–43.

Larsen, M. A., & Searle, M. J. (2017). International service learning and critical global citizenship: A cross-study of a Canadian teacher education alternative practicum. *Teaching and Teacher Education, 63,* 196–205. doi:10.1016/j.tate.2016.12.011

Larson, R. B., & Heimrich, C. R. (2015, June). *Characteristics of several religiosity measures.* Paper presented at the 40th Annual Macromarketing Conference, Chicago, IL.

Lawrence, S. J. (2012). *Consumer xenocentrism and consumer cosmopolitanism: The development and validation of scales of constructs influencing attitudes towards foreign product consumption* (Doctoral dissertation). Retrieved from ProQuest Dissertations and Theses. (No. 1272344163)

Lawthong, N. (2003). A development of the global-mindedness scale in Thai socio-cultural context. *Journal of Institutional Research South East Asia, 1,* 57–70.

Le, Q. V., & Raven, P. V. (2015). An assessment of experiential learning of global poverty issues through international service projects. *Journal of Teaching in International Business, 26,* 136–158. doi:10.1080/08975930.2015.1051692

Leach, C. W., van Zomeren, M., Zebel, S., Vliek, M. L. W., Pennekamp, S. F., Doosje, B., & Ouwerkerk, J. W. (2008). Group-level self-definition and self-investment: A hierarchical (multicomponent) model of in-group identification. *Journal of Personality and Social Psychology, 95,* 144–165. doi:10.1037/0022–3514.95.1.144

Leduc, R. (2013). Global citizenship instruction through active participation: What is being learned about global citizenship? *The Educational Forum, 77,* 394–406. doi:10.1080/00131725.2013.822038

Lee, K. (2011). Understanding Hong Kong adolescents' environmental intention: The roles of media exposure, subjective norm, and perceived behavioral control. *Applied Environmental Education and Communication, 10,* 116–125. doi:10.1080/1533015X.2011.575733

Lee, R. B., Baring, R., Maria, M. S., & Reysen, S. (2017). Attitude toward technology, social media usage, and grade point average as predictors of global citizenship identification in Filipino university students. *International Journal of Psychology, 52,* 213–219. doi:10.1002/ijop.12200

Leek, J. (2016). Global citizenship education in school curricula. A Polish perspective. *Journal of Social Studies Education Research, 7,* 51–74.

Lentz, T. F. (1950). The attitudes of world citizenship. *The Journal of Social Psychology, 32,* 207–214. doi:10.1080/00224545.1950.9919047

Leung, A. K.-Y., Koh, K., & Tam, K.-P. (2015). Being environmentally responsible: Cosmopolitan orientation predicts pro-environmental behaviors. *Journal of Environmental Psychology, 43,* 79–94. doi:10.1016/j.jenvp.2015.05.011

Levine, M., Prosser, A., Evans, D., & Reicher, S. (2005). Identity and emergency intervention: How social group membership and inclusiveness of group boundaries shape helping behavior. *Personality and Social Psychology Bulletin, 31,* 443–453. doi:10.1177/0146167204271651

Levy, O., Beechler, S., Taylor, S., & Boyacigiller, N. A. (2007). What we talk about when we talk about 'global mindset': Managerial cognition in multinational corporations. *Journal of International Business Studies, 38,* 231–258. doi:10.1057/palgrave.jibs.8400265

Levy, S. R., Chiu, C., & Hong, Y. (2006). Lay theories and intergroup relations. *Group Processes & Intergroup Relations, 9,* 5–24. doi:10.1177/1368430206059855

Levy, S. R., West, T. L., & Ramirez, L. (2005). Lay theories and intergroup relations: A social-developmental perspective. *European Review of Social Psychology, 16,* 189–220. doi:10.1080/10463280500397234

Lilley, K., Barker, M., & Harris, N. (2015). Exploring the process of global citizen learning and the student mind-set. *Journal of Studies in International Education, 19,* 225–245. doi:10.1177/1028315314547822

Lilley, K., Barker, M., & Harris, N. (2017). The global citizen conceptualized: Accommodating ambiguity. *Journal of Studies in International Education, 21,* 6–21. doi:10.1177/1028315316637354

Lin, C.-P., Lyau, N.-M., Tsai, Y.-H., Chen, W.-Y., & Chiu, C.-K. (2010). Modeling corporate citizenship and its relationship with organizational citizenship behaviors. *Journal of Business Ethics, 95,* 357–372. doi:10.1007/s10551-010-0364-x

Lin, Y.-C., & Wang, K.-Y. (2016). Local or global image? The role of consumers' local-global identity in code-switched ad effectiveness among monolinguals. *Journal of Advertising, 45,* 482–497. doi:10.1080/00913367.2016.1252286

Lindahl, J. (2013). *What does it mean to be a global citizen? A qualitative interview study with Indian and Nepalese young adults concerning their perceptions of global citizenship* (Unpublished undergraduate thesis). Jönköping University, Jönköping, Sweden.

Linklater, A. (1998). *The transformation of political community.* Cambridge: Polity Press.

Lisak, A., & Erez, M. (2015). Leadership emergence in multicultural teams: The power of global characteristics. *Journal of World Business, 50,* 3–14. doi:10.1016/j.jwb.2014.01.002

Livingstone, A., & Haslam, S. A. (2008). The importance of social identity content in a setting of chronic social conflict: Understanding intergroup relations in Northern Ireland. *British Journal of Social Psychology, 47,* 1–21. doi:10.1348/014466607X200419

Logsdon, J. M., & Wood, D. J. (2002). Business citizenship: From domestic to global level of analysis. *Business Ethics Quarterly, 12,* 155–187. doi:10.2307/3857809

Logsdon, J. M., & Wood, D. J. (2005). Global business citizenship and voluntary codes of ethical conduct. *Journal of Business Ethics, 59,* 55–67. doi:10.1007/s10551-005-3411-2

Long, T. E. (2013). From study abroad to global studies: Reconstructing international education for a globalized world. *Frontiers: The Interdisciplinary Journal of Study Abroad, 22,* 25–36.

Longhofer, W. A. (2011). *Foundations of global giving* (Doctoral dissertation). Retrieved from ProQuest Dissertations and Theses. (No. 917715182)

Lough, B. J., & McBride, A. M. (2013). Navigating the boundaries of active global citizenship. *Transactions of the Institute of British Geographers, 39,* 457–469. doi:10.1111/tran.12035

Lough, B. J., Sherraden, M. S., McBride, A. M., & Xiang, X. (2014). The impact of international service on the development of volunteers' intercultural relations. *Social Science Research, 46,* 48–58. doi:10.1016/j.ssresearch.2014.02.002

Lovvorn, A. S., & Chen, J.-S. (2011). Developing a global mindset: The relationship between an international assignment and cultural intelligence. *International Journal of Business and Social Science, 2,* 275–283.

Luke, M. A. & Maio, G. R. (2009). Oh the humanity! Humanity-esteem and its social importance. *Journal of Research in Personality, 43,* 586–601. doi:10.1016/j.jrp.2009.03.001

Maignan, I., Ferrell, O. C., & Hult, G. T. M. (1999). Corporate citizenship: Cultural antecedents and business benefits. *Journal of the Academy of Marketing Science, 27,* 455–469. doi:10.1177/0092070399274005

Malsch, A. M. (2005). *Prosocial behavior beyond borders: Understanding a psychological sense of global community* (Doctoral dissertation). Available from ProQuest Dissertations and Theses database. (UMI No. 3175058)

Mansoory, S. (2012). *Exploring global identity in emerging adults* (Unpublished master's thesis). Stockholm University, Stockholm, Sweden.

Maringe, F. (2010). The meanings of globalization and internationalization in HE: Findings from a world survey. In F. Maringe & N. Foskett (Eds.), *Globalization and internationalization in higher education: Theoretical, strategic and management perspectives* (pp. 17–34). London: Continuum International Publishing.

Markus, H. R., & Kitayama, S. (1991). Culture and the self: Implications for cognition, emotion, and motivation. *Psychological Review, 98,* 224–253. doi:10.1037/0033–295X.98.2.224

Markus, H. R., & Nurius, P. (1986). Possible selves. *American Psychologist, 41,* 954–969. doi:10.1037/0003–066X.41.9.954

Marshall, H. (2007). Global education in perspective: Fostering a global dimension in an English secondary school. *Cambridge Journal of Education, 37,* 355–374. doi:10.1080/03057640701546672

Martin, M. M. (2014). *The effects of the many global cultures program upon students' global citizenship* (Doctoral dissertation). Retrieved from ProQuest Dissertations and Theses. (UMI No. 3581060)

Maslow, A. H. (1943). A theory of human motivation. *Psychological Review, 50,* 370–396. doi:10.1037/h0054346

Maslow, A. H. (1954). *Motivation and personality.* New York: Harper & Row.

Massey, K. D. (2013). *An investigation of global citizenship education in one geography course: The students' perspective* (Master's thesis). Retrieved from ProQuest Dissertations and Theses. (No. 1511459631)

Mather, N. (2015). Attitudes toward gay men and lesbians among college students at a Christian university: Examining in-group social influence, attitude functions, and ally identity. *Undergraduate Journal of Psychology, 28,* 9–19.

McCutcheon, L. E., Pope, T. J., Garove, A. R., Bates, J. A., Richman, H., & Aruguete, M. (2015). Religious skepticism and its relationship to attitudes about celebrities, identification with humanity, and the need for uniqueness. *North American Journal of Psychology, 17,* 45–58.

McDougall, H. R. (2005). *From the individual to the world: Global citizenship in education, thought, and practice* (Doctoral dissertation). Available from ProQuest Dissertations and Theses database. (UMI No. 3183505)

McFarland, S., & Hornsby, W. (2015). An analysis of five measures of global human identification. *European Journal of Social Psychology, 45,* 806–817. doi:10.1002/ejsp.2161

McFarland, S., Webb, M., & Brown, D. (2012). All humanity is my ingroup: A measure and studies of identification with all humanity. *Journal of Personality and Social Psychology, 103,* 830–853. doi:10.1037/a0028724

McLean, B. (2017). 'Who killed the world?' Religious paradox in *Mad Max: Fury Road. Science Fiction Film and Television, 10,* 371–390. doi:10.3828/sfftv.2017.25

McLean, L. R., & Cook, S. A. (2016). Rethinking global citizenship resources for new teachers: Promoting critical thinking and equity. *Journal of Global Citizenship and Equity Education, 5,* 1–24.

McLean, L. R., Cook, S. A., & Crowe, T. (2008). Imagining global citizens: Teaching peace and global education in a teacher-education programme. *Citizenship Teaching and Learning, 4,* 50–64.

Mignolo, W. D. (2000). The many faces of cosmo-polis: Border thinking and critical cosmopolitanism. *Public Culture, 12,* 721–748. doi:10.1215/08992363–12–3–721

Miyahara, M., Sawae, Y., Wilson, R., Briggs, H., Ishida, J., Doihata, K., & Sugiyama, A. (2018). An interdependence approach to empathic concern for disability and accessibility: Effects of gender, culture, and priming self-construal in Japan and New Zealand. *Journal of Pacific Rim Psychology, 12,* e11. doi:10.1017/prp.2017.19

Moghaddam, F. M. (2014). Editorial: The new global American dilemma. *Peace and Conflict, 20,* 54–67. doi:10.1037/pac0000015

Moizumi, E. M. (2010). *Examining two elementary-intermediate teachers' understandings and pedagogical practices about global citizenship education* (Master's thesis). Retrieved from ProQuest Dissertations and Theses. (No. 869527840)

Miller, C. D. (2014). Global citizenship: Fostering concern of nihilism? *Global Studies Journal, 6,* 67–76.

Moffa, E. D. (2016). Fostering global citizenship dispositions: The long-term impact of participating in a high school global service club. *The Social Studies, 107,* 145–152. doi:10.1080/00377996.2016.1148004

Montaigne, M. (1958). *The complete essays of Montaigne*, ed. and trans. D. M. Frame. Stanford, CA: Stanford University Press.

Morais, D. B., & Ogden, A. C. (2011). Initial development and validation of the global citizenship scale. *Journal of Studies in International Education, 15,* 445–466. doi:10.1177/1028315310375308

Morton, A. T., & Postmes, T. (2011a). Moral duty or moral deference? The effects of perceiving shared humanity with the victims of ingroup perpetrated harm. *European Journal of Social Psychology, 41,* 127–134. doi:10.1002/ejsp.751

Morton, T, A., & Postmes, T. (2011b). What does it mean to be human? How salience of the human category affects responses to intergroup harm. *European Journal of Social Psychology, 41,* 866–873. doi:10.1002/ejsp.831

Murphy, D., Sahakyan, N., Yong-Yi, D., & Magnan, S. S. (2014). The impact of study abroad on the global engagement of university graduates. *Frontiers: The Interdisciplinary Journal of Study Abroad, 24,* 1–24.

Myers, J. P. (2010). 'To benefit the world by whatever means possible': Adolescents' constructed meanings for global citizenship. *British Educational Research Journal, 36,* 483–502. doi:10.1080/01411920902989219

Needham, J. (1943). *Time: The refreshing river*. London: George Allen & Unwin.

Neff, K. D., Pisitsungkagarn, K., & Hsieh, Y. (2008). Self-compassion and self-construal in the United States, Thailand, and Taiwan. *Journal of Cross-Cultural Psychology, 39,* 267–285. doi:10.1177/0022022108314544

Ng, K. Y., Van Dyne, L., & Ang, S. (2012). Cultural intelligence: A review, reflections, and recommendations for future research. In A. M. Ryan, F. T. L. Leong, & F. L. Oswald (Eds.), *Conducting multinational research: Applying organizational psychology in the workplace* (pp. 29–58). Washington D.C.: American Psychological Association.

Ngcoya, M. (2015). Ubuntu: Toward an emancipatory cosmopolitanism? *International Political Sociology, 9,* 248–262. doi:10.1111/ips.12095

Nguyen, T. T. A. (2013). Towards skillful global citizenship education. *Paideusis, 21,* 26–38.

Nickerson, A. M., & Louis, W. R. (2008). Nationality versus humanity? Personality, identity, and norms in relation to attitudes toward asylum seekers. *Journal of Applied Social Psychology, 38,* 796–817. doi:10.1111/j.1559–1816.2007.00327.x

Niens, U., & Reilly, J. (2012). Education for global citizenship in a divided society? Young people's views and experiences. *Comparative Education, 48,* 103–118. doi:10.1080/03050068.2011.637766

Niessen, C., Weseler, D., & Kostova, P. (2016). When and why do individual craft their jobs? The role of individual motivation and work characteristics for job crafting. *Human Relations, 69,* 1287–1313. doi:10.1177/0018726715610642

Nijssen, E. J., & Douglas, S. P. (2008). Consumer world-mindedness, social-mindedness, and store image. *Journal of International Marketing, 16,* 84–107. doi:10.1509/jimk.16.3.84

Nijssen, E. J., & Douglas, S. P. (2011). Consumer world-mindedness and attitudes toward product positioning in advertising: An examination of global versus foreign versus local positioning. *Journal of International Marketing, 19,* 113–133. doi:10.1509/jimk.19.3.113

Norris, P., & Inglehart, R. (2009). *Cosmopolitan communications: Cultural diversity in a globalized world.* Cambridge: Cambridge University Press.

Nussbaum, M. C. (1997). Kant and Stoic cosmopolitanism. *The Journal of Political Philosophy, 5,* 1–25. doi:10.1111/1467–9760.00021

Oakes, P. J., Haslam, S. A., & Turner, J. C. (1998). The role of prototypicality in group influence and cohesion: Contextual variation in the graded structure of social categories. In S. Worchel, J. F. Morales, D. Paez, & J.-C. Deschamps (Eds.), *Social identity: International perspectives* (pp. 75–92). London: Sage.

O'Byrne, D. J. (2003). *The dimensions of global citizenship: Political identity beyond the nation-state.* London: Frank Cass. doi:10.4324/9780203009321

Oceja, L., & Salgado, S. (2013). Why do we help? World change orientation as an antecedent to prosocial action. *European Journal of Social Psychology, 43,* 127–136. doi:10.1002/ejsp.1925

Ogden, A., C. (2010). *Education abroad and the making of global citizens: Assessing learning outcomes of course-embedded, faculty-led international programming* (Doctoral dissertation). Retrieved from ProQuest Dissertations and Theses. (UMI No. 3420254)

Onraet, E., Van Assche, J., Roets, A., Haesevoets, T., & Van Hiel, A. (2017). The happiness gap between conservatives and liberals depends on country-level threat: A worldwide multilevel study. *Social Psychological and Personality Science, 8,* 11–19. doi:10.1177/1948550616662125

Onwuegbuzie, A. J., & Leech, N. L. (2005). On becoming a pragmatic research: The importance of combining quantitative and qualitative research methodologies. *International Journal of Social Research Methodology, 8,* 375–387. doi:10.1080/13645570500402447

Orlitzky, M., Schmidt, F. L., & Rynes, S. L. (2003). Corporate social and financial performance: A meta-analysis. *Organization Studies, 24,* 403–441. doi:10.1177/017084 0603024003910

O'Rourke, K. H., & Williamson, J. G. (2002). When did globalisation begin? *European Review of Economic History, 6,* 23–50. doi:10.1017/S1361491602000023

Osler, A., & Vincent, K. (2002). *Citizenship and the challenge of global education.* Stoke-on-Trent, UK: Trentham Books.

Ott, D. L., & Michailova, S. (in press). Cultural intelligence: A review and new research avenues. *International Journal of Management Reviews.* doi:10.1111/ijmr.12118

Oxfam. (1997). *A curriculum for global citizenship.* Oxford, UK: Oxfam.

Oxfam. (2006). *Education for global citizenship: A guide for schools.* Oxfam, UK: Oxfam.

Oxley, L., & Morris, P. (2013). Global citizenship: A typology for distinguishing its multiple conceptions. *British Journal of Educational Studies, 61,* 301–325. doi:10.1080/00071005.2013.798393

Oyserman, D. (2017). Culture three ways: Culture and subcultures within countries. *Annual Review of Psychology, 68,* 435–463. doi:10.1146/annurev-psych-122414–033617

Ozer, S., & Schwartz, S. J. (2016). Measuring globalization-based acculturation in Ladakh: Investigating possible advantages of a tridimensional acculturation scale. *International Journal of Intercultural Relations, 53,* 1–15. doi:10.1016/j.ijintrel.2016.05.002

Palasinski, M., Abell, J., & Levine, M. (2012). Intersectionality of ethno-cultural identities and construal of distant suffering outgroups. *The Qualitative Report, 17,* 1–17.

Pangle, T. L. (1998). Socratic cosmopolitanism: Cicero's critique and transformation of the stoic ideal. *Canadian Journal of Political Science, 31,* 235–262. doi:10.1017/S0008423900019788

Pareles, J. (2012, October 1). Turning up the volume on global poverty. *The New York Times,* p. C1.

Parkerson, S., & Reysen, S. (2015). Illusion of explanatory depth and global citizenship identification. *International Journal of Humanities and Social Science, 5,* 43–49.

Parts, O., & Vida, I. (2011). The effects of consumer cosmopolitanism on purchase behavior of foreign vs. domestic products. *Managing Global Transitions, 9,* 355–370.

Pasha, A. (2015). Global citizenship in Pakistan. *International Journal of Development Education and Global Learning, 7,* 33–52. doi:10.18546/IJDEGL.07.1.03

Pavey, L., Greitemeyer, T., & Sparks, P. (2011). Highlighting relatedness promotes prosocial motives and behavior. *Personality and Social Psychology Bulletin, 37,* 905–917. doi:10.1177/0146167211405994

Perdue, J. L. (2014). *Passports, global citizenship, and the Black student: A qualitative study uncovering the dispositions of undergraduate African American students regarding global citizenship* (Unpublished doctoral dissertation). Western Kentucky University, Bowling Green, KY.

Peters, M. A. (2014). Problematizing liberal cosmopolitanisms: Foucault and neoliberal cosmopolitan governmentality. *Contemporary Readings in Law and Social Justice, 6,* 13–37.

Phelps, J. M., Eilertsen, D. E., Türken, S., & Ommundsen, R. (2011). Integrating immigrant minorities: Developing a scale to measure majority members' attitudes toward their own proactive efforts. *Scandinavian Journal of Psychology, 52,* 404–410. doi:10.1111/j.1467–9450.2011.00876.x

Pieterse, J. N. (2006). Emancipatory cosmopolitanism: Towards an agenda. *Development and Change, 37,* 1247–1257. doi:10.1111/j.1467–7660.2006.00521.x

Pike, G. (2008). Citizenship education in global context. *Brock Education, 17,* 38–49. doi:10.26522/brocked.v17i1.100

Pike, G. & Selby, D. (1988). *Global teacher, global learner.* London: Hodder & Stoughton.

Pitty, R., Stokes, G., & Smith, G. (2008). Globalization and cosmopolitanism: Beyond populist nationalism and neoliberalism. In G. Stokes, R. Pitty, & G. Smith (Eds.), *Global citizens: Australian activists for change* (pp. 200–211). Cambridge, UK: Cambridge University Press.

Plaks, J. E., Levy, S. R., & Dweck, C. S. (2009). Lay theories of personality: Cornerstones of meaning in social cognition. *Social and Personality Psychology Compass, 3,* 1069–1081. doi:10.1111/j.1751–9004.2009.00222.x

Plante, C. N., Reysen, S., Roberts, S. E., & Gerbasi, K. C. (2016). *FurScience! A summary of five years of research from the International Anthropomorphic Research Project.* Waterloo, Ontario: FurScience.

Plante, C. N., Roberts, S., Reysen, S., & Gerbasi, K. C. (2014). "One of us": Engagement with fandoms and global citizenship identification. *Psychology of Popular Media Culture, 3,* 49–64. doi:10.1037/ppm0000008

Postmes, T., Haslam, S. A., & Jans, L. (2013). A single-item measure of social identification: Reliability, validity, and utility. *British Journal of Social Psychology, 52,* 597–617. doi:10.1111/bjso.12006

R. C. (1944). An embryologist looks at adults. *The Journal of Heredity, 35,* 118–121. doi:10.1093/oxfordjournals.jhered.a105363

Raman, K. R. (2007). Community-Coca-Cola interface: Political-anthropological concerns on corporate social responsibility. *Social Analysis, 51,* 103–120. doi:10.3167/sa.2007.510305

Rapoport, A. (2010). We cannot teach what we don't know: Indiana teachers talk about global citizenship education. *Education, Citizenship and Social Justice, 5,* 179–190. doi:10.1177/1746197910382256

Rapoport, A. (2013). Global citizenship themes in the social studies classroom: Teaching devices and teachers' attitudes. *The Educational Forum, 77,* 407–420. doi:10.1080/00131725.2013.822041

Rawwas, M. Y. A., Rajendran, K. N., & Wuehrer, G. A. (1996). The influences of worldmindedness and nationalism on consumer evaluation of domestic and foreign products. *International Marketing Review, 13,* 20–38. doi:10.1108/02651339610115746

Regan, R. (1982, June 17). *Remarks in New York City before the United Nations general assembly special session devoted to disarmament.* Retrieved from http://www.presidency.ucsb.edu/ws/?pid=42644

Reese, G., & Kohlmann, F. (2015). Feeling global, acting ethically: Global identification and fairtrade consumption. *The Journal of Social Psychology, 155,* 98–106. doi:10.1080/00224545.2014.992850

Reese, G., Proch, J., & Cohrs, J. C. (2013). Individual differences in responses to global inequality. *Analyses of Social Issues and Public Policy, 14,* 217–238. doi:10.1111/asap.12032

Reese, G., Proch, J., & Finn, C. (2015). Identification with all humanity: The role of self-definition and self-investment. *European Journal of Social Psychology, 45,* 426–440. doi:10.1002/ejsp.2102

Reimer, K., & McLean, L. R. (2009). Conceptual clarity and connections: Global education and teacher candidates. *Canadian Journal of Education, 32,* 903–926.

Renger, D., & Reese, G. (2017). From equality-based respect to environmental activism: Antecedents and consequences of global identity. *Political Psychology, 38,* 867–879. doi:10.1111/pops.12382

Reysen, S., & Branscombe, N. R. (2010). Fanship and fandom: Comparisons between sport fans and non-sport fans. *Journal of Sport Behavior, 33,* 176–193.

Reysen, S., & Hackett, J. (2016). Further examination of the factor structure and validity of the identification with all humanity scale. *Current Psychology, 35,* 711–719. doi:10.1007/s12144-015-9341-y

Reysen, S., & Hackett, J. (2017). Activism as a pathway to global citizenship. *The Social Science Journal, 54,* 132–138. doi:10.1016/j.soscij.2016.09.003

Reysen, S., & Katzarska-Miller, I. (2013a). A model of global citizenship: Antecedents and outcomes. *International Journal of Psychology, 48,* 858–870. doi:10.1080/00207594.2012.701749

Reysen, S., & Katzarska-Miller, I. (2013b). Intentional worlds and global citizenship. *Journal of Global Citizenship and Equity Education, 3,* 34–52.

Reysen, S., & Katzarska-Miller, I. (2015). Inclusive identities: From humans to global citizens. In B. R. Nelson (Ed.), *New developments in social identity research* (pp. 1–21). Hauppauge, NY: Nova.

Reysen, S., & Katzarska-Miller, I. (2017a). Superordinate and subgroup identities as predictors of peace and conflict: The unique content of global citizenship identity. *Peace and Conflict: Journal of Peace Psychology, 23,* 405–415. doi:10.1037/pac0000208

Reysen, S., & Katzarska-Miller, I. (2017b). Media, family, and friends: Normative environment and global citizenship identification. *Journal of International and Global Studies, 9,* 38–55.

Reysen, S., & Katzarska-Miller, I. (2017c). [Global university perceptions]. Unpublished raw data.

Reysen, S., & Katzarska-Miller, I. (2018a). [Associations between global citizenship identification and measures related to employee work environment]. Unpublished raw data.

Reysen, S., Katzarska-Miller, I., Gibson, S. A., & Hobson, B. (2013). World knowledge and global citizenship: Factual and perceived world knowledge as predictors of global citizenship identification. *International Journal of Development Education and Global Learning, 5,* 49–68. doi:10.18546/IJDEGL.05.1.04

Reysen, S., Katzarska-Miller, I., Gibson, S., Mohebpour, I., & Flanagan, J. (2017). Global citizenship identification and willingness to protest unethical corporations. *International Journal of Business and Globalisation, 18,* 480–492. doi:10.1504/IJBG.2017.084352

Reysen, S., Katzarska-Miller, I., Nesbit, S. M., & Pierce, L. (2013). Further validation of a single-item measure of social identification. *European Journal of Social Psychology, 43,* 463–470. doi:10.1002/ejsp.1973

Reysen, S., Katzarska-Miller, I., Salter, P. S., & Hirko, C. (2014). Blurring group boundaries: The impact of subgroup threats on global citizenship. *Cultural Encounters, Conflicts, and Resolutions, 1*(2). Retrieved from http://engagedscholarship.csuohio.edu/cecr/vol1/iss2/5/

Reysen, S., Larey, L. W., & Katzarska-Miller, I. (2012). College course curriculum and global citizenship. *International Journal of Development Education and Global Learning, 4,* 27–39. doi:10.18546/IJDEGL.04.3.03

Reysen, S., & Lloyd, J. D. (2012). Fanship and fandom in cyber space. In Z. Yan (Ed.), *Encyclopedia of cyber behavior* (pp. 292–300). Hershey, PA: IGI Global. doi:10.4018/978-1-4666-0315-8.ch025

Reysen, S., Pierce, L., Spencer, C., & Katzarska-Miller, I. (2013). Exploring the content of global citizenship identity. *The Journal of Multiculturalism in Education, 9,* 1–31.

Reysen, S., Pierce, L., Mazambani, G., Mohebpour, I., Puryear, C., Snider, J. S., Gibson, S., & Blake, M. E. (2014). Construction and initial validation of a dictionary for global citizen linguistic markers. *International Journal of Cyber Behavior, Psychology and Learning, 4,* 1–15. doi:10.4018/ijcbpl.2014100101

Reysen, S., Plante, C. N., Roberts, S. E., & Gerbasi, K. C. (2016). Optimal distinctiveness and identification with the furry fandom. *Current Psychology, 35,* 638–642. doi:10.1007/s12144-015-9331-0

Richardson, M., Abraham, C., & Bond, R. (2012). Psychological correlates of university students' academic performance: A systematic review and meta-analysis. *Psychological Bulletin, 138,* 353–387. doi:10.1037/a0026838

Ridout, T. N., Grosse, A. C., & Appleton, A. M. (2008). News media use and Americans' perception of global threat. *British Journal of Political Science, 38,* 575–593.

Riefler, P., & Diamantopoulos, A. (2009). Consumer cosmopolitanism: Review and replication of the CYMYC scale. *Journal of Business Research, 62,* 407–419. doi:10.1016/j.jbusres.2008.01.041

Riefler, P., Diamantopoulos, A., & Siguaw, J. A. (2012). Cosmopolitan consumers as a target group for segmentation. Journal of International Business Studies, 43, 285–305. doi:10.1057/jibs.2011.51

Robbins, M., Francis, L. J., & Elliott, E. (2003). Attitudes toward education for global citizenship among trainee teachers. *Research in Education, 69,* 93–98. doi:10.7227/RIE.69.8

Rock, T. C., Polly, D., & Handler, L. (2016). Preparing elementary teacher candidates to use global content: An action research study. *Social Studies Research Practice, 11,* 31–44.

Roddick, M. A. (2008). *Forming engaged global citizens: A case study of the WUSC international seminar* (Master's thesis). Retrieved from ProQuest Dissertations and Theses. (No. 304436420)

Rosenmann, A., Reese, G., & Cameron, J. E. (2016). Social identities in a globalized world: Challenges and opportunities for collective action. *Perspectives on Psychological Science, 11,* 202–221. doi:10.1177/1745691615621272

Russell III, W. B., & Waters, S. (2013). "Reel" character education: Using film to promote global citizenship. *Childhood Education, 89,* 303–309. doi:10.1080/00094056.2013.830901

Salgado, S., & Oceja, L. (2011). Towards a characterization of a motive who ultimate goal is to increase the welfare of the world: Quixoteism. *The Spanish Journal of Psychology, 14,* 145–155. doi:10.5209/rev_SJOP.2011.v14.n1.12

Sampson, D. L., & Smith, H. P. (1957). A scale to measure world-minded attitudes. *The Journal of Social Psychology, 45,* 99–106. doi:10.1080/00224545.1957.9714290

Saran, A., & Kalliny, M. (2012). Cosmopolitanism: Concept and measurement. *Journal of Global Marketing, 25,* 282–291. doi:10.1080/08911762.2012.779196

Schäfer, M. S., Ivanova, A., & Schmidt, A. (2014). What drives media attention for climate change? Explaining issue attention in Australian, German and Indian print media from 1996 to 2010. *The International Communication Gazette, 76,* 152–176. doi:10.1177/1748048513504169

Schattle, H. (2005). Communicating global citizenship: Multiple discourses beyond the academy. *Citizenship Studies, 9,* 119–133. doi:10.1080/13621020500049077

Schattle, H. (2008). *The practices of global citizenship.* Lanham, MD: Rowman & Littlefield.

Schattle, H. (2009). Global citizenship in theory and practice. In R. Lewin (Ed.), *The handbook of practice and research in study abroad: Higher education and the quest for global citizenship* (pp. 3–18). New York: Routledge.

Schattle, H. (2014). Mediating love of humanity, love of country, and love of culture: A comparison of normative debates on global citizenship in South Korea and the United States. *Korea Journal, 54,* 5–32.

Schattle, H. (2015). Global citizenship as a national project: The evolution of segye shimin in South Korean public discourse. *Citizenship Studies, 19,* 53–68. doi:10.1080/13621025.2014.883835

Scholte, J. A. (2014). Reinventing global democracy. *European Journal of International Relations, 20,* 3–28. doi:10.1177/1354066111436237

Schmiers, T. (2017). *Getting Europe back on track? Learning experiences during Interrail and how a free Interrail ticket could foster global citizenship* (Unpublished master's thesis). Uppsala University, Uppsala, Sweden.

Schroy, C., Plante, C. N., Reysen, S., Roberts, S. E., & Gerbasi, K. C. (2016). Different motivations as predictors of psychological connection to fan interest and fan groups in anime, furry, and fantasy sport fandoms. *The Phoenix Papers, 2,* 148–167.

Schuiling, I., & Kapferer, J.-N. (2004). Executive insights: Real differences between local and international brands: Strategic implications for international marketers. *Journal of International Marketing, 12,* 97–112. doi:10.1509/jimk.12.4.97.53217

Schulman, D., & Godard, E. (2010). In Phish fans donate over one million dollars [Press release]. Retrieved from http://mbird.org/2010/08/mbird-mff/

Schutte, I. W., Kamans, E., Wolfensberger, M. V. C., & Veugelers, W. (2017). Preparing students for global citizenship: The effects of a Dutch undergraduate honors course. *Education Research International,* Article ID 3459631. doi:10.1155/2017/3459631

Schwartz, S. H. (1992). Universals in the content and structure of values: Theory and empirical tests in 20 countries. In M. Zanna (Ed.), *Advances in experimental social psychology* (Vol. 25, pp. 1–65). New York: Academic Press. doi:10.1016/S0065-2601(08)60281-6

Scotto, T. J., Sanders, D., & Reifler, J. (2018). The consequential nationalist-globalist policy divide in contemporary Britain: Some initial analyses. *Journal of Elections, Public Opinion and Parties, 28,* 38–58. doi:10.1080/17457289.2017.1360308

Selby, D. (1999). Global education: Towards a quantum model of environmental education. *Canadian Journal of Environmental Education, 4,* 125–141.

Sen, S., & Bhattacharya, C. B. (2001). Does doing good always lead to doing better? Consumer reactions to corporate social responsibility. *Journal of Marketing Research, 38,* 225–243. doi:10.1509/jmkr.38.2.225.18838

Seo, H. (2016). *A study on secondary school teachers' global citizenship type and perceptions of global citizenship education* (Unpublished master's thesis). Seoul National University, Seoul, South Korea.

Seppälä, P., Mauno, S., Feldt, T., Hakanen, J., Kinnunen, U., Tolvanen, A., & Schaufeli, W. (2008). The construct validity of the Utrecht work engagement scale: Multisample and longitudinal evidence. *Journal Happiness Studies, 10,* 459–481. doi:10.1007/s10902-008-9100-y

Sevincer, A. T., Varnum, M. E. W., & Kitayama, S. (2017). The culture of cities: Measuring perceived cosmopolitanism. *Journal of Cross-Cultural Psychology, 48,* 1052–1072. doi:10.1177/0022022117717030

Shadowen, N. L., Chieffo, L. P., & Guerra, N. G. (2015). The global engagement measurement scale (GEMS): A new scale for assessing the impact of education abroad and campus internationalization. *Frontiers: The Interdisciplinary Journal of Study Abroad, 26,* 231–247.

Sherman, P. D. (2017). *The emergent global citizen: Cultivating global citizenship identity and engagement within Soka education* (Unpublished doctoral dissertation). Lancaster University, Lancaster, UK.

Shultz, L. (2007). Educating for global citizenship: Conflicting agendas and understandings. *The Alberta Journal of Educational Research, 53,* 248–258.

Shweder, R. A. (1990). Cultural psychology—what is it? In J. Stigler, R. Shweder, & G. Herdt (Eds.), *Cultural psychology: Essays on comparative human development* (pp. 1–46). Cambridge, UK: Cambridge University Press.

Sim, H. R. (2016). Global citizenship education in South Korea through civil society organizations: Its status and limitations. *Asian Journal of Education, 17,* 107–129.

Singh, M., & Jing, Q. (2013). *21st century international-mindedness: An exploratory study of its conceptualization and assessment.* Washington, DC: International Baccalaureate.

Sklad, M., Friedman, J., Park, E., & Oomen, B. (2016). 'Going glocal': A qualitative and quantitative analysis of global citizenship at a Dutch liberal arts and sciences college. *Higher Education, 72,* 323–340. doi:10.1007/s10734-015-9959-6

Smith, L. G. E., Thomas, E. F., & McGarty, C. (2015). "We must be the change we want to see in the world": Integrating norms and identities through social interaction. *Political Psychology, 36,* 543–557. doi:10.1111/pops.12180

Smith, W. C., Fraser, P., Chykina, V., Ikoma, S., Levitan, J., Liu, J., & Mahfouz, J. (2016). Global citizenship and the importance of education in a globally integrated world. *Globalisation, Societies and Education, 15,* 648–665. doi:10.1080/14767724.2016.1222896

Snider, J. S., & Reysen, S. (2014). Effect of framing of reentry program on perceptions of ex-offenders. *World Journal of Social Science Research, 1,* 68–88. doi:10.22158/wjssr.v1n1p68

Snider, J. S., Reysen, S., & Katzarska-Miller, I. (2013). How we frame the message of globalization matters. *Journal of Applied Social Psychology, 43,* 1599–1607. doi:10.1111/jasp.12111

Sobol, K., Cleveland, M., & Laroche, M. (2017). Globalization, national identity, biculturalism and consumer behavior: A longitudinal study of Dutch consumers. *Journal of Business Research, 82,* 340–353. doi:10.1016/j.jbusres.2016.02.044

Song, G. (2016). Shifting global citizenship education: Broadening citizenship education through global events in China. *Asian Journal of Education, 17,* 81–105.

Soongbeum, A. (2017). Resistance to a posthuman and retrograde oughtopia: Exploring the narrative of South Korea's sci-fi animation, *Wonder Kiddy. Animation: An Interdisciplinary Journal, 12,* 45–61. doi:10.1177/1746847716686544

Sparks, H., & Gore, J. S. (2017). My religion and my people: Levels of ingroup identification and Christian religious orientation. *Kentucky Journal of Undergraduate Scholarship, 1,* 100–120.

Sperandio, J., Grudzinski-Hall, M., & Stewart-Gambino, H. (2010). Developing an undergraduate global citizenship program: Challenges of definition and assessment. *International Journal of Teaching and Learning in Higher Education, 22,* 12–22.

Standish, A. (2012). *The false promise of global learning: Why education needs boundaries.* London: Continuum.

Stavrova, O., & Siegers, P. (2014). Religious prosociality and morality across cultures: How social enforcement of religion shapes the effects of personal religiosity on prosocial and moral attitudes and behaviors. *Personality and Social Psychology Bulletin, 40,* 315–333. doi:10.1177/0146167213510951

Stein, S. (2015). Mapping global citizenship. *Journal of College and Character, 16,* 242–252. doi:10.1080/2194587X.2015.1091361

Stewart, C., Wall, A., & Marciniec, S. (2016). Mixed signals: Do college graduates have the soft skills that employers want? *Competition Forum, 14,* 276–281.

Stone, D. L., & Deadrick, D. L. (2015). Challenges and opportunities affecting the future of human resource management. *Human Resource Management Review, 25,* 139–145. doi:10.1016/j.hrmr.2015.01.003

Streitwieser, B., & Light, G. (2016). The grand promise of global citizenship through study abroad: The student view. In E. Jones, R. Coelen, J. Beelen, & H. de Wit (Eds.), *Global and local internationalization* (pp. 67–73). Rotterdam, The Netherlands: Sense Publishers. doi:10.1007/978-94-6300-301-8_10

Strizhakova, Y., & Coulter, R. A. (2013). The "green" side of materialism in emerging BRIC and developed markets: The moderating role of global cultural identity. *International Journal of Research in Marketing, 30,* 69–82. doi:10.1016/j.ijresmar.2012.08.003

Strizhakova, Y., Coulter, R. A., & Price, L. L. (2008). Branded products as a passport to global citizenship: Perspectives from developed and developing countries. *Journal of International Marketing, 16,* 57–85. doi:10.1509/jimk.16.4.57

Strizhakova, Y., Coulter, R. A., & Price, L. L. (2011). Branding in a global marketplace: The mediating effects of quality and self-identity brand signals. *International Journal of Research in Marketing, 28,* 342–351. doi:10.1016/j.ijresmar.2011.05.007

Stürmer, S., Rohmann, A., van der Noll, J. (2016). Mobilizing the global community to combat Ebola: Psychological effects of the Band Aid 30 campaign. *The Journal of Social Psychology, 156,* 291–304. doi:10.1080/00224545.2015.1108898

Tajfel, H. (1978). Social categorization, social identity, and social comparison. In H. Tajfel (Ed.), *Differentiation between social groups: Studies in the social psychology of intergroup relations* (pp. 61–76). London: Academic Press.

Tajfel, H., & Turner, J. C. (1979). An integrative theory of intergroup conflict. In W. Austin & S. Worchel (Eds.), *The social psychology of intergroup relations* (pp. 33–47). Monterey, CA: Brooks/Cole.

Taneja, S. S., Taneja, P. K., & Gupta, R. K. (2011). Researches in corporate social responsibility: A review of shifting focus, paradigms, and methodologies. *Journal of Business Ethics, 101,* 343–364. doi:10.1007/s10551–010–0732–6

Tarrant, M. A. (2010). A conceptual framework for exploring the role of studies abroad in nurturing global citizenship. *Journal of Studies in International Education, 14,* 433–451. doi:10.1177/1028315309348737

Tarrant, M. A., Lyons, K., Stoner, L., Kyle, G. T., Wearing, S., & Poudyal, N. (2013). Global citizenry, educational travel and sustainable tourism: Evidence from Australia and New Zealand. *Journal of Sustainable Tourism, 22,* 403–420. doi:10.1080/09669582.2013.815763

Tarrant, M. A., Rubin, D. L., & Stoner, L. (2014). The added value of study abroad: Fostering a global citizenry. *Journal of Studies in International Education, 18,* 141–161. doi:10.1177/1028315313497589

Tausczik, Y. R., & Pennebaker, J. W. (2010). The psychological meaning of words: LIWC and computerized text analysis methods. *Journal of Language and Social Psychology, 29,* 24–54. doi:10.1177/0261927X09351676

Thanosawan, P., & Laws, K. (2013). Global citizenship: Differing perceptions within two Thai higher education institutions. *Journal of Higher Education Policy and Management, 35,* 293–304. doi:10.1080/1360080X.2013.786861

Their, M. (2016). *Maturing measurement: Validity and reliability trials of a measure of global citizenship for high school students.* Unpublished manuscript, Educational Policy Improvement Center University of Oregon, Eugene, OR.

Thomas, E. F., McGarty, C., Lala, G., Stuart, A., Hall, L. J., & Goddard, A. (2015). Whatever happened to Kony2012? Understanding a global Internet phenomenon as an emergent social identity. *European Journal of Social Psychology, 45,* 356–367. doi:10.1002/ejsp.2094

Topçu, U. C., & Kaplan, M. (2015). Willingness to buy foreign products in relation to ethnocentric tendencies and worldminded attitudes of consumers. *Procedia – Social and Behavioral Sciences, 207,* 157–164. doi:10.1016/j.sbspro.2015.10.166

Toukan, E. V. (2018). Educating citizens of 'the global': Mapping textual constructs of UNESCO's global citizenship education 2012–2015. *Education, Citizenship and Social Justice, 13,* 51–64. doi:10.1177/1746197917700909

Tran, T. B. H., Oh, C. H., & Choi, S. B. (2016). Effects of learning orientation and global mindset on virtual team members' willingness to cooperate in: The mediating role of self-efficacy. *Journal of Management & Organization, 22,* 311–327. doi:10.1017/jmo.2015.37

Tripodi, S. J., Kim, J. S., & Bender, K. (2010). Is employment associated with reduced recidivism? *International Journal of Offender Therapy and Comparative Criminology, 54,* 706–720. doi:10.1177/0306624X09342980

Tu, L., Khare, A., & Zhang, Y. (2012). A short 8–item scale for measuring consumers' lo-cal–global identity. *International Journal of Research in Marketing, 29,* 35–42. doi:10.1016/j.ijresmar.2011.07.003

Tuazon, A. P., & Claveria, J. G. (2016). Global education and students' acquisition of global perspectives in social sciences. *Asia Pacific Higher Education Research Journal, 3,* 1–13.

Tung, R. L. (2014). Requisites to and ways of developing a global mind-set: Implications for research on leadership and organizations. *Journal of Leadership & Organizational Studies, 21,* 329–337. doi:10.1177/1548051814549249

Tung, R. L. (2016). New perspectives on human resource management in a global context. *Journal of World Business, 51,* 142–152. doi:10.1016/j.jwb.2015.10.004

Turban, D. B., & Greening, D. W. (1997). Corporate social performance and organizational attractiveness to prospective employees. *Academy of Management Journal, 40,* 658–672. doi:10.2307/257057

Türken, S., & Rudmin, F. W. (2013). On psychological effects of globalization: Development of a scale of global identity. *Psychology and Society, 5,* 63–89.

Turner, J. C., Hogg, M. A., Oakes, P. J., Reicher, S. D., & Wetherell, M. (1987). *Rediscovering the social group: A self-categorization theory.* Oxford: Blackwell.

Uchida, Y., Townsend, S. S. M., Markus, H. R., & Bergsieker, H. B. (2009). Emotions as within or between people? Cultural variation in lay theories of emotion expression and inference. *Personality and Social Psychology Bulletin, 35,* 1427–1439. doi:10.1177/0146167209347322

Van Camp, D., Barden, J., & Sloan, L. (2016). Social and individual religious orientations exist within both intrinsic and extrinsic religiosity. *Archive for the Psychology of Religion, 38,* 22–46. doi:10.1163/15736121–12341316

Van Droogenbroeck, F., Spruyt, B., Siongers, J., & Keppens, G. (2016). Religious quest orientation and anti-gay sentiment: Nuancing the relationship between religiosity and negative attitudes toward homosexuality among young Muslims and Christians in Flanders. *Journal for the Scientific Study of Religion, 55,* 787–799. doi:10.1111/jssr.12303

Van Gent, M., Carabain, C., De Goede, I., Boonstoppel, E., & Hogeling, L. (2013). The development of the global citizenship inventory for adolescents. *International Journal of Development Education and Global Learning, 5,* 71–86. doi:10.18546/IJDEGL.05.2.05

van Veelen, R., Eisenbeiss, K. K., & Otten, S. (2016). Newcomers to social categories: Longitudinal predictors and consequences of ingroup identification. *Personality and Social Psychology Bulletin, 42,* 811–825. doi:10.1177/0146167216643937

Veugelers, W. (2011). The moral and the political in global citizenship: Appreciating differences in education. *Globalisation, Societies and Education, 9,* 473–485. doi:10.1080/14767724.2011.605329

Veugelers, W., de Groot, I., & Nollet, F. (2014). Higher education and citizenship development. In A. Teodoro & M. Guilherme (Eds.), *European and Latin American higher education between mirrors* (pp. 179–196). Rotterdam, The Netherlands: Sense Publishers. doi:10.1007/978–94–6209–545–8_13

Vinson, T., & Ericson, M. (2014). The social dimensions of happiness and life satisfaction of Australians: Evidence from the world values survey. *International Journal of Social Welfare, 23,* 240–253. doi:10.1111/ijsw.12062

Vonk, J., & Pitzen, J. (2017). Believing in other minds: Accurate mentalizing does not predict religiosity. *Personality and Individual Differences, 115,* 70–76. doi:10.1016/j.paid.2016.06.008

Waddock, S., & Smith, N. (2000). Relationships: The real challenge of corporate global citizenship. *Business and Society Review, 105,* 47–62. doi:10.1111/0045–3609.00064

Waldron, J. (2000). What is cosmopolitan? *The Journal of Political Philosophy, 8,* 227–243. doi:10.1111/1467–9760.00100

Walker, L., Leviston, Z., Price, J., & Devine-Wright, P. (2015). Responses to a worsening environment: Relative deprivation mediates between place attachments and behaviour. *European Journal of Social Psychology, 45,* 833–846. doi:10.1002/ejsp.2151

Walters, R., & Zeller, B. (2017). A comparative study of Australia and Slovenia's private international laws and the application of citizenship and residence. *Liverpool Law Review, 38,* 325–338. doi:10.1007/s10991–017–9204–8

Wang, J., Leung, K., & Zhou, F. (2014). A dispositional approach to psychological climate: Relationships between interpersonal harmony motives and psychological climate for communication safety. *Human Relations, 67,* 489–515. doi:10.1177/0018726/13495423

Wang, Y. (2015). Globalization and territorial identification: A multilevel analysis across 50 countries. *International Journal of Public Opinion Research, 28,* 401–414. doi:10.1093/ijpor/edv022

Wang, Z. (2017). *A double degree program in international communication: An exemplary case of global citizenship* (Unpublished master's thesis). The University of Western Ontario, London, Ontario, Canada.

Westjohn, S. A. (2009). *Global consumption orientation: An investigation of antecedents and consequences* (Doctoral dissertation). Retrieved from ProQuest Dissertations and Theses. (UMI No. 3383238)

Westjohn, S. A., Singh, N., & Magnusson, P. (2012). Responsiveness to global and local consumer culture positioning: A personality and collective identity perspective. *Journal of International Marketing, 20,* 58–73. doi:10.1509/jim.10.0154

Whitley, B. E., Jr. (2009). Religiosity and attitudes toward lesbians and gay men: A meta-analysis. *The International Journal for the Psychology of Religion, 19,* 21–38. doi:10.1080/10508610802471104

Wilson, R., & Keil, F. (1998). The shadows and shallows of explanation. *Minds and Machines, 8,* 137–159. doi:10.1023/A:1008259020140

Wohl, M. J. A., & Branscombe, N. R. (2005). Forgiveness and collective guilt assignment to historical perpetrator groups depend on level of social category inclusiveness. *Journal of Personality and Social Psychology, 88,* 288–303. doi:10.1037/0022–3514.88.2.288

Wohl, M. J. A., Branscombe, N. R., & Klar, Y. (2006). Collective guilt: Emotional reactions when one's group has done wrong or been wronged. *European review of Psychology, 17,* 1–37. doi:10.1080/10463280600574815

Wood, D. J. (2010). Measuring corporate social performance: A review. *International Journal of Management Reviews, 12,* 50–84. doi:10.1111/j.1468–2370.2009.00274.x

Woolf, M. (2010). Another mishegas: Global citizenship. *Frontiers: The Interdisciplinary Journal of Study Abroad, 19,* 47–60.

Xin, Z., Yang, Z., & Ling, X. (2017). Interdependent self-construal matters in the community context: Relationships of self-construal with community identity and participation. *Journal of Community Psychology, 45,* 1050–1064. doi:10.1002/jcop.21910

Young, J. M. (2010). Problems with global education: Conceptual contradictions. *The Alberta Journal of Educational Research, 56,* 143–156.

Young, M., & Commins, E. (2002). *Global citizenship: The handbook for primary teaching.* Oxford, UK: Oxfam.

Yu, Y. (2018). Using 'classic reading instruction' to raise students' gender awareness: Students' perceptions of their learning experiences at a Taiwanese university. *Asian Journal of Women's Studies, 24,* 88–105. doi:10.1080/12259276.2017.1421292

Zeller, E. (1889). *Outlines of the history of Greek philosophy,* trans. S. F. Alleyne & E. Abbott. New York: Henry Holt and Company.

Zeller, E. (1962). *The Stoics, Epicureans, and Sceptics,* trans. O. J. Reichel. New York: Russell & Russell.

Zepeda, L., & Reznickova, A. (2017). Innovative millennial snails: The story of slow food university of Wisconsin. *Agriculture and Human Values, 34,* 167–178. doi:10.1007/s10460–016–9701–8

Zeugner-Roth, K. P., Žabkar, V., & Diamantopoulos, A. (2015). Consumer ethnocentrism, national identity, and consumer cosmopolitanism as drivers of consumer behavior: A social identity perspective. *Journal of International Marketing, 23,* 25–54. doi:10.1509/jim.14.0038

Zhang, R., Hsu, H.-Y., & Wang, S.-K. (2010). Global literacy: Comparing Chinese and US high school students. *Multicultural Education & Technology Journal, 4,* 76–98. doi:10.1108/17504971011052304

Zhang, Y., & Khare, A. (2009). The impact of accessible identities on the valuation of global versus local products. *Journal of Consumer Research, 36,* 524–537. doi:10.1086/598794

Zhao, Y., Lin, L., & Hoge, J. D. (2007). Establishing the need for cross-cultural and global issues. *International Education Journal, 8,* 139–150.

Zhou, M. (2016). Social and individual sources of self-identification as global citizens: Evidence from the interactive multilevel model. *Sociological Perspectives, 59,* 153–176. doi:10.1177/0731121415579281

Index

About the Authors

Iva Katzarska-Miller is an associate professor of psychology at Transylvania University in Lexington, Kentucky. She teaches classes related to cultural psychology, social justice, and diversity. Her research interests focus on privilege and oppression, interpersonal relationships, and global citizenship.

Stephen Reysen is an associate professor of psychology at Texas A&M University-Commerce. He teaches classes related to social psychology, intergroup relations, and multicultural diversity. His research interests include topics related to personal (e.g., fanship) and social identity (e.g., global citizenship).